$6.00
cdA

(64-13554) 7-31-64

THE
NEGRO
IN NORTH
CAROLINA
1876-1894

THE
NEGRO
IN NORTH
CAROLINA
1876-1894

BY FRENISE A. LOGAN

Chapel Hill
The University of North Carolina Press

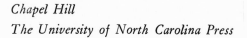

PRINTED BY SEEMAN PRINTERY, DURHAM, N. C.

To my beloved wife Mary

Preface

The period between 1876 and 1894 constitutes a lacuna in the history of North Carolina. There is no published or manuscript study of Bourbon Democracy for these years. There continues to be a need for expanding the research and writing in the area of business and entrepreneurial history, and definitive studies of the farmer and laboring classes are wanting. Definitive biographies of Zebulon B. Vance and Matt W. Ransom have not been prepared. There are still considerable opportunities for research and writing on the role of the Republican party in state politics for this period.

Many facets of this epoch, therefore, have been neglected. This study is an attempt to fill a gap in one phase of state history for these years, a narrative of the Negro group. This effort becomes all the more challenging in view of the fact that the return of "home rule" in 1876 following a decade of "reconstruction" in the state did not, as is generally assumed by laymen, result immediately in repression of the Negroes. During the late seventies, and throughout the eighties and into the nineties, North Carolina Negroes continued to vote in large numbers. Even the physical separation and segregation of the races which were so prominent in the first decades of the twentieth century were not legalized or codified and were often ignored by whites and Negroes alike.

This effort, then, can be viewed also as as attempt to explore Negro-white relations during a period that contributes to a solution of present-day race tensions. There is much historical truth in the bold statement of Professor C. Vann Woodward that segregation and white supremacy, certainly as they pertain to North Carolina, are products of twentieth-century Southern-white mentality. In the years between 1865 and 1898 North Carolina witnessed only a few of "the policies of proscription, segregation, and disfranchisement" which were later to characterize Negro-white relations in that state.

Any attempt to explain the long absence of a study of the Negro in post-Reconstruction North Carolina is purely conjectural and, therefore, perhaps to many scholars and laymen alike, will prove unsatisfactory and unconvincing. None the less, one factor that merits consideration in seeking an answer is the difficulty of ferreting out the primary material from which a narrative of the Negro during the period must be fashioned. It is widely dispersed, sometimes resting in the most unsuspected places, or it is found scattered among bulky collections of "extraneous" materials. To seek out and exploit these sources is not a challenge for the fainthearted.

I have selected for use in this study a method of presentation that is, in the main, topical rather than chronological. Within each topical grouping, the chronological organization is followed. The reason for this choice is that such a mode of treatment will enable the reader to obtain a more concrete picture of the Negroes' existence during the years under examination. I have also decided to utilize, with great liberality in some cases, the exact words, phrases, extracts of letters, and remarks of contemporaries, both Negro and white. It would seem that either the wisdom or the prejudice would be reflected best in their own words, rather than in any effort of mine to interpret and paraphrase them. The utterances of these individuals will certainly give a freshness and an illusion of contemporaneousness that a more thorough secondhand version would lack.

In gathering this material, I have incurred obligations that I gladly take this opportunity to acknowledge: the American Association for State and Local History, whose financial assistance made it possible for me to complete the research for this book; the staff of the Library of The University of North Carolina at Chapel Hill, especially Mr. William S. Powell and his associates in the North Carolina Room; the Duke University Library; the North Carolina State Department of Archives and History; the North Carolina State Library; and the Library of Congress. I should also like to note special obligations to the staff of the Library of The University of North Carolina at Greensboro; the staff of the Library of the Agricultural and Technical College of North Carolina for many courtesies, to Mrs. Loreno Marrow and Professor Darwin T. Turner of the English Department of the Agricultural and Technical College of North Carolina for their courage and stamina in wading through what must have been for them an arduous task, and to Professors George B. Tindall and Richard Bardolph for their many helpful suggestions. However, I must bear full responsibility for any errors either of fact or interpretation which may come to light.

I wish especially to express my sincere appreciation to Professors Richard Walser and Harvey Wish, for convincing me that this study should be made, and to Professor Joseph F. Steelman, for his readings of the manuscript and for his many helpful suggestions.

Finally, to my wife, Mary Whitfield Logan, I offer especial acknowledgment for her patience, cooperation, sacrifices, and untiring support throughout the long stages of my labors.

Contents

THE
NEGRO
IN NORTH
CAROLINA
1876-1894

In Retrospect:

The Negro Up to 1876

> It is a great mistake to suppose that the Southern
> white man has any hostility to the Negro as a race.
> In his place, in a menial or servile relation, he is
> liked and appreciated.
> Winston REPUBLICAN, June 6, 1878.

In 1699 five white men in the Albemarle region
of the colony of North Carolina appeared in court to "prove their
rights to land" by the importation of eight slaves. This is the first
positive record of the presence of Negroes in North Carolina, although
the institution was recognized by the "Fundamental Constitutions of
Carolina" as early as 1669. Indeed, before the latter date, the Lords
Proprietors encouraged the development of slavery by granting fifty
acres of land for each slave over fourteen years old brought into the
colony. Undoubtedly, it was on the basis of this act that the five
white men in 1699 based their claim.[1]

The number of slaves in North Carolina did not grow rapidly
during the early period, and most of those who were imported came
from Virginia and South Carolina. John Hope Franklin points out
that the strong resistance of the Indians in the first decades of the
eighteenth century, the economic impracticability of the plantation

1. William L. Saunders, ed., Colonial Records of North Carolina (Raleigh, 1890),
I, 86, 204.

system in some sections of North Carolina, and the sturdy resistance offered by some groups possessing religious scruples against the institution contributed to its slow development in the colony.[2] Although conflicting, the estimates of population in the colonial period, however, show clearly the growth of the number of slaves. In 1712 it was 800, in 1730 it was 6,000, in 1756 it was 19,000, and in 1775 it was 80,000.[3] In 1755, as later, the eastern counties were the stronghold of slavery. New Hanover had 1,374 slaves, Craven 934, Edgecombe 924, Northampton 834, and Beaufort 567.[4] In the first census of the United States (1790), white inhabitants outnumbered the Negro slaves 288,204 to 100,572. By 1860, the figures were 629,942 and 331,059 respectively.[5]

Slavery in colonial North Carolina, although never attaining the degree of importance that it did in South Carolina, played an important part in shaping the conditions under which Negroes lived. The early years of the colony's life witnessed the granting to the slaveholders of absolute power and authority over their Negro slaves. King George III, however, after purchasing the colony in 1927, attempted to mitigate the ofttimes harsh slave policy of masters and overseers by instructing the first royal governor to press for the enactment of a law providing the death penalty for the willful killing of Negro slaves, "and a fit penalty be imposed for the maiming of them."[6] In spite of this royal order and subsequent efforts to enact it into law, it was not until 1774 that the legislature passed such a measure. Even then the penalty for the first offense was only twelve months' imprisonment.[7]

Other laws on the matter of slavery are indicative of the purpose of their white designers. Ordinary courts were not open to slaves. A law of 1715 required that slaves charged with crimes be tried by three justices of the precinct court and three freeholders, the majority of whom were slaveholders. A 1741 law increased to four the number of freeholders. Trial by jury was not extended to slaves until 1793, and then only in cases in which the penalty extended to "life, limb, or member." Slaves were not allowed to testify against whites.[8]

2. John Hope Franklin, *The Free Negro in North Carolina, 1790-1860* (Chapel Hill, 1943), p. 8.
3. Hugh T. Lefler, *History of North Carolina* (New York, 1956), I, 133.
4. Saunders, ed., *Colonial Records of N.C.*, V, 575.
5. John S. Bassett, *Slavery in the State of North Carolina* (Baltimore, 1899), p. 77.
6. Saunders, ed., *Colonial Records of N.C.*, IV, 660, 666, 676.
7. *State Records,* ed. Walter Clark, Vol. XXIII, p. 64.
8. *North Carolina History Told by Contemporaries*, ed. Hugh T. Lefler (Chapel Hill, 1934), pp. 263-64.

It is needless to observe that these laws afforded ample opportunity for the practice of cruelty. Many barbarous punishments were inflicted upon slaves convicted of crimes. Negroes guilty of rape were often castrated; there were a few cases reported of slaves, convicted of murder, being burned at the stake by order of the court.[9]

After 1800 there was a downward trend in the growth of the slave population. The migration of many North Carolina slaveholders into the cotton kingdom of the lower South and the demand for slaves in that region tended to drain away the slaves of the older areas. Indeed, by 1850, 73 per cent of the families in North Carolina owned no slaves, and by 1860 more than two-thirds of the slaveholders had no more then ten slaves.[10]

Perhaps the comparatively smaller number of slaves in the total population of the state contributed to their better treatment at the hands of the whites. Frederick Law Olmsted noted that in some ways the condition of the slave in North Carolina was "less lamentable" than in other parts of the South and that the institution had "more of a patriarchal character."[11] Hinton Rowan Helper, the anti-slavery protagonist, and Thomas Ruffin, a leading jurist who owned over one hundred slaves, expressed similar views.[12]

However, it must be stressed that though the general aspects of slavery in North Carolina were more humanitarian and moderate than in most southern states, the rise of a strong anti-slavery opposition after 1830 resulted in a hardening of the pro-slavery attitude in North Carolina similar to that elsewhere in the South. The fear of slave revolts, the rise of abolitionist sentiment in the North, the growth of the free Negro element in the state, contests over the expansion of slavery into the territories in the West, and the publication of anti-slavery works like Helper's *Impending Crisis* undoubtedly solidified pro-slavery thought in the state.

In the colonial period, the people of the rice and tobacco growing area of the coastal plain of the colony owned the most slaves. The years after 1800, however, witnessed the movement of the slave population westward into the northern and southern Piedmont as a

9. R. D. W. Connor, *North Carolina: Rebuilding an Ancient Commonwealth* (Chicago, 1929), I, 183-84.

10. Cornelius O. Cathey, *Agricultural Developments in North Carolina, 1783-1860* (Chapel Hill, 1956), p. 53.

11. Frederick L. Olmsted, *A Journey in the Seaboard Slave State in the Years 1853-1854* (New York, 1856), p. 367.

12. Hinton R. Helper, *The Impending Crisis of the South: How to Meet It* (New York, 1857), p. 218; *Arator*, I (November, 1855), 249, quoted in Cathey, *Agricultural Developments*, p. 57.

result of the extension of the area of tobacco and cotton cultivation. The planters of the latter area, however, never owned as many slaves as those of the East.[13] The average slaveholdings for Edgecombe, for example, were 15.4; for Bertie, 17.4; for Halifax, 14.8. The largest holdings in the Piedmont were in the tobacco producing counties of Granville and Caswell, where the average holdings were 11.2 and 12.3 respectively.[14]

Whether they lived in the coastal or Piedmont area, Negro slaves of the state, as I have already noted, felt the adverse effects of the laws and practices imposed upon them by the dominant white group. Fortunately their lot was made easier by the activities of religious sects. As early as 1763, the members of the Anglican church were fostering educational institutions for Indians and Negroes. Not only the Episcopalians, but later the Presbyterians and Methodists, promoted education among the slaves of western North Carolina.[15] Of all the denominations, however, the Quakers were the most successful in educating the Negroes of ante-bellum North Carolina.[16]

The attention to religious instruction of the slaves by whites was not always motivated by purely spiritual considerations. In their quest for an instrument that would sustain the status quo, the slaveholders of North Carolina, as of other states, turned to religion and established the church as an institution that supported, sometimes with unnecessary zeal, the slavocracy.[17] Although it was possible for slaves and free Negroes to have the benefit of separate religious instruction, the prevailing practice was to include the free Negro as well as the slave in the religious activities of the whites. This was achieved either by creating an exclusive section in which Negroes sat at the regular services or by providing them with special services at the end of the regular ones.[18]

An interesting facet of Negro life in ante-bellum North Carolina was the position and role of the free Negroes. The free Negroes in North Carolina, unlike those of other southern states, were not characteristically an urban group. According to Franklin, they, like most

13. Rosser H. Taylor, *Slaveholding in North Carolina: An Economic View* (James Sprunt Historical Publications; University of North Carolina Press: Chapel Hill, 1926), pp. 35-36.

14. *Ibid.*

15. Franklin, *Free Negro*, pp. 165-66.

16. Carter G. Woodson, *Education of the Negro* (Associated Publishers, n.d.), p. 46.

17. W. S. Jenkins, *Pro-Slavery Thought in the Old South* (Chapel Hill: University of North Carolina Press, 1936), p. 207.

18. Franklin, *Free Negro*, p. 174.

other North Carolinians, were rural, and, therefore, agricultural.[19]

Despite the fact that most of the Negroes of the state were slaves even in the colonial period, there were some "free persons of color," as they were designated, as early as 1700, if not earlier.[20] And although their number had increased considerably by 1800, generally they were an unwanted class. As the colonial period came to an end, more and more restrictions were imposed on their freedom. Many slaveholders felt that the presence of the free Negroes exercised an unfavorable influence on the slaves. Indeed, John Taylor wished to impose a kind of apartheid between the free Negroes and slaves and to require those slaves receiving freedom by manumission to quit the state immediately.[21]

As a group in the society of ante-bellum North Carolina, the free Negroes were circumscribed by a number of laws and practices that operated to their disadvantage and discomfort. Notwithstanding the fact that they were, as Franklin states, "within physical proximity" to the socio-economic and political transformations taking place, they were severely hampered in their efforts to participate in those transformations.[22] A case in point is the exercise of the ballot. Between 1776 and 1835 there was no legal disfranchisement of free Negroes. Dissatisfaction of many white citizens with free Negro voting, however, was a contributing factor in the call for a constitutional convention in 1835, and also a factor in that convention's decision by a narrow margin to abrogate the suffrage rights of the free Negro.[23]

The passage of the Thirteenth Amendment in December, 1865, signaled not only the freedom of all former slaves but also their possible re-emergence as participants in North Carolina politics. The freedmen, however, were compelled to wait until the passage of the Reconstruction Act of Congress in the spring of 1867 before being admitted to the electorate. In that year, North Carolina, with South Carolina, made up the Second Military District, and in November, 1867, General Edward Canby, the commander of the district, ordered an election of delegates to a convention that was to write a new constitution for the state. For the first time since 1835, Negroes were granted the right to register as voters. Some 73,000 registered and

---

19. *Ibid.*, pp. 6-7.
20. Lefler, *History of N.C.*, I, 133.
21. Cathey, *Agricultural Development*, p. 61.
22. Franklin, *Free Negro*, p. 163.
23. *Ibid.*, pp. 108-13.

were instrumental in electing 107 Republicans, 15 of whom were Negroes, to the Constitutional Convention of January 14, 1868.[24]

This convention, in the course of fifty-five days of deliberation, wrote a constitution that was to stand for a scant eight years although portions of it are still included in the constitution of the state. Despite the fact that the convention was elected on the basis of biracial suffrage, it did not concede readily to the congressional requirement of universal manhood suffrage, white and Negro. The thirteen Conservative (Democratic) delegates objected, without much success, to the enfranchisement article. This was, perhaps, the convention's most radical innovation. Some of the other significant changes were the elimination of all property and religious qualifications for voting and office holding, except the disbarment of atheists from public office; and the authorization of a system of public schools with tuition free to the children of the state between six and twenty-one years of age.

Changes were also made in the machinery of government. Popular election was made mandatory for all state and county officials, judicial as well as executive. The county court system was abolished, and the township-county commission form of local government was adopted. A present-day state historian has described the constitution objectively. "Many of the changes," writes Hugh T. Lefler, "were modern, progressive, liberal, and democratic."[25]

In April, 1868, in an election that was also marked by the election of a Republican governor and legislature, the constitution, including the universal manhood suffrage clause, was ratified by popular vote of 93,084 for and 74,015 against. The Constitution of 1868 was shortly thereafter approved by Congress, and North Carolina's senators and representatives, all Republicans except one, took their seats in Washington. The new state legislature met in Raleigh on July 1, 1868, and on July 2 ratified the Fourteenth Amendment. General Canby followed this action by a declaration ending military rule. Civil government under Republican auspices had come to North Carolina.

Republican dominance, however, was to have a comparatively short life in North Carolina. In 1870 that party lost control of both houses of the state legislature. By 1874 the Republicans had become so reduced in strength that they failed to defeat a bill calling for a constitutional convention to be held the following year. The avowed aim of the Democrats in calling the convention was to alter the Con-

24. William A. Mabry, "The Negro in North Carolina Politics Since Reconstruction," *Trinity College Historical Society Papers*, XIII (1940), 12.
25. Lefler, *Hist. of N.C.*, I, 554.

stitution of 1868. Therefore, in the campaign for members both parties waged a determined and at times a virulent canvass. The election, held in August, 1875, was won narrowly by the Democrats. As a consequence, it became evident after the opening session on September 6 that there would be no general overhauling of the Constitution of 1868. Of the thirty amendments adopted, only three directly affected the participation of Negroes in the political life of the state. The first authorized the General Assembly to elect and to control the justices of the peace. The second provided that persons desiring to vote must reside in a county ninety days. This particular amendment also stipulated that any person convicted of a felony would be disfranchised. Perhaps the most far-reaching was the third amendment, which granted to the General Assembly the power "to modify, change, or abrogate county government." As I shall point out in subsequent chapters, the Constitutional Convention of 1875, incidentally, provided all future legislative assemblies with a powerful weapon in their effort to control the Negro vote.

It does not lie within the scope of this study to detail the role the Negro played in the Reconstruction period. Some brief comments on the period, however, are necessary for the narrative that is to follow. The most obvious fact is that at no time before 1876 was there Negro rule in North Carolina. At no time did the number of Negro voters approximate the number of white voters, nor did Negro officeholders occupy the highest elective offices in the state. Notwithstanding the fact that each session of the legislature between 1868 and 1876 included Negro members, never were they in a majority as they were for six years in the lower house of the South Carolina legislature.

Unfortunately, pointing out the deficiencies of the Republican rule in North Carolina between 1868 and 1876 has been a habit of most partisan historians. Its accomplishments, on the other hand, are slow to be recognized. It supervised, for example, the legal transformation of the Negroes from freedmen to first-class citizens; it established the right of all citizens to attend public schools at state expense, and it established the principle of the equality of all men before the law. One somewhat partisan historian begrudgingly admitted that the 1868 constitution "was considerably more democratic than the one it replaced and in many ways was a sound document."[26]

Republican rule in North Carolina, according to many historians, ended in the aftermath of the election of 1876. In reality, however, the state did not become solidly Democratic until 1879, when the

26. Mabry, "Negro in N.C. Politics," *Trinity College Papers,* p. 10.

Democrats captured the judiciary. Nonetheless, 1876 is recognized in North Carolina as the date of resumption of "home rule."

The campaign that brought this about has been described by North Carolina historians as the greatest political battle in the history of the state.[27] The Democratic gubernatorial nominee, Zebulon B. Vance, set the tone of the Democrats' campaign when he characterized the Republican party as "begotten by a scalawag out of a mulatto and born in an outhouse."[28] Democrats, with telling effect, continually harped on the "Negro-dominates-the-Republican-party" theme throughout the months of the torrid campaign. Despite a strong canvass by the Republican nominee for governor, Thomas Settle, the Republicans could not overcome the charge of Negro domination. The voters gave Vance a majority of approximately thirteen thousand.[29] All the constitutional amendments were ratified, and the incoming state legislature was assured a Democratic majority. White supremacy had come to North Carolina, but not to the heavily Negro populated counties of the East. The task of freeing this area from "Negro rule," however, had been assigned to the legislature by the Constitutional Convention of 1875. As we have noted, the ratification of the amendments proposed by that convention provided all future legislative assemblies with the weapons necessary to render less potent Negro political activity in eastern North Carolina. How well the legislatures made use of these weapons will be examined in some detail in the next several chapters.

27. See J. G. de R. Hamilton, *North Carolina Since 1860* (*History of North Carolina*, Vol. III [Chicago, 1919]), p. 189, 190; R. D. W. Connor, *North Carolina: Rebuilding an Ancient Commonwealth* (Chicago, 1929), I, 350; *History of North Carolina*, ed. S. A. Ashe (Raleigh, 1925), II, 1179.

28. Robert W. Winston, *It's a Far Cry* (New York, 1937), p. 84. See also Wilmington *Morning Star*, July 17, 1876.

29. See Wilmington *Morning Star*, November 11, 1876; Raleigh *News and Observer*, November 28, 1880.

Part One

Politics

2

"The Great Political
Parties of This State"

*. . . the . . . great political parties of this State [have]
declared in their respective platforms and otherwise
that they believe in maintaining and securing forever
the political rights, the educational rights, and all
other rights . . . belonging to the colored people of
this union.*

From William H. Moore's "Resolution in Favor
of the Working People" (1876).

In North Carolina, there existed throughout the
period a native white mountain and Piedmont element that allied
itself politically with the Negroes in the eastern counties. As a consequence, the Republican party in the state cannot be characterized as
"the Negro party." Leaders in that party came from both groups.
White citizens such as Oliver Dockery, of Richmond County; Daniel
L. Russell, of New Hanover County; and Jeter C. Pritchard, of Madi-
son County, joined forces with such Negro Republicans as James H.
Harris, of Wake County; James E. O'Hara, of Halifax County;
Henry P. Cheatham, of Vance County; and George H. White, of
Edgecombe County.

One historian has shown most conclusively the role geography
has played in the development of the Republican party in North
Carolina. Ten solidly Republican counties in the western third com-

bined with sixteen in the center and east and with forty-seven frequently Republican counties scattered throughout the state to establish
the Republican party in North Carolina as a solid competitor.[1]

Despite a small number of Negro Democrats, many of them
temporary converts, the politically conscious Negroes were inclined
to remain loyal to the Republican party. They did this for several
reasons. In the first place, the Republican party had been instrumental in removing the chains of slavery and extending the franchise
to the ex-slaves; in the second place, it had been directly responsible
for organizing them into a potent political force in the state. Nonetheless, the relationship between white and Negro Republicans was
not always amicable. The disturbing factor, the color line, was usually
drawn by white Republicans, and the Negro Republicans reacted to it
with extreme vehemence and bitterness. The frequent refusal of
white Republicans to support Negro office-seekers, for example, led to
acrid and lengthy factional conflict that considerably weakened the
party in its battles with a reasonably unified Democratic party. A
white Republican told a Northern white man who was visiting the
state that he favored voting for Negroes but that he was strongly
against their demands for holding office. "I will not vote to make a
Negro my ruler," he declared with feeling; "I am a Republican, but I
was a white man before I was a Republican."[2] Little wonder that a
white Democrat in the town of Littleton could prophesy on the eve of
the 1890 congressional elections: "None of the white Republicans
[here] will vote for [the Negro candidate Henry] Cheatham."[3]

Although it was the general practice of white Republicans to
award the more important appointive federal offices to white Republicans, some members of this group even went as far as to express
opposition to the selection of Negro postmasters. A white Republican,
in urging the retention of a Democratic postmaster of Hamilton, in
Martin County, wrote Senator Matt W. Ransom that while they
differed in politics, he was convinced that there was not a single
Negro Republican in the county "fit for a postmaster."[4] The appointment of a Negro postmaster at Fayetteville in 1891 was received
with much rejoicing by the Negroes of the state. However, there were

1. Helen Edmonds, *The Negro and Fusion Politics in North Carolina, 1895-1901*
(Chapel Hill, 1951).
2. Frank Hitch to Matt W. Ransom, March 18, 1889. Matt W. Ransom Papers,
University of North Carolina Library, Chapel Hill.
3. John E. Woodward to Matt W. Ransom, April 14, 1889. Matt W. Ransom
Papers, University of North Carolina Library, Chapel Hill.
4. Charles N. Hunter to Oliver Hunter, March 26, 1881. Charles N. Hunter
Papers, Duke University Library, Durham.

"a few white men calling themselves Republicans who gritted their teeth in madness," noted a Negro newspaper of Raleigh.[5]

Another issue resulting in widespread friction between the two groups was the opposition of some white Republicans to the employment of Negro speakers by the Executive Committee of the state Republican party during political campaigns. R. Beverly Frayser argued that such a course would greatly harm the party's chances of victory. Not only would it be futile to send out Negro canvassers with the expectation of making additions to the party, but, he added, "I do not believe that a white man in the South can be gained by that mode of electioneering, while thousands would be lost, and it would beget a supineness and indifference with those who are true White Republicans."[6]

Indeed, many white Republicans were made unhappy by the "over-presence" of Negroes in the state conventions of that party. One such party affiliate from the western part of North Carolina, after attending the Republican State Convention in 1888, withdrew from the party. He gave as his reason the fact that Negroes were too much in evidence. Two Negroes acted as secretaries; a Negro during a portion of the meeting acted as presiding officer. Two of the four delegates to the National Republican Convention in Chicago were Negroes. "Altogether, there was too much Negro in the convention to suit me," he concluded, "and although I have been a Republican, I am a white man and believe in white men ruling North Carolina."[7] The prominent presence of the Negro at party gatherings undoubtedly incensed many white Republicans, but political expediency caused them to tolerate the Negro members.

White Republicans, in some instances, successfully opposed Negro Republicans who sought elective positions. A recital of two cases will suffice. Elected to the national House of Representatives in 1874 from the second Congressional District, John A. Hyman sought re-election in 1876. However, the Republican convention, meeting in Goldsboro, failed to nominate him. Instead, that gathering selected a white Republican. The rejection of Hyman was used effectively against the Republicans by the Democratic press. The Warrenton *Gazette,* in mock sympathy, stated,

5. Raleigh *Gazette,* October 17, 1891.
6. R. Beverly Frayser to Daniel Russell, July 5, 1882. Daniel L. Russell Papers, University of North Carolina Library, Chapel Hill.
7. "A Disgruntled Republican," North Carolina State Democratic Executive Committee pamphlet (1888), University of North Carolina Library, Chapel Hill.

The Negro has been treated badly by his white allies. . . . In a word, they have been made tools of by a few white men who joined their party to get votes. Eighty thousand colored voters and seventeen thousand white radicals over the State and yet not a single colored man on the State ticket!! Now every intelligent colored man knows this is true. They have been treated shamefully, badly, and if they had that self-respect that every free man ought to possess, they would quit the men who have so insulted and abused them.[8]

The Warrenton paper reported in a subsequent editorial that Hyman was defeated at Goldsboro because several prominent white Republicans "publicly avowed that if a Negro were nominated, it would hurt the State ticket." Indeed, one white Republican was quoted as saying that the $5,000 congressional salary was entirely too much for a "kinky head."[9]

Ever alert to opportunities to spread greater disunity within the Republican ranks, the editor of the Wilson *Advance,* in a letter to Ransom on the rebuff of Hyman at the Goldsboro convention, suggested that the Democrats could "make something for our side" in the Second District. He proposed to circulate among the Negro voters the idea that the gathering at Goldsboro was run by white office-seekers.[10]

The defeat of Stewart Ellison for the state legislature in Wake County caused "universal" dissatisfaction among the colored voters of that county. "Their denunciation of the men who planned and effected his overthrow is ominous of future evil to the unity of the Republican party in the metropolitan county of the State," warned a Negro paper of Raleigh. "There is no use in disguising the fact," it continued heatedly, "the Negro voters of Wake County have been sold out by some of their pretended white friends."[11]

The continued failure of Republicans to name Negroes to state tickets led the Negroes of Wilson County in 1882 to demand their inclusion. Since they constituted the Republican party of the county, and since they had men among them as capable of holding office as their white countrymen, the Negroes refused to vote unless a Negro was placed on the county ticket.[12] A similar demand was made by the Negroes in Nash County.[13]

8. Warrenton *Gazette*, July 28, 1876; see also *ibid.*, May 9, 1884.
9. *Ibid.*, August 4, 1876.
10. H. Williams to Matt W. Ransom, July 28, 1876. Ransom Papers.
11. Raleigh *North Carolina Republican*, November 12, 1880.
12. Wilson *Advance*, September 8, 1882.
13. Fayetteville *Examiner*, July 27, 1882.

E. H. Sutton, of the First Congressional District, sought the Republican nomination for Congress, but he was turned down for a white man. Sutton, obviously angry and disappointed, is reported to have said: "What have they [the Republican party] ever given us [Negroes]? We who number 13,000 voters in this district to *their* 1,400? We are nearly ten to their one, and yet for nearly twenty years we have been voting solidly for white men for Congress, and when a Negro asks to be allowed one chance in twenty, he is denounced, brow-beaten, bull-dozed, and told he is too fresh!"[14]

The Negroes of the Fifth Congressional District, frustrated and disappointed by the refusal of white Republicans to support the nomination of Negroes for office, decided in 1890 to nominate a man of their own race to Congress. C. L. Davis, who was nominated, was a school principal in Greensboro and was described by one of the local white papers of that city as a man of intelligence and considerable ability.[15]

The feeling on the part of the Negroes that they were being denied the right to share in the offices resulted in their calling a state-wide colored convention in Raleigh in 1890. The expressed purpose of this gathering was to demand more federal offices for Negroes. Pointing with a great deal of satisfaction to the convention as a sign of disunity in the Republican ranks, the *News and Observer* stated editorially that "all work and no office is not satisfactory to the darkeys, who are no longer so manageable as they were."[16]

In spite of these objections and the efforts of the white Democrats to exploit them, even to the point of urging the Negroes to join the the Democratic party, most Negroes remained in the Republican party. Perhaps the classic answer to the white man's plea that the Negro join the Democratic party and "let them damn yankees alone" was given by Robert Hill, an ex-slave, in January, 1881. "Take away all the laws in our favor that 'them damn Yankees' have made," noted Hill, "and what would be left?"[17] Charles Price, district attorney of the western district of North Carolina, was quoted as saying that the basis of the Democratic party was prejudice against the Negro. "It is

14. Wilson *Advance,* November 16, 1883. The First Congressional District in 1883 comprised Beaufort, Camden, Chowan, Carteret, Currituck, Dare, Gates, Hertford, Hyde, Martin, Pamlico, Pasquotank, Pitt, Tyrrell, and Washington counties.

15. *Ibid.,* April 10, 1890.

16. Raleigh *News and Observer,* August 31, 1890.

17. Helen M. Chestnutt, *Charles Waddell Chestnutt* (Chapel Hill: University of North Carolina Press, 1952), p. 27.

therefore impossible," he concluded, "for the Negro to be anything but a Republican. . . ."[18]

Statistics, unfortunately, are sketchy on the number of Negro Republicans. Estimates were made by the supporters of each party. The Negro editor of the *North Carolina Republican,* James H. Harris, noted in 1880 that there were 90,000 colored voters.[19]   In the same year, the Democratic *News and Observer* declared that there were 105,018 Negro voters.[20]   In 1882 another Democratic paper, the Wilson *Advance,* also listed the Negro voting strength as 105,000.[21]   One of the chief Negro newspapers stated in 1896 that in 1890 there had been 109,000 colored voters in the state.[22]   One of the leading Democratic representatives, Thomas J. Jarvis, stated in 1896 that the Republican party was "composed of about 100,000 Negro voters and about 10,000 white voters who want office."[23]   From these conflicting figures it is apparent that any effort to determine the approximate number of Negro voters is nearly impossible.

Likewise, estimates of the number of Negro Republican voters in particular counties and cities of the state are useful though not conclusive.   In Guilford County in 1871 the Republican party was composed of 1,191 Negroes and "less than 500 bonafide white voters."[24] In Wilmington in 1881 there were 1,604 registered Negro voters to 1,246 white registered voters.[25]   According to a Democratic leader in Littleton, the town was evenly divided between white and Negro voters, 112 each.   "We have 2 or 3 white Republicans," he said, "and 1 or 2 colored Democrats which makes us about even."[26]   It becomes quite obvious that no precise number of Negro voters can be assigned. It is true, on the other hand, that the Negro did form a sizable segment of the Republican party and that his affiliation with that party did provide grist for the Democratic propaganda mill.

The prominent presence of numerous Negroes at Republican party gatherings provided much ammunition for the Democratic charge that the Republican party was Negro dominated.   The Democratic

18. Raleigh *News and Observer,* August 29, 1890.
19. Raleigh *North Carolina Republican,* November 12, 1880.
20. Raleigh *News and Observer,* August 26, 1883.
21. Wilson *Advance,* September 8, 1882.
22. Raleigh *Gazette,* October 31, 1896.
23. Thomas J. Jarvis to Edward Chambers Smith, April 13, 1896.   Edward Chambers Smith Papers, Duke University Library, Durham.
24. Greensboro *Patriot,* August 18, 1871.
25. Wilmington *Daily Review,* March 24, 1881.
26. M. E. Newsome to Marmaduke J. Hawkins, October 27, 1890. Marmaduke J. Hawkins Collection, State Department of Archives and History, Raleigh.

press never failed to emphasize the seemingly dominant role the Negro played at the state Republican conventions. At the 1888 convention, for example, not only did the Democratic *State Chronicle* talk about "big black buck Negroes in long dusters and beavers drinking mean liquor and smoking bad cigars," but it also noted that ten of the fourteen "chief managers" of the body were Negroes.[27] At the Republican state convention of 1890, the *News and Observer* placed emphasis upon the selection of a Negro, E. E. Smith, as temporary chairman and upon the predominance of Negroes in all activities of the meeting.[28]

Thus the Democrats were quick to realize the political harvest that might be theirs by convincing the white voters that the Republican party was a "Negro party." Cries such as "And what results would follow our defeat, . . . Negro magistrates and Negro constables!"[29] were sufficient to convince the average white voter that his best interests lay with the Democrats. Indeed, the repeated use of the "Negro domination" theme in the political campaigns of the state led one Republican to ejaculate with much disgust, "Nigger, nigger, nigger is its [the Democratic party's] only cry."[30]

Although leaders of both parties were well aware that the fear of Negro domination, within and without the Republican party, was but a scarecrow, a ruse, a political trick to frighten the whites into voting the Democratic ticket,[31] it forced the Republicans to consider the wisdom of nominating state tickets in some election years. J. J. Mott, a prominent Republican leader, for example, opposed a Republican state ticket in 1892 on the grounds that the Democrats would capitalize on the idea of Negro domination. He said the Negro was more "prominent" than the whites in the Republican state convention of that year. It would, therefore, be just what the Democrats wanted because they could then point to the large Negro element in the convention and present the Republicans "as traitors to our race, aliens, an infamous, degraded set trying to put the state under Negro rule." Daniel L. Russell had voiced a similar opinion on the eve of the 1888 campaign.[32]

27. Raleigh *State Chronicle*, May 23, 1888.
28. Raleigh *News and Observer*, August 28, 1890.
29. *Ibid.*, October 13, 1892; October 18, 1890.
30. Robert W. Winston, *It's a Far Cry* (New York: Henry Holt and Co., 1937), p. 57.
31. See, for example, the Winston *Union Republican*, August 14, 1890; Greensboro *North Carolinian*, August 17, 1892; Greensboro *North State*, February 9, 1888.
32. Theron P. Jones, "The Gubernatorial Election of 1892 in North Carolina" (Unpublished master's thesis, University of North Carolina, 1949), p. 50, quoting the Winston *Union Republican*, July 28, 1892. See also Rosalie F. McNeill, "The

The ever present specter of a Republican victory in each election campaign caused the Democrats to raise the cry of a white man's government. Although public utterances tended to be somewhat contemptuous of the Republicans, many Democratic leaders privately professed great fear of the outcome of the elections. In the campaign preceding the election of 1888, for example, a Democratic leader wrote Senator Matt W. Ransom that "the present aspect is alarming. . . . A great deal of work must be done in the Negro counties in Eastern N.C."[33] In the same campaign another Democratic leader warned that North Carolina was not in a "satisfactory condition."[34]

In order to cope with Republican ascendancy and the threat that party posed to its supremacy, the Democratic party resorted to many "saving" devices. One such method was the purchase of Negro votes. "Am buying Negro votes," candidly wrote a Democratic worker in Montgomery County in 1888, "and using all our efforts to give at least one-hundred majority."[35] In Fayetteville in the same year, Democratic success was threatened by a combination of Democrats and Republicans called the Union Labor Party. "To meet this unexpected opposition, we must of necessity draw from the colored vote," warned Thomas H. Sutton, "and we cannot do this without spending money among them."[36]

Sutton spared no efforts to bring home to Democratic leaders the seriousness of the political situation in Fayetteville in 1888. In a letter to Senator Ransom, he suggested that only the purchase of Negro votes could save the Democrats from defeat.

My heart is in the cause of Democratic success, and I will do, and dare anything to accomplish it. . . . Now to be plain, we must spend money among the colored people. We must get votes from them to counteract and off-set votes we will certainly lose from other sources that we have heretofore been getting. To do this we must have money to spend among them, right here and as soon as possible. Don't stand on technicalities by sending it through devious channels, but send it to me and I will turn it over to our treasurer who will send you his receipt and account for every cent.[37]

First Fifteen Months of Governor Daniel Lindsey Russell's Administration" (Unpublished master's thesis, University of North Carolina, 1939), p. 121.

33. F. H. Busbee to Matt W. Ransom, September 12, 1888. Ransom Papers.

34. Thomas H. Sutton to Matt Ransom, September 15, 19, 1888. Ransom Papers. See also T. C. Davis to Ransom, September 20, 1888. Ransom Papers.

35. J. A. McAvery to Matt Ransom, July 3, 1888. Ransom Papers.

36. Thomas H. Sutton to Calvin S. Bruce, October 3, 1888. Ransom Papers.

37. Thomas H. Sutton to Ransom, October 4, 1888. Ransom Papers.

In analyzing the chances of a Democratic victory in 1892, a Democrat from Salisbury observed soberly that only a "little money" among the Negroes would achieve the desired end and that "nothing else will do."[38]

In many instances Negroes became willing collaborators in such schemes. Negro leaders in at least two of the townships of Warren County in 1894 "volunteered to carry" them for the Democratic nominees for twenty-five dollars.[39]

Another method employed by the Democrats in a predominantly Negro Republican area was to encourage the entry of several Negroes for the same office. Usually, the Democrats could not hope to win a plurality of votes. Their only hope was to "divide and win." The election of a Register of Deeds for Warren County in 1894 is a case in point. J. G. Newsome, a white Democrat, sought unsuccessfully to put a second Negro against the Republican nominee, a Negro named Mansfield Thornton.[40] Following John A. Hyman's rejection by the Republicans in their 1876 Second Congressional District convention, the Democrats seriously considered urging the rejected Negro "to bolt and run" for Congress as an independent.[41]

Although the record does not reveal that the Democrats of North Carolina ever elected or named Negroes to public offices in the state, there are numerous examples of Negro participation in Democratic politics. In the 1876 campaign, Garland H. White, a Baptist minister, "stumped the state against Republicans." At a Democratic mass meeting in Wentworth on September 25, 1886, several Negroes were in attendance. The New Bern *Daily Journal* proudly informed its readers of "the colored teachers who voted with the Democrats in the election of 1886." A Negro minister of Durham, Andrew J. Chambers, offered his services to the Democrats in the 1892 campaign. "While it may not be judicious for me to go on the stump in this state owing to my color," he said, he was of the opinion that he could be most effective in Ohio where he had been reared, in Indiana where he had been married, in Connecticut where he had pastored a church, and in New York state where he had canvassed for William J. Tilden in 1876.[42]

38. F. B. Arendell to Matt Ransom, July 25, 1892. Ransom Papers.

39. Walter B. Faulcon to Marmaduke J. Hawkins, November 3, 1894. Marmaduke J. Hawkins Collection, State Department of Archives and History, Raleigh.

40. J. G. Newsome to Marmaduke J. Hawkins, September 21, 1894. Marmaduke J. Hawkins Collection, State Department of Archives and History, Raleigh.

41. H. Williams to Matt Ransom, July 28, 1876. Ransom Papers.

42. Warrenton *Gazette,* July 14, 1876; R. J. Lewllyn to Alfred M. Scales, September 25, 1886. Governors' Papers, State Department of Archives and History, Raleigh.

Showing little of the party loyalty of Negro Republicans, many
Negroes joined the Democratic party merely to procure a job or to
attempt to gain favor with the white community. Garland H. White,
for example, was successful, not only in serving his own economic
interests by supporting the Democratic party but also in securing
menial jobs in Washington for other Negroes who supported that
party. "The best thing for the colored people to do," he wrote Senator
Ransom in 1894, "is to unite with the governing class of white people
of this section which are Democrats whom we have to depend upon
in every emergency." He assured Ransom that this theme would be
vigorously advanced as he campaigned before the Negroes of North
Carolina.[43]

Negro Democrats were usually referred to by white Democrats
as "very intelligent and conservative," but were generally regarded by
Negro Republicans as "poisonous rattle-snakes or copper-heads
crawling about trying to bite or poison the minds of their Republican
sentiments."[44]

Frequently, Negro Democrats were socially ostracized or physically
threatened by other Negroes. A Negro in Warrenton was expelled
from his church because he would not apologize for voting the
Democratic ticket. Henry Mumford, a Negro butcher of Wilmington,
was threatened by a crowd of Negro Republicans for voting with the
Democrats. The police probably saved him from bodily harm. In
New Bern in the 1886 state elections, Negro Republicans snatched
tickets from Negroes who attempted to vote for the Democratic
party. Indeed, it was reported that threats were made that if they
voted Democratic, they could not continue to live in that community.
In Goldsboro during the 1892 election a Negro, Owen W. Parrott,
who had been instrumental in persuading Negroes "who never voted
the Democratic ticket before to go up openly and do so," was threatened by a mob of other Negroes.[45]

In most, if not all, of the elections held in North Carolina between
1876 and 1894, Negroes who voted with Democrats were subjected
to ostracism by their own race. They were jeered and hooted at

See also New Bern *Daily Journal*, January 6, 1887; Andrew J. Chambers to Matt
Ransom, August 2, 1892. Ransom Papers.

43. Garland H. White to Matt Ransom, April 11, 1892. Ransom Papers.

44. Raleigh *Republican*, November 30, 1867.

45. Warrenton *Gazette*, November 17, 1876; New Bern *Daily Journal*, November 6,
1876; Wilmington *Star*, November 14, 1884; Owen W. Parrott to M. Burrett, October
4, 1893. Ransom Papers. See also W. C. Fields to Matt Ransom, October 22, 1893.
Ransom Papers.

when casting their ballots and were isolated in their social and religious life.

Not only did Negro Republicans criticize Negro Democrats but many white Democrats did not favor Negro adherents. The words of a Henderson Democratic leader indicate the trend in white thinking toward Negro Democrats in the late eighties and early nineties: ". . . it is fast assuming shape that no Negro is to be allowed to vote the Democratic ticket. We cannot prevent him putting it in the ballot box, and having it counted with the rest, but he cannot expect to receive any recognition for it."[46]

The emergence of the Populist party in North Carolina in the late eighties and the resultant defection of large numbers of Democratic voters presented a serious challenge to the continued supremacy of the Democratic party in state politics. Basically rural, the movement was a protest against governmental indifference to the interest and welfare of the farmers. By the early nineties the Democrats of the state were greatly concerned about the role the new party was to play in state politics. Especially did they deplore any suggestion that the Populists would ally themselves with the Republicans. The Democratic press, especially the *News and Observer,* throughout the 1890 and 1892 campaigns, in an effort to counter such thoughts, continuously announced the theme, "the white people of the state must stand close together in this day and hour." Openly appealing to the white farmer's fear of Negro domination, the press argued for Democratic unity. Editorializing in this vein, the Greensboro *Daily Record* noted that "in the face of the overshadowing . . . danger of Negro domination, the [state] cannot afford to fall apart or divide. Nobody knows this better than the farmers. They have had, and they are having their little third party recreation; . . . but when the proper time arrives, they will promptly fall into line and renew and strengthen the organization which stands for white supremacy."[47] Prominent Democratic leaders such as Zebulon Vance and William H. Kitchin also pleaded for "harmony and united action among the white people during the crisis."[48]

That the threat of a third party or "Fusionist" victory was a real one can be seen in the correspondence of Democratic leaders during the 1892 campaign. From all sections of the state, letters poured into the office of Senator Matt Ransom emphasizing the fact that the

46. O. R. Smith to Matt Ransom, October 14, 1893. Ransom Papers.
47. Greensboro *Daily Record,* August 19, 1892. See the Raleigh *News and Observer,* July 10, September 10, 13, 1890.
48. See Raleigh *News and Observer,* September 21, 1890.

political situation was "about as bad as it can be and is getting no better."[49]

In desperation, the Democrats resorted to any and all devices that might bring them victory, including the cultivation of Negro voters. The importance of securing Negro votes, as well as other Democratic campaign strategy, is revealed in the following letter a Democratic leader sent to Senator Ransom in September, 1890:

> I feel so much concern about the election that I may be excused for a little suggestion. . . . Our sole reliance now to win with votes, is in Republican defection and we must be prepared to use all there is in that. Go on with your real or seeming confidence, but don't forget to impress trusty men with the gravity of affairs and try in some way to get it to be discreetly understood that every ironclad Democrat must vote *one* Negro through. It is entirely a matter of practical detail and thousands of votes can be had in this way. . . . Republican defection leaders will make Negro indifference, and we can by patience and due cultivation make many voters on this line and we must have them. It ought to be worked so as not to call too much attention to it.[50]

Another Democratic leader was not as pessimistic of a Democratic defeat and expressed the conviction that the Negro, aware that the Populist party in North Carolina was composed of a class of whites that historically had been hostile to him, would not support the new party. He predicted, therefore, that the colored vote in the state would support the Democratic party in preference to a combination of Republicans and Populists.[51]

These sanguine hopes were not to be realized. Democratic supremacy in North Carolina was brought to an end in 1894 by the Fusionists, or as the Democrats of the state described them, a "hybrid party made up of old well-cured, well-soaked Republicans, raw Democrats and sour Negroes." Indeed, when a Fusionist leader, in announcing the overthrow of the Democratic party, "planted himself in the midst of his black followers," a new era in North Carolina history was launched.[52] The Republican party, then, came into power in North Carolina as a consequence of fusion with an organized group of dissatisfied whites. The fateful, frightful aftereffects of that marriage are detailed in Dr. Helen Edmond's very fine study.[53]

49. F. M. Simmons to Matt Ransom, July 23, 1892. Ransom Papers. See also M. H. Pennix to Ransom, July 18, 1892; J. A. Ashe to Ransom, July 17, 1892; and John A. Barringer to Ransom, July 18, 1892. *Ibid*.

50. James A. Lockhart to Matt Ransom, September 28, 1892. Ransom Papers.

51. E. D. Hall to Matt Ransom, February 2, 1894. Ransom Papers.

52. Raleigh *News and Observer,* October 21, November 8, 1894.

53. Edmonds, *Fusion Politics.* Full citation for this study is given earlier in this chapter.

3

"Respect the Rights of My People"

God speed the day when Carolina shall be free from . . . Negro haters. . . . I have never spoken in this chamber unless aroused by flings at the Negro race. The sooner the whites of this state learn to respect the rights of my people, then will come the joyful day for us all.

From speech of Henry Eppes before the Senate of North Carolina, 1887.

Although the Republican party was the minority party in the state, Negro Republicans held local and legislative positions in at least seventeen counties of eastern North Carolina during the period. Unlike the skimpy representation of Negroes from North Carolina in the United States Congress, the General Assembly of the state was more generously sprinkled with members of this group. In an overview of the legislative careers of these Negro members, several factors merit attention. First, many of them had college or normal school training; a still larger number possessed a public school education; and the few who had no formal schooling had become educated to the extent that they were fairly literate. Second, as a consequence of their educational background, there was a generous proportion of teachers, preachers, and lawyers among them. Third, with few exceptions, they had enjoyed long years of public service prior to their election to the General Assembly. Fourth, the Negro members were almost without influence in legislatures dominated by white Democrats, but they were allowed the customary privileges of a minority, including service on several important committees. Fifth, in purely local legislative proposals dealing with their own counties or districts, they were able to see many, with the support of the white members of both parties, enacted into law. Sixth, the Negro members were generally inactive participants in legislative proposals and debates except on matters affecting the race, such as legislation designed to improve and expand the educational facilities available to the Negroes of North Carolina, registrations, election and county government laws, laws dealing with convict labor, and labor contracts.

Although the Negroes of the state were elated to see members of their race in both houses of the state legislature, they were especially proud of the fifteen who served in the upper house during the period under consideration. For similar to membership in the United States Congress, membership in the state Senate carries with it greater prestige, affluence, and stature than does membership in the House. That a majority of the Negro electorate and a minority of the white electorate made this colored representation in the North Carolina Senate possible may be seen from an examination of the senatorial districts from which these representatives came. With few exceptions, the "blacker" the district, the more frequent its colored representation in the Senate. Thus the Third (Bertie and Northampton), the Fourth (Halifax), the Fifth (Edgecombe), the Eighth (Craven), the Twelfth (New Hanover), the Nineteenth (Warren), and the Twenty-first (Granville) districts were responsible for *all* the Negroes who served in the North Carolina Senate between 1876 and 1894.

Among the prominent Negro legislators elected to the state Senate was William P. Mabson of the Fifth Senatorial District of Edgecombe County. Mabson was educated at Lincoln University, Chester County, Pennsylvania. In addition to his service in the 1876-1877 Senate, he had served one previous term in that body (1874), and one in the House (1872); he was also a member of the Constitutional Convention of 1875. A former school teacher, Mabson was considered the leader of the Republican party in Edgecombe County. That both parties respected his ability is attested by his being selected to serve on the important Proposition and Grievance Committee.[1]

1. Tarboro *Southerner*, December 1, 1876; R. A. Shotwell and Natt Atkinson, *Legislative Record, Sketches of the Lives of the Members, 1877* (Raleigh, 1877), p. 9; *Senate Journal, 1876-1877*, p. 26.

Another Negro state senator was George Allen Mebane, born in Bertie County of parents who were slaves. Mebane represented the Third Senatorial District of Bertie and Northampton for two terms, 1876-1877 and 1883. During the Civil War, Mebane managed to escape to the Union lines, where he attempted to enlist in Company A, of the 85th New York Regiment, under the command of one Lieutenant Strickland. Because he was only thirteen years old, Mebane was considered too young to be a soldier; but the regimental commander agreed to enlist him as a mess boy. In the latter part of 1864, Lieutenant Strickland sent Mebane to McKean County, Pennsylvania, where he attended public school. He remained there until 1871. Returning to his native county of Bertie during the early part of 1871, he adopted school teaching as his profession. Although urged to enter politics shortly after his return to the state, Mebane held out until 1876. In addition to the two terms he served in the state Senate, he was nominated (but later withdrew) as a candidate for the United States Congress in the Second Congressional District in 1888.[2]

Henry Eppes of Halifax was a native of his county. He "never went to school any of his life," but through self-help and study secured a fair education. He was a minister of the Methodist church, as well as a brick-mason and plasterer. Eppes represented Halifax County in the Constitutional Convention of 1868 and was a member of the National Republican Convention that nominated Ulysses S. Grant for president in 1872. In all he served a total of sixteen years, or eight terms, in the Senate of North Carolina. He was described as "having the respect of all who knew him, white and colored, and especially that of his own race." He was considered "a faithful and careful representative and [one who] looks well to the interests of his constituency." Eppes was easily the most outstanding Negro in the senate during the period under survey. Certainly he was the dean of Negro senators in terms of senatorial tenure, experience, and legislative initiative and activities.[3]

George H. White was unquestionably the most brilliant Negro in

2. Shotwell and Atkinson, *Legislative Record,* p. 9; statements by Rev. John Mebane, son of George A. Mebane, personal interview, Tarboro, North Carolina, December 26, 1952; New Bern *Daily Journal,* May 31, September 23, 27, 1888; John Mebane to Charles N. Hunter, February 20, 1885. Charles N. Hunter Papers, Duke University Library, Durham.

3. J. S. Tomlinson, *Tar Heel Sketch Book: A Brief Biographical Sketch of the Members of the General Assembly, 1879* (Raleigh News Steam Book and Job Print, 1879), p. 9; *Legislative Biographical Sketch Book, 1887,* State Department of Archives and History, Raleigh, p. 4; statements by R. Faulkner Eppes, son of Henry Eppes, personal interview, Greenville, North Carolina, December 30, 1952.

public life during the period. A native of Bladen County, he attended normal school at Lumberton. Later, he enrolled and graduated from Howard University in 1877. He served as principal of a graded school, a parochial school, and the State Normal School for Negroes. His biographer states that "few men of his race have better education than he." White read law under Walter Clark, judge of the Superior Court, and later, judge and chief justice of the Supreme Court of North Carolina. White began practice in 1879. He was considered "successful in his profession." He served in the House in 1881, and as a member of the Senate of 1885 he worked "with the zeal and tenacity of a Charles Sumner." That his associates of both parties respected his presence in the Senate may be seen from his appointment to the Judiciary Committee. White was also elected as solicitor for the Second Judicial District of the state in 1886 as well as a member of the United States Congress in 1896.[4]

The overwhelming majority of the fifty-two Negroes elected to the lower house of the North Carolina legislature between 1876 and 1894 were sent there from counties that boasted a Negro population of 50 per cent and over. The single exception was Wake County. Here the Negro minority comprised approximately 48 per cent of the total population. As might be expected, the largest representation in the lower house came from the counties with large Negro concentrations, such as Edgecombe, Warren, New Hanover, and Caswell. Significantly, however, some of the "black counties" in eastern North Carolina contributed a surprisingly small number of Negro legislators. Conspicuous among this group were Halifax, Craven, and Northampton counties. Hertford and Richmond, each having a Negro population exceeding 55 per cent, sent no Negro representatives to the General Assembly.

Negro legislators in the lower house reached a peak number of fifteen after the election of 1887 and declined to three after the election of 1891. Several of them merit close examination.

John H. Williamson, elected from Franklin County in 1876, was born in Covington, Georgia, but came to Franklin when he was only thirteen years old. He had no educational advantages except what he acquired by his own efforts. He was a member of the Constitutional Convention of 1868 and had served several previous terms in the House. He was a delegate to the National Republican Convention at Philadelphia in 1872, as well as to the 1884 convention, which

4. *Peoples' Advocate* (New Bern), July 31, 1886; New Bern *Daily Journal,* June 20, 1886; Tomlinson, *Tar Heel Sketch Book,* 1885, p. 7.

nominated James G. Blaine. Williamson served as a justice of the peace in Louisburg and was editor of several newspapers. In 1876 he was elected to the legislature for the first of two terms during the period under study. Even his Democratic opponents labeled him as a natural speaker who "frequently makes a telling point. . . . He is naturally pleasant and affable in manner." A Republican newspaper of the state described him as "one of the recognized leaders" in the lower house, and his urbanity of manners and deportment "commanded the respect of the entire body of members, Democratic and Republicans. . . ."[5]

Stewart Ellison, elected from Wake County in 1879, never attended formal school, but was educated by attending night school. A carpenter by trade, he served as a Raleigh city alderman for eight years and as director of the penitentiary for four years. Although nominated by the Republicans of Wake County as a candidate for the House in 1876 after having served several previous terms in that body, Ellison declined by stating that it "was not the proper time for colored men to be put forward." However, he apparently considered the next session propitious, for he accepted the nomination and was elected. Ellison's biographer considered him "far above the average of his race as to intelligence. . . ."[6]

James H. Harris, "the black war-horse of Raleigh," was "Mr. Politician" among Negro public figures of the period. Generally considered the finest statesman of his color in North Carolina, he was born in Granville County and was self-educated. He was a member of the Constitutional Convention of 1868, and had served one previous term in the House and one in the senate before his election to the legislature in 1883. He had been a member of the Raleigh Board of Aldermen and the director for the Institution for the Deaf, Dumb and Blind for four years, as well as a United States deputy collector. Harris was recognized as "one of the leading members of the Republican party, and for the chances generally afforded colored men, he was well posted on political matters and a good speaker."[7]

In many of the county elections of eastern North Carolina, Negro voters exercised a significant influence. As noted in an earlier chapter, the 1877 legislature instituted a county government system that lasted

5. Shotwell and Atkinson, *Legislative Record*, p. 33; Tomlinson, *Tar Heel Sketch Book*, p. 28; Greensboro *Patriot*, February 14, 28, 1877; Raleigh *Signal*, February 3, March 10, 1887.

6. Tomlinson, *Tar Heel Sketch Book*, p. 123; Tarboro *Southerner*, September 22, 1876.

7. Tarboro *Southerner*, November 17, 1876; Raleigh *Register*, October 4, 1877.

for eighteen years. Justices of the peace, appointed by the General Assembly, were the most important county officers. Indeed, with two exceptions, the Register of Deeds and the Surveyor, all county officers were appointive.[8] Despite Democratic determination to restrict colored office holding on the county level as exemplified by the system of county government, Negro citizens in a number of eastern counties were given representation by that party in the local government.

Such action evoked severe criticism from white Democrats. The 1876-1877 General Assembly's selection of thirty Negro justices of the peace for some of the eastern counties, for example, resulted in strong protest from western as well as eastern Democrats. The comments of the editor of the Concord *Sun* are typical of the western attitude toward "this outrage."

In the matter of Magistrates, we consented to give up our much-loved right of electing Magistrates by the people, so that incompetent carpet-baggers and Negroes would have to stand aside and make way for those whose interests were with the people. But in numbers of Eastern Counties, Negroes were recommended to the Legislature for Magistrates and got their appointments, after howling for twelve years about being *under Negro* rule.[9]

A similiar feeling was expressed by several of the Democratic eastern newspapers. The editor of the Goldsboro *Messenger* indignantly declared in the spring of 1877: "The election . . . in some instances of Negro magistrates for some of the Eastern counties by the General Assembly . . . shows a gross disregard of the people's wishes. The impudent transaction is without parallel."[10] The Republican Raleigh *Register,* on the other hand, calmly remarked that "the election of competent colored men to be magistrates is nothing more or less than an act of simple justice."[11]

Despite these outcries by angry party members, local Democrats continued to recommend Negro justices of the peace until after 1887. The white clerk of the Superior Court in Tarboro, Bryan J. Keech, urged the appointment of N. B. Bellamy. On the other hand, he sought the rejection of another Negro, Frank L. Dancy, when he "learned something derogatory" about him.[12]

8. Helen Edmonds, *The Negro and Fusion Politics in North Carolina, 1895-1901* (Chapel Hill, 1951), p. 118.
9. Quoted in the Tarboro *Southerner,* March 30, 1877.
10. Quoted in the Raleigh *Register,* April 6, 1877.
11. Raleigh *Register,* April 10, 1877.
12. Keech to Governor Alfred M. Scales, May 12, 1887. Governors' Papers, State Department of Archives and History, Raleigh.

In local elections for registers of deeds in "Negro" counties, Negro candidates were generally successful. John C. Dancy held that post in Tarboro in 1882 and subsequently sought re-election. In support of his candidacy, the Republican Wilmington *Post* noted, "The Republicans of Edgecombe, white and colored, could not reflect more credit upon themselves than in re-nominating and re-electing Mr. Dancy, as he is a young man as capable, intellectually and morally, of filling his present position as any man in the state."[13] In 1891 James B. Dudley was serving as register of deeds for New Hanover County.[14] Thomas Eaton was elected register of deeds for Vance County in 1888 and served continuously in that capacity for ten years.[15]

Raleigh, New Bern, Wilmington, Warrenton, and Tarboro were among the cities of eastern North Carolina which elected Negroes as aldermen. In the municipal election held in Raleigh in the spring of 1887, for example, three of the seventeen successful aspirants were Negroes.[16] The records reveal that at least one Negro between 1876 and 1894 held the highest municipal office. In 1881, Franklin D. Dancy was elected mayor of Tarboro "to the surprise of everyone."[17] A blacksmith by trade, Dancy was considered "a fine specimen of his race in appearance."

Specific evidence as to the capabilities of the city and county Negro officeholders is not available. In the absence of harsh or desultory criticism in the Democratic newspapers, it is reasonably safe to assume that Negro officers were no better or worse than their white counterparts.

13. Wilmington *Post*, August 6, 1882; Wilson *Advance*, September 8, 1882.

14. See letter of protest from thirteen Republicans, February 9, 1891. Ransom Papers.

15. Edmonds, *Fusion Politics*, p. 122.

16. *State Chronicle* (Raleigh), May 5, 1887.

17. MSS in possession of Mrs. Lillian Reid, Salisbury, North Carolina.

4

"The Black Second"

> If the colored people in a [congressional] district
> where they have a 12,000 majority . . . have not
> manhood to send one of their own race to Congress
> they do not deserve the political sympathy of
> anybody.
>
> Hillsboro ORANGE COUNTY OBSERVER, August 19,
> 1882, quoting the Greensboro STATE.

It is a most significant political fact that the four
Negroes who represented North Carolina in the United States Congress were elected from the predominantly Negro-controlled Second
Congressional District of the state.[1] Described contemptuously by
eastern North Carolina Democrats as the "Black Second," the boun-
daries of the district remained almost unchanged between 1876 and
1894. A relatively minor modification occurred in 1883 when the
North Carolina General Assembly, through a legislative enactment of
that year, excluded Wayne and Jones counties and added the counties
of Bertie and Vance. Thus the Second Congressional District after
1883, in addition to the two cited above, comprised the counties of
Craven, Edgecombe, Greene, Halifax, Lenoir, Northampton, Warren,
and Wilson. In commenting on the changes brought by the law of
1883, a white New Bern daily newspaper probably voiced the sentiments of a large proportion of the Democrats of the state when it
caustically declared that the district was "made blacker than ever,"

1. The four were John A. Hyman, James E. O'Hara, Henry P. Cheatham, and
George H. White.

and predicted that no Democrat would "ever again find his way to Washington through [that] impenetrable blackness."[2] The prophecy proved erroneous, for of the nine congressional elections between 1877 and 1893, Negro candidates were victorious in only four, James E. O'Hara and Henry P. Cheatham serving two terms each.

The first of these men, O'Hara, was born in New York City on February 26, 1844. At the age of six he was taken by his parents to the West Indies where he remained until early manhood. Returning to the United States, he received "an academical education," and studied law both in North Carolina and at Howard University. O'Hara was admitted to the bar by the North Carolina General Assembly of 1868.[3]

In consequence of the highly questionable actions of the Democratic canvassing boards in the Second Congressional District after the November, 1878, elections, the congressional seat that O'Hara contested was awarded to the Democratic candidate William H. Kitchin. The decision of the Second District Executive Committee of the Republican party to nominate Orlando Hubbs rather than O'Hara as its standard bearer in 1880 again denied the latter an opportunity to represent the "Black Second." O'Hara's supporters, if judged by their actions at the nominating convention of the Second District in 1882, were determined that their candidate would not be deprived of his "rightful place" a third time.[4] Meeting at Weldon on July 19 and 20, 1882, the convention nominated two white men, Congressman Orlando Hubbs, the pre-convention favorite, and L. W. Humphrey, and two Negroes, James E. O'Hara and I. B. Abbott. Since twenty-six of the thirty-two delegates present were in favor of one of the two white candidates, motions to adjourn were made by O'Hara supporters but were voted down. When the convention started balloting for a candidate, the secretary, S. N. Hill, was directed by the chairman, L. G. Estes, to call the roll. George T. Wassom, a Negro alternate from Wayne County, and apparently without recognition from the chairman, mounted a table and, announcing that he was authorized to withdraw the name of L. W. Humphrey, asked the supporters of the latter to vote for O'Hara. "Without waiting for anyone and in defiance of all parliamentary law and usage," so went the report of

2. New Bern *Daily Journal,* March 8, 1883.

3. *Congressional Directory,* Forty-eighth Congress, First Session (Washington, 1884), p. 65. The New Bern *Daily Journal,* carrying the obituary of O'Hara on September 17, 1905, listed his birth as March 23, 1844.

4. See *O'Hara vs. Kitchin.* Forty-sixth Congress, Third Session, House of Representatives Miscellaneous Document Number 7 (January 6, 1881), pp. 1-29; House of Representatives Report from the Committee on Elections, report number 263, pp. 1-6; *Union Republican* (Winston), January 2, 1879.

Estes and Hill, [and] "flagrantly usurping the functions of the chair, Wassom appealed to the outside mass on a *viva voce* vote, which was a rabble yell, and thereupon he [Wassom] declared O'Hara nominated."[5]

The supporters of Hubbs refused to accept the results of the Weldon convention and claimed that their candidate was the regular nominee. Throughout the months of August and September both men maintained publicly that each was the regular nominee, with the followers of O'Hara the most articulate and outspoken. Asked by a reporter of the New Bern *Daily Journal* to predict the outcome of the O'Hara-Hubbs contest, one O'Hara supporter declared boldly that if the Republican state Executive Committee decided against O'Hara, the decision would be ignored, and if another convention were called, O'Hara followers would have nothing to do with it. "O'Hara," he concluded, "has been regularly nominated and we are going to have him elected, and those who fail to stand up to the rack will get no fodder in this District."[6] Faced with such determination and resistance, Hubbs publicly stated in October, 1882, that he was withdrawing from the congressional contest "because a continued struggle will give the District to the enemy."[7] In commenting on the withdrawal of Hubbs, the Tarboro *Southerner,* a Democratic newspaper of eastern North Carolina, made the arresting observation that "while we are opposed to O'Hara and think him unfit for the position, candor compels us to say that he will make a better representative than [Orlando Hubbs] his immediate predecessor."[8]

After the retirement of the only possible active Republican opposition to O'Hara, the Democrats of the Second District held a convention and decided that it was "not expedient to nominate a candidate or to have a volunteer candidate." Despite some grass-roots opposition to the decision,[9] it remained unchanged, and O'Hara was elected overwhelmingly to the Forty-eighth Congress, receiving 18,-531 of the 19,944 votes cast.[10]

Appointment of O'Hara to the Committees on Mines and Mining and Expenditures on Public Buildings caused the chief Negro newspaper of Washington, D.C., to remark caustically that the Negro

5. Report of L. G. Estes and S. N. Hill, as quoted in the New Bern *Daily Journal,* July 28, 1882. See also New Bern *Daily Journal,* August 6, 1882.

6. New Bern *Daily Journal,* August 1, 1882.

7. Greensboro *Patriot,* as quoted in the Lenoir *Topic,* October 25, 1882.

8. Tarboro *Southerner,* October 19, 1882.

9. See, for example, the New Bern *Daily Journal,* October 17, 19, 1882.

10. *Congressional Directory,* Forty-eighth Congress, First Session (Washington, 1884), p. 65.

Congressman would "see that North Carolina and the rest of the South get a dollar or two for public buildings."[11] Although rather active, O'Hara was unsuccessful in his legislative efforts. Most of his measures, local in nature, failed to receive committee recommendation. Despite failure, it is notable that the majority of O'Hara's bills in the early sessions of the Forty-eighth Congress were non-racial. His effort to insert amendments in the Rivers and Appropriation bill to improve the navigation of the Moccasin and Trent rivers in eastern North Carolina as well as his bill to pay certain expenses of the Eastern Band of Cherokee Indians in North Carolina are cases in point.[12]

O'Hara was re-elected to the Forty-ninth Congress, receiving 22,309 votes against 15,699 votes for Fred A. Woodward, his Democratic opponent.[13] If many of his measures in the first session of the Forty-eighth Congress were non-racial in character, the majority of his bills and amendments in the Second Session of that Congress and the subsequent Forty-ninth Congress were decidedly racially oriented. Two cases in point will suffice. In the debate on the interstate commerce bill, O'Hara offered on December 16, 1884, an amendment providing that any person having purchased a ticket to be conveyed from one state to another, or having paid the required fare, should receive the same treatment and be afforded accommodations equal to those furnished all other persons holding tickets of the same class, without discrimination. O'Hara correctly reasoned that since Congress had the right to say how property moving between states could be carried, Congress should have the right to say how persons traveling on interstate railroads should be treated. In answer to the charge from an Alabama representative that his amendment was designed to "raise a political issue," O'Hara countered by declaring that he was not in the habit of raising a political issue two years before a campaign began. "All I ask of the American Congress," he said, "is that . . . you shall . . . give voice and expression to the protection of the

11. Washington *Bee*, January 5, 1884.

12. *Congressional Record*, Forty-eighth Congress, Second Session, Part 5, pp. 4950, 4981-4982. *Ibid.*, Part 1, First Session, p. 347.

13. *Congressional Directory*, Forty-ninth Congress, First Session, p. 69. In view of the relative closeness of the final results, the pre-election day note of extreme pessimism voiced both by some Democratic newspapers of the Second District as well as by Woodward himself is surprising. The Wilson *Advance* of June 20, 1884, for example, in evaluating the chances of Woodward to unseat O'Hara, stated: "There is no probability of his election." Woodward, in a speech at Snow Hill on September 13, 1884, declared that he was the leader of a forlorn hope, that he knew he could not be elected. . . ." See Wilson *Advance*, September 19, 1884. Of course, this pessimistic pre-election forecast could have been Democratic campaign strategy to rally and rouse white support.

rights of American colored citizens.[14]   The Washington *Bee,* while
describing O'Hara's amendment as "a masterly piece of statesman-
ship," was severely critical of the Washington *Post* for insinuating
that O'Hara was not responsible for the successful passage of the
amendment.   "Little enough is accorded the Negro," it complained,
"and when that little is well done, he ought to have the credit."[15]

As a result of the murder of Negro citizens by a mob of whites
on March 18, 1886, in Carrollton, Mississippi, and the subsequent failure of the governor of that state to take effective measures to bring
the murderers to justice, as well as the inaction of a grand jury in
Carrol County, Mississippi, to bring the murderers before the courts
to answer for their crimes, O'Hara introduced a resolution for
the appointment of a five-man committee to investigate the murders
and "to report, by bill or otherwise, such measures as will check or
prevent in future the wanton and barbarous destruction of human
life."   O'Hara also urged that the proposed committee, when appointed, be empowered to subpoena witnesses, administer oaths, and
appoint a subcommittee to visit Mississippi to take testimony.   The
resolution was rejected.[16]

In June of 1886, despite these and other attempts on behalf of the
Negroes of North Carolina and the country at large,[17] it appeared that
some Negroes of the Second District, dissatisfied with the work of
O'Hara in Congress, were actively trying to defeat him in the fall
elections of that year and to replace him with a white Republican,
L. J. Moore.   The charges that were made against O'Hara were that
he failed to have Negroes appointed to "prominent" places in Washington; that he failed to recognize his constituents; and that he was a
foreigner.   In an attempt to answer these charges, the *Bee* angrily
observed that they illustrated "the weaknesses of the colored people."
"Mr. O'Hara," it continued, "has made a good representative and we
doubt very much whether Mr. Moore will do more for the colored
people of the South than Mr. O'Hara has done or will do."   This important Negro newspaper of the nation's capital concluded its criticism
with the assertion that O'Hara was an American citizen and not a
foreigner and that he or "some other colored man" should be elected

14. *Congressional Record,* Forty-eighth Congress, Second Session, Part 1, 1884-
1885, p. 317; Raleigh *News and Observer,* December 18, 19, 1884.

15. Washington *Bee,* December 27, 1884.

16. *Congressional Record,* Forty-ninth Congress, First Session, Part 3, pp. 2897,
3123.

17. See Samuel D. Smith, *The Negro in Congress, 1870-1901* (Chapel Hill: University of North Carolina Press, 1940), pp. 118-19.

to Congress from the Second Congressional District of North Carolina.[18] Such was not to be the case, for Furnifold Simmons, the Democratic candidate, defeated O'Hara and another Negro aspirant, I. B. Abbott, in the congressional election of 1886. There is no question that had there not been a division of the Negro vote, O'Hara would have been re-elected inasmuch as he lost by some 2,098 votes.[19] O'Hara subsequently returned to North Carolina and engaged in the practice of law.

The other Negro congressman to represent North Carolina during the eighteen years covered by this study was born in North Carolina. Unlike O'Hara, according to one historian, he always identified himself with the better class of white people."[20] Henry P. Cheatham's political career really began at Weldon on May 30, 1888, at the Second District Republican convention. A division of sentiment resulted in the splitting of that body and the nomination of both Cheatham and another Negro, George A. Mebane. Taking note of the division, the New Bern *Daily Journal* wrote: "We understand from those who know that both of these men are well worthy of the confidence imposed in them by their friends. . . . The minority [white] vote in the district should be glad that while they [the Negro majority] insist on the color line in the selection of their candidates, they do use good judgment in taking men of good repute and abilities such as we learn both of these nominees to be."[21]

The fact that a staunch Democratic paper of eastern North Carolina would openly speak so highly of Negro candidates of the opposite party was perhaps refreshing, but did little to resolve the question as to which candidate was entitled to be the regular nominee. Feelings over the matter were heightened when at a Harrison-Dockery-Cheatham club meeting in Tarboro on July 18, 1888, a resolution endorsing the latter as the only Republican nominee of the Second Congressional District "was received with a roar of deafening applause." The club also denounced the "demagogism of the opposition would-be candidate from Bertie and his political henchmen."[22] A week later, Mebane, taking advantage of the fact that Cheatham was in New Bern, suggested to Cheatham that the two of them engage in a public discussion of the issues between them. Cheatham, in reply, declared that he could not recognize any Republican nominee

18. Washington *Bee*, June 26, 1886.
19. *Congressional Directory*, Fiftieth Congress, Second Session, p. 80.
20. Smith, *Negro in Congress*, p. 121.
21. New Bern *Daily Journal*, May 31, June, 1888.
22. Greensboro *North State*, July 26, 1888.

in the district except himself, and since the party did not countenance bolters, he could not accept Mebane's request. The latter, obviously chagrined by the terseness of Cheatham's note, fired back: "The question is not what *you* know, but what the people want to know. If you have any confidence in your position, you cannot fail to recognize the importance of a joint discussion. However, the people shall hear the truth before the campaign shall have closed. If you dodge now, you cannot dodge them on election day, and all true Republicans will see you do not defeat the wishes of the party."[23]

The *Daily Journal,* of New Bern, interestingly enough, went to great pains to pay compliments to Mebane. On August 5, 1888, the strong Democratic newspaper praised him "as an intelligent, working man who takes every occasion to inform himself about the wants and needs of his people, so as to be able to represent their interests in the Congress of the United States." Although confident that Simmons would be re-elected, the editor, nevertheless, confessed that he liked what he heard about Mebane.[24]

Then, with dramatic suddenness, the voters of the Second District learned of Mebane's withdrawal from the congressional race. Since no public explanation came from Mebane, rumors circulated that he had been bought off by the supporters of Cheatham.[25] It would appear from the above that Mebane's withdrawal was prompted partly at least by a conviction that this alone would insure a Republican victory at the polls in November. If this were the strategy, it nearly proved disastrous for Cheatham. L. W. Humphrey, one of the Republican leaders in Goldsboro, was confident that the move would benefit the Democratic candidate, Furnifold Simmons. In a letter to Senator Matt Ransom, he noted that

Mebane's withdrawal has not affected him [Simmons] seriously as I thought it would. The prejudices against Cheatham caused by Mebane's candidacy is very great and will not down; the buying Mebane off by Cheatham, as they say, provokes greater feeling and the Mebane followers will vote for Mr. Simmons. A prominent colored man from Warren writes to know when he can come to see [and] says that the Mebane men will not vote for Cheatham [and] that Mr. Simmons can get a large colored vote in Warren. Just at this moment a delegation from Edgecombe of six men, one white and the others colored, here-to-fore of both factions, all for Mr. Simmons outright.[26]

23. Quoted in the New Bern *Daily Journal,* August 4, 1888.
24. *Ibid.,* August 5, 11, 1888.
25. See the Raleigh *News and Observer,* September 21, 1888; New Bern *Daily Journal,* September 23, 27, 1888, October 3, 4, 1888.
26. L. W. Humphrey to Matt Ransom, September 27, 1888. Ransom Papers.

As a consequence of the defection of both Negro and white Republicans, Cheatham was severely handicapped in the election. His victory was a narrow one, 16,704 to 16,051.[27] Unquestionably, the support given the Democratic aspirant by both Negro and white Republicans resulted in the close election count.

Born in Granville County, December 27, 1857, Cheatham attended public and private schools near the town of Henderson, and in 1882 he received the B.A. degree from Shaw University. He became principal of the Plymouth State Normal School immediately after graduation and served in that capacity until 1885, when without serious opposition he was elected Register of Deeds of Vance County.[28]

Though Cheatham was not a "talking" member during his first term as congressman, he was still able to secure appointments of "over 86 of his constituents, including postmasters, special mail agents and clerks."[29] Indeed, the Washington *Bee* went so far as to declare that more Negroes were appointed by Cheatham than by any other congressman from the Second District and predicted that in the fall elections of 1890, he would be returned to Congress by a large majority.[30]

Cheatham, apparently, experienced no serious difficulty in securing renomination, for on August 14, 1890, he telegraphed a friend in New Bern that he had "just been re-nominated by acclamation amid great enthusiasm.[31] The Democrats, on the other hand, were not as successful in choosing a candidate. The first nominee, W. J. Rogers, withdrew from the contest on October 7, 1890, because of physical disability. For several weeks it appeared as though the Democrats would not or could not find a replacement.

Thus the Democrats of the Second District greeted with considerable relief the news that James M. Mewborne of Lenoir County had announced himself as a "self-made" Democratic nominee for Congress. "Now," shouted the *Journal* of New Bern to the white voters of Craven County, "which shall you choose: on one side is a North Carolinian . . . who loves the land of his nationality, a true Democrat, an upright honorable Christian gentleman. . . . On the other side is an incompetent Negro, an inconsiderate, fanatical demagogue. . . ."[32] Not only did the *Daily Journal* preach with undisguised

27. *Congressional Directory,* Fifty-first Congress, First Session, pp. 84-85.
28. *Ibid.*
29. Washington *Bee,* June 8, 1889.
30. *Ibid.,* September 27, 1890.
31. Quoted in the New Bern *Daily Journal,* August 21, 1890.
32. *Ibid.,* July 26, 1890.

zeal the cult of white supremacy, but it also attacked Cheatham's greatest political weapon, his successful appointment record. Seizing upon the fact that one of the Negro's appointees, an assistant post-mistress at Halifax, was allegedly responsible for $1,500 shortage in her accounts, the paper gleefully declared that "Congressman Cheatham's appointees, about whom he boasts so with the colored people, are like himself, short and growing shorter."[33]

Despite strong and spirited opposition, Cheatham was re-elected, receiving 16,943 votes against 15,713 votes for Mewborne.[34] Signifi-cantly, Cheatham was the sole Negro member of the Fifty-second Congress. Undoubtedly, it was this fact that prompted the *Bee* to make the observation on December 20, 1890, that Cheatham would be very lonely in the in-coming Congress.[35] Perhaps Cheatham's most notable work during this Congress was the introduction of a bill requesting that $100,000 be appropriated "for the purpose of collecting, preparing, and publishing facts and statistics pertaining to the moral, industrial, and intellectual development and progress of the colored people of African descent residing in the United States." The result was to be published as a part of the United States government's exhibit at the World's Columbian Exposition in Chicago. Com-menting on this bill, a Negro religious quarterly suggested that Cheatham's bill merited immediate passage, "for the [Negro] race is entitled to the consideration which it contemplates . . . and though tardy, such treatment as this measure proposed would go far toward correcting the mistake already made."[36] The measure died in com-mittee.

Cheatham unsuccessfully sought re-election in 1892 and 1894. In each instance a significant factor in his defeat was the growing oppo-sition of large numbers of Negroes in the Second District. It is reasonably clear that had the Negroes been favorably inclined to support him, even the fraudulent election practices of the Democrats, especially in the 1892 balloting, would have been to no avail. "Cheatham is very unpopular in Warren and Halifax," wrote John Graham to Cyrus Thompson after the 1894 fall elections. [Fred A. Woodward] received many Negro votes."[37] It is difficult to explain

33. Quoted from the Tarboro *Southerner*, in the New Bern *Daily Journal*, October 9, 1890.
34. *Congressional Directory*, Fifty-second Congress, First Session, p. 78.
35. Washington *Bee*, December 20, 1890.
36. *African Methodist Episcopal Zion Church Quarterly* (July, 1892), p. 415.
37. John Graham to Cyrus Thompson, November 15, 1894. Cyrus Thompson Papers, University of North Carolina Library, Chapel Hill.

the declining popularity of Cheatham. Possibly the Negroes expected too much from him by way of appointments and similar favors. They little realized the very difficult obstacles he had to overcome to secure what meager federal patronage he was able to control. Their failure to comprehend this elementary political fact led them, perhaps unfairly, to label him a "white folk's nigger."

In evaluating Cheatham's work in Congress, however, the Raleigh *Signal* reflected the sentiments of white and some Negro Republicans of the state when it described him as "a faithful public servant who has done all that he could do for the whole state. . . ." The Raleigh newspaper concluded by saying that during his four years in Congress he had "reflected great credit on his race, the Republican party and himself."[38] These observations could very well apply to the congressional record of O'Hara. The two men met the criteria for office holding of their day, both in the matter of prior public service experience and educational training.

38. Raleigh *Signal*, April 21, 1892.

5

The Fruits of Federal Patronage

We are much distressed over a rumored change in our postmaster at this place, and indications are that a Negro will be appointed. . . . Now is there anything you can do to prevent a Negro being put in. You understand the humiliation and mortification that must be experienced by us if such a thing happens.
    T. E. Gilman to Matt Ransom, April 30, 1889.

Federal patronage proved to be one of the most attractive sources of public office for the Negroes of the state. Although the national administrations of both political parties appointed Negroes as federal officeholders, the more important posts awarded by each party were filled by whites. In other offices, especially the ministries to Liberia and Haiti, as well as postmasterships and railroad mail agencies, Negroes were appointed in large numbers, notably by Republican administrations.

The appointment of Negroes as ministers to Haiti and Liberia evoked little or no white opposition from each party. "No white man desires these appointments," observed the *State Chronicle*. "And besides," it continued, "it is conceded by all that a Negro ought to represent our government in a Negro country."[1] In the period under con-

1. Raleigh *State Chronicle*, October 26, 1888.

sideration, two of the Negro ministers of Liberia, John H. Smyth and E. E. Smith, were North Carolinians at the time of their appointments. Smyth was a Republican; Smith was a Democrat. Both were appointed upon the recommendation of Matt Ransom, a Democrat, who served as United States senator from North Carolina between 1876 and 1894.

John H. Smyth, residing in North Carolina at the time of his appointment in 1876, was a native of Virginia. By working as a clerk in federal bureaus in Washington, he was able to put himself through the law school at Howard University. After graduation he was appointed cashier of the Wilmington branch of the Freedman's Bank. When that institution collapsed, Smyth practiced law. An active Republican, his efforts as a campaigner in the election of 1876 netted him the ministership to Liberia.[2] After his appointment had become official, Smyth remembered the support Ransom had given him. "Your influence," said Smyth in a letter to the Senator in 1878, "was potent in attaining that end."[3]

In February, 1888, J. C. Price, the president of Livingstone College, was offered the Liberian ministership, but he refused. The chairman of the college's trustee board, Bishop J. W. Hood, in a letter to Senator Ransom, proposed E. E. Smith of the State Normal School, Fayetteville. The Bishop described Smith as "a Christian gentleman, strictly temperate, free from the use of tobacco, neat and genteel in his personal appearance." Bishop Hood concluded his recommendation with these interesting remarks: "He is neither arrogant nor timid, and can entertain without telling all he knows."[4] Smith was later confirmed by the United States senate and after his arrival in Monrovia, expressed to Ransom his "sense of gratitude . . . for the important part you kindly took in effecting my appointment to this post of trust."[5]

In the course of his three-year stay in Liberia, Smith apparently found the work and world of a diplomat quite satisfying. In December, 1894, Smith wrote B. F. Aycock of his wish to return to that African country. Aycock's subsequent letter to Ransom in behalf of Smith is most significant in that it illustrates the extent to which the Democrats of the state were inclined to reward some Negro politicians for their services, not only as a matter of insuring increased allegiance

2. Richard Bardolph, *The Negro Vanguard* (New York, 1959), pp. 73-74.

3. John H. Smith to Matt Ransom, May 16, 1878. Ransom Papers, University of North Carolina Library, Chapel Hill.

4. J. W. Hood to Grover Cleveland, February 28, 1888. Ransom Papers.

5. E. E. Smith to Matt Ransom, March 4, 1889. Ransom Papers.

but also to flatter and attract the Negro vote. "He [Smith] did faithful work in the last campaign," Aycock reminded Ransom, "and though we went under we must not forget our Negroes."[6] Despite the efforts of Ransom, Smith was passed over, and the Liberian post went to a South Carolinian, William H. Heard.

Other Negroes unsuccessfully sought Ransom's support for diplomatic and consular service posts. Garland H. White, a Democrat of long standing, based his qualifications for the Liberian appointment on his loyalty and devotion to the party's interest: "I have for the last ten or twelve years fought for the success of the [Democratic] party telling my people that you and others of your political opinion would do all in their power to promote our interest."[7]

Although he candidly confessed to Ransom in 1876 that they owed allegiance to different political faiths, John H. Collins solicited the latter's aid in his quest for the Haitian ministership. "Since a Negro will receive the place," Collins noted blandly, "our senators will prefer one from North Carolina [in] preference to any other state."[8]

The postal service probably took more Negro appointees than did any other branch of the federal service. They were employed as postmasters, mail clerks, and route agents, mainly in the eastern part of the state. Although white opposition to Negro postal workers was general, Negro postmasters were prime targets. The appointment of a Negro postmaster at Fayetteville in October, 1891, during the Harrison administration, is a case in point. Though the Negroes of the state hailed it "with gladness,"[9] many of the whites were quite put out with the appointment and continued to harp against it, especially after the advent of the Cleveland administration in 1893. John G. Shaw, a well-known lawyer in Fayetteville, wrote despairingly to Ransom in late 1893: "As a Democrat I desire to say to you that leaving a Negro Republican in our post office this long is an insult to the Democrats of this entire section."[10]

Senator Ransom, then, was severely criticized by some whites of Fayetteville for his inability or seeming reluctance to have the Negro postmaster removed. "The white Democrats are swearing at you," wrote H. L. Evans, a local businessman in August, 1894, "and saying bad things about you." He went on to urge Ransom to direct all his efforts towards removing the colored postmaster. "It ought to

6. B. F. Aycock to Matt Ransom, December 26, 1894. Ransom Papers.
7. Garland H. White to Matt Ransom, March 27, 1888. Ransom Papers.
8. John H. Collins to Matt Ransom, March 15, 1877. Ransom Papers.
9. Raleigh *Gazette*, October 17, 1891.
10. John G. Shaw to Matt Ransom, October 28, 1893. Ransom Papers.

make no difference whether he is objectionable or not," concluded Evans, "the fact that he is a Negro is enough."[11]

The continued presence of the Negro postmaster in Fayetteville became a source of embarrassment to Ransom. Indeed, some Democrats in that city in the summer of 1894 freely predicted that unless the Negro were removed, the Democrats could expect little support in the fall elections.[12] It is quite possible that this was a contributing factor in the defeat of the Democrats at the polls in Fayetteville in 1894.

The extent of white opposition to Negro postmasters can also be seen in their resistance to the appointment of a member of that race to the post office in Wilson. Henry P. Cheatham, revealed in April of 1889 that he desired to have a Negro, S. H. Vick, appointed postmaster at Wilson. John E. Woodward, a powerful political figure in eastern North Carolina, became the spokesman for the white opposition. In a determined bid to block the appointment, Woodward turned to Senator Ransom. "We would esteem it a great favor," Woodward wrote Ransom, "if you would do all in your power to prevent the appintment of Vick and secure the appointment of . . . some efficient, unobjectionable white man."[13]

Not only were the whites unable to prevent the appointment of Vick, but they faced similar setbacks in other cities of the Second Congressional District. "It seems that our colored Representative, Mr. Cheatham," wrote W. H. Jones in the spring of 1889, "is *bent* on turning out all the old Democratic postmasters in this District."[14] Making due allowance for bias, it appears that there was more truth than fiction in the observation of Jones. Although in office barely a month, Cheatham was reported to have procured appointments for seven Negroes as postmasters.[15]

Widespread white opposition to Negro postmasters was based on economic jealousy as well as racial antipathy. A postmaster's position in a city the size of Fayetteville, Wilson, or Wilmington, for example, paid $1,800 and upwards. Such salaries provided economic grounds for the whites of the state to protest the appointment or to demand continuously the removal of Negroes from these positions. A white businessman in Fayetteville, for example, complained most bitterly in 1894: "When we reflect that this young colored Republican, without

11. H. L. Evans to Matt Ransom, August 6, 1894. Ransom Papers.
12. A. B. Andrew to Matt Ransom, June 21, 1894. Ransom Papers.
13. John E. Woodward to Matt Ransom, April 14, 1889. Ransom Papers.
14. W. H. Jones to Matt Ransom, March 5, 1889. Ransom Papers.
15. John E. Woodward to Matt Ransom, April 14, 1889. Ransom Papers.

a family, enjoys an office paying $1,800 per annum and consider how many scores of Democrat heads of families there are in this community, who during this depression can scarcely secure the necessaries of life, it seems indeed hard and cruel."[16]

On the other hand, some post offices, such as the one at Mt. Gilead, paid less than twenty-five dollars a month.[17] Nevertheless, the local whites voiced objections to a Negro postmaster. It is extremely doubtful that the average white man, even in the nineties, was interested economically in a position that paid only three hundred dollars per year. The basis, then, of white protest to this and similarly situated offices held by Negroes was purely racial. One white woman expressed most succinctly the general prevailing white attitude when she said, ". . . it makes our blood boil to see a Negro PM. . . ."[18]

The strain and tension under which Negro postmasters worked was also experienced by Negro mail agents on the railroads of the state. Vigorous white opposition was especially vocal during the Democratic administration of Grover Cleveland. Attacks on the Negro mail agent from Goldsboro to Greensboro evidence the opposition. "He passes here [Selma] everyday," wrote A. M. Noble, "and the people of Johnston County think it an outrage that he is kept in office more than two years after a Democratic administration is in power." Noble admonished Ransom that it would be most difficult at best to gain the county's support in the next election, "but it will be a heavy load to carry a Negro mail agent and win the race."[19] Similar reactions were expressed by whites in other areas of the state.

Probably the most important post held by a Negro as a result of federal patronage during the period was the collector of customs at the port of Wilmington. The Republican administration of Harrison provided the interesting spectacle of two North Carolina Negroes vying for the position. Initially, James H. Young appeared the most likely to receive the appointment, but strong opposition from some prominent Republicans of Wilmington resulted in the selection of John C. Dancy.[20] The latter's salary was approximately $4,000 per annum, a sum in excess of that paid to many of the top state officials including the governor. It is, therefore, not surprising that the whites

16. H. R. Horne to James D. McNeil, April 20, 1894. Ransom Papers.

17. C. W. Wooley to Matt Ransom, February 19, 1889. Ransom Papers.

18. Nannie G. Fisher to Matt Ransom, December 14, 1894. Ransom Papers.

19. A. M. Noble to Matt Ransom, May 16, 1887. Ransom Papers. See W. E. Kyle to Ransom, May 23, 1879; H. McDuffie to Ransom, April 1, 17, 1879. *Ibid.*

20. Protest of thirteen Republicans to Matt Ransom, February 9, 1891. Ransom Papers.

of North Carolina vehemently disapproved of a Negro's holding such a position. Incidentally, Dancy, in addition to serving as collector of customs under Harrison, also held that post under the administration of McKinley, from 1897 through 1901.

The federal officeholders mentioned above naturally stirred the pride of the Negroes of the state. Most North Carolina Negroes, holding federal jobs, however, were laborers, charwomen, spittoon cleaners, and other menials.[21] Throughout the period it was the general practice to award these jobs, usually in Washington, to deserving Negro Democrats as a consequence of their services to the party during political campaigns. Following the fall elections of 1878, for example, one Negro Democrat sought Senator Ransom's aid in employing his "worthy Democratic colored friend" for the position of policeman at the capital.[22]

Federal patronage for Negroes, then, was not a monopoly of the Republican party. In all fairness to that party, however, it must be stated that the Republicans more frequently than the Democrats, rewarded Negroes with positions higher than menial labor. At no time during a Democratic administration, for example, was a Negro appointed a collector of customs or a postmaster.

21. T. B. Womack to Matt Ransom, February 27, 1889; Garland H. White to Ransom, December 2, 1892; D. A. G. Crockett to Ransom, October 14, 1893; White to Ransom, February 2, 1894. Ransom Papers.
22. Garland H. White to Matt Ransom, December 10, 1875. Ransom Papers.

6

"The Day the Democrats Took Charge"

They [the amendments of 1875 to the North Carolina Constitution] give us enlarged powers. Many of our colored fellow-citizens . . . fear it will be used to their detriment. Let our acts teach them there will be no cause for such fears, and that all their rights will be held sacred by us.

Address of Lieutenant Governor Jarvis before the North Carolina Senate, January 2, 1877.

The colored people will now have the opportunity to learn that the Democratic Party has no design against their liberties, we shall invade none of their rights, or interfere with none of their privileges. . . . We shall give them peace, prosperity and protection. The laws will be impartially executed respecting white and colored people. . . . We shall afford him every possible facility for the education of his children. We shall afford the colored man opportunity for bettering his condition.

Raleigh SENTINEL, November 9, 1876.

O fficials who are elected by popular vote usual-
ly reflect the sentiments and thinking of the citizens whose votes
placed them in office. The members of the legislative body of North
Carolina during the period under survey were no exception to this

rule. Nearly all of the members of each session of the General Assembly had lived all their lives among the people whom they represented and, therefore, had been exposed to all the influences of local associations and atmosphere. Consequently, with respect to the Negroes, it would be expected that these officeholders would affirm the large general views of their communities, which, if judged by the political campaigns between 1876 and 1894, were anti-Negro and anti-Republican.

Yet, in 1876, immediately after the election results were official, the Democratic press of the state, together with the newly elected Democratic legislature and state party leaders, attempted to assure the apprehensive Negroes, who had been led to believe that a Democratic victory meant re-enslavement, that the new regime would not be "hostile to their rights and interests." On November 8, 1876, the day following the sweeping Democratic victory, the editor of the Greensboro *Patriot,* for example, wrote: "The Negro need not be alarmed. He will not lose a single right or privilege he has enjoyed. Instead of being reduced to slavery again he will be fully emancipated. . . . The day that Democracy takes charge of this government will be the brightest the Negro ever saw. He need have no fears. His old friends will be his friends again, and his future will be better and brighter."[1]

A Democrat from Person County, speaking for his party, promised the Negroes that the legislature would "seek to inspire all its citizens with an absolute confidence in its justice, [and] in its good will."[2] However, despite these solemn pledges that the destinies of the Negroes and whites were the same and that the white people of North Carolina would protect the liberties of the Negroes even with their "heart's blood"; and in spite of the plea by Lieutenant Governor Thomas Jarvis before the members of the upper house of the state legislature on January 2, 1877, to treat the Negro equitably and justly, "and to hold his rights . . . sacred," these men immediately thereafter set in motion legislation aimed at partially disfranchising the Negroes of North Carolina.[3]

The first decisive move in this direction by the General Assembly was the passage on February 27, 1877, of an act to establish county government. This law abolished the right of the people to select

1. Greensboro *Patriot,* November 8, 1876.
2. *Ibid.,* January 10, 1877.
3. Tarboro *Southerner,* November 17, 1876. See also the address of Lieutenant Governor Jarvis before the Senate of North Carolina, January 2, 1877, in the *State Journal,* 1877, p. 25.

justices of the peace for counties, cities, and towns, and transferred that privilege to the General Assembly.[4] Thus, the legislature by this action guaranteed to the white minorities of the "Negro counties" a controlling voice in county government, for the law stated that justices of the peace, who were appointed by a Democratic dominated legislature, were to appoint the county commissioners, who in turn were empowered to establish county courts.[5] In effect, then, this act nullified the strength of the Negroes at the ballot box in the eastern counties by denying them the right to elect the county officials who controlled their personal and civil liberties. Even a staunch supporter of rule by "the more conservative and better elements of the population," was forced to admit that this system was anything but democratic.[6]

William H. Moore, spearheading the futile Republican opposition in the state Senate, argued that since all just powers of government were derived from the consent of the governed, no laws should be passed by the legislature of the state which would in any way fetter the people in their free exercise of the right of suffrage. Moore declared that by denying the Negroes the right to elect their justices of the peace, the franchise was, in effect, taken from them. He also reminded the Democrats that in the campaign of 1876 they had gone on record as saying that they would take away no rights from the Negroes. He therefore urged that the people continue to elect the justices of the peace. His request was rejected by a vote of twenty-six to eleven.[7] In the lower house, John T. Reynolds, Negro Republican, in leading his minority supporters, based his opposition to the county government bill on the belief that all officers should be elected by the people. Especially should this be the case, he emphasized, "where they levy the taxes upon the people."[8]

As the law applied to all of the counties in the state, there was considerable doubt whether the whites in the sparsely Negro-populated regions of western North Carolina would accept it. Indeed, a little over a month before its passage, a Greensboro newspaper predicted disapproval on the part of the mountain whites toward the county government bill when it said that "the protection of the rights and

4. *Public and Private Laws and Resolutions of the State of North Carolina, 1876-1877,* c. 141, sec. 4. Act of February 27, 1877.
5. *Ibid.,* sec. 5.
6. Stephen B. Weeks, "The History of Negro Suffrage in the South," *Political Science Quarterly,* IX (December, 1894), 692.
7. Raleigh *Observer,* February 6, 1877.
8. Legislative Papers, 1876-1877. State Department of Archives and History, Raleigh.

interests of the white people . . . of the East, without making changes in municipal government undesirable in the West" was a matter of great difficulty.[9] However, after much talk "about ridding the eastern counties of ignorant Negro rule and black domination," the western members of the 1876-1877 legislature hesitantly embraced the county government bill.

Having, therefore, made this "supreme sacrifice," the mountain whites were infuriated as a result of the 1876-1877 General Assembly's selection of thirty Negro justices of the peace for some of the eastern counties. The comments of the editor of the Concord *Sun* are typical of their attitude toward "this outrage."

Look at the East was the campaign cry from one end of the state to the other, and so often were the words that we of the West began to think that no sacrifice, no matter how great, was too much for their relief. In the matter of Magistrates, we consented to give up our much-loved right of electing Magistrates by the people, so that incompetent carpet-baggers and Negroes would have to stand aside and make way for those whose interests were with the people. But in numbers of the Eastern Counties, Negroes were recommended to the Legislature for Magistrates and got their appointments, after howling for twelve years about being under Negro rule.[10]

A similar feeling was expressed by several of the Democratic eastern and near-eastern newspapers. The editor of the Goldsboro *Messenger,* for example, indignantly declared: "The election . . . in some instances of Negro magistrates for some of the Eastern counties by the General Assembly just adjourned, shows a gross and palpable disregard of the people's wishes. . . . The impudent transaction is without parallel. We cannot find language strong enough to condemn so flagrant a disregard of the hopes and wishes of our Eastern people."[11]

The Republican Raleigh *Register,* on the other hand, calmly remarked that "the election of competent colored men to be magistrates was nothing more or less than an act of simple justice."[12]

Not only did the white voters and newspapers of the mountain counties and the Democratic press of the East feel that they had been deceived, but several members of the North Carolina legislature in the 1876-1877 session from the coastal and Piedmont counties also

9. Greensboro *Patriot,* January 10, 1877.

10. Quoted in the Tarboro *Southerner,* March 30, 1877.

11. Quoted in the Raleigh *Register,* April 6, 1877. See also the editorial opinion of the Fayetteville *Gazette,* and the Durham *Herald* as quoted in the Raleigh *Register,* April 6, and 13, 1877.

12. Raleigh *Register,* April 10, 1877.

joined in the protest against the selection of Negro justices of the peace. Their protest is of sufficient merit and revelation to justify a full quotation. The protesting group declared they

. . . respectfully but earnestly protest against the policy which appears to have been approved by a majority of the Democratic members of this General Assembly in the election of colored magistrates in and for certain counties of this state. We believe that in the said election of magistrates by the General Assembly, a record to some extent has been made for the Democratic-Conservative party of North Carolina, inconsistent with the principles and purposes of the party as expressed during the recent and previous campaigns, in its party platforms and as expressed by its thousands of speakers upon the stump, who asserted the superiority by nature and education of the white race over the colored, and the consequent greater fitness of the former for public office as rulers and dispensers of justice—aye, more than that, who maintained unhesitatingly, freely and repeatedly, that the colored people, especially as citizens of the same county and government with white people, were absolutely unfit for these public positions. We believe that in the late campaign the appeals made by the press and speakers of the Democratic Conservative party to the pride and sympathy of the white race in behalf of its own color, to secure its rescue from Negro domination, was in every part of the state, one of the strongest and most effective means used for obtaining the success of our cause.

We express the belief now, that these principles and opinions asserted by our party, and the grounds upon which we based our appeal to our white brethren, all being in harmony, are just and reasonable and true, and, that if the Democratic-Conservative party varies from its position in behalf of white supremacy, it will, to some extent, lose that strength, solidity and unity of purpose resulting from devotion to principle. We believe that in the black Republican counties of the eastern portion of this state, or wherever they may be found in this state, the fidelity of the white people to their political principles, and the material aid they give in swelling the aggregate vote for all officers elected by the state at large, and the high taxes they pay to carry on state government, and for other purposes which we forbear to mention, entitle them to the same consideration from their party friends in the General Assembly which Democratic counties receive through their members elect.

While we would exercise and advocate the right and practice of choosing white men for offices in preference to colored men, we hereby distinctly disclaim a desire to deny the colored race the equal rights before the law guaranteed to them by the 14th and 15th amendments to the Constitution of the United States.

Our feelings toward the colored people are kind and humane in every particular, and we believe the ultimate effect of the course we advocate, if pursued by our party, will be best for the country, for the people, both

white and black, and if the latter are not flattered and blinded by advocates
of the mistaken policy we oppose, we believe many of them will be able
to see the situation as we do, and thus, by their better understanding, we
may hope the antagonisms between the white and colored races will sub-
side, and their differences will be settled upon a somewhat reliable basis,
with less prospect of disturbance than if we abandon the principles and
policy which our party has heretofore maintained.

If the Democrats do what they persistently abused and condemned
Republicans for doing, how can they hope to escape just censure?
We protest in sorrow rather than in anger, against the action of our
political associates, who we believe with pure motives have acted unwisely.[13]

Shortly after the adjournment of the General Assembly in 1877,
this and similar protests by the whites of eastern North Carolina
gradually eased and finally ceased. However, unlike these short-lived
grumblings from the East, western North Carolina's dissatisfaction
with the county government system continued throughout the period.
This was reflected, either in the adverse opinion expressed by the
mountain whites or in the perennial pleadings by the eastern Democrats for western support. As a result, in the Democratic state convention of 1882, many delegates from the mountain counties were
openly hostile towards the county government system and insisted
upon its repeal. However, the eastern representatives persisted that it
was necessary "in order to keep the Negroes from getting county
offices."[14] In an official party publication, the Democrats in the same
year declared that they stood for control over county government
on the simple premise "that white men and not Negroes" should
dominate North Carolina politics. Then, in a direct appeal to the
voters in the western counties, the state Executive Committee asked,
"White men of North Carolina, will you go with the Negroes, or will
you side with your own blood and your own color?"[15]

In the 1884 political campaign, the editor of the Wilmington *Star*
stoutly informed the white voters of western North Carolina that the
county government system was "an absolute necessity." He went on
to say that without it "twenty-five or twenty-six" eastern counties
were "at the mercy of ignorant Negroes who have never learned to
distinguish between mine and thine."[16] Also in the same year, the

13. *Journal of the House of the General Assembly of the State of North Carolina,
1876-1877*, pp. 872-74.

14. New York *Daily Tribune*, July 6, 1882.

15. *Democracy vs. Radicalism*, The Democratic State Executive Committee, 1884,
pp. 42, 43. See also Appleton's *Annual Cyclopedia*, N.S. (1882), VII, 630.

16. Quoted in the Charlotte *Home Democrat*, August 15, 1884.

Democratic state Executive Committee, in a very strange bit of logic and reasoning, declared that "the white voters of the West are safe under any form of county government, and will, *from a mere sense of justice,* see to it that the present or some similar form of county government is maintained for *their* protection. [Italics mine.]"[17]

A near victory by the Republican party in the election of 1886 led Josephus Daniels, an ardent Democrat, who in 1894 assumed the editorship of the powerful and anti-Negro Raleigh *News and Observer,* to send letters to many of the foremost Democratic leaders in the state, asking them to explain the causes of the near defeat. Among the answers received, the overwhelming number coming from the leaders of western North Carolina listed two reasons. In the first place, their section was dissatisfied with the county government system that prevented the West from electing its local officials, and in the second place, the western section was dissatisfied with the refusal of the Democratic party in the state to agree to end its practice of injecting the perennial cry of "save Eastern North Carolina from Negro rule."[18] However, instead of catering to the demands of the West to "let up" on these two issues, the Democratic party of North Carolina in the election campaigns between 1888 and 1894 redoubled and intensified their efforts, apparently convinced that these issues, and these issues alone, could insure Democratic victories election year after election year.[19]

The Republicans of the state were quick to realize that western dissatisfaction was a weak spot in the defensive armor of the Democrats, and throughout the period constantly urged the West to "revolt against the despotism of Bourbon Democracy." In practically every election year the Republican platform demanded the repeal of "the iniquitous county government system," and extended sympathy to the western farmers "in their effort to throw the despotic yoke of Bourbon tyranny."[20] The editor of the Winston *Union-Republican* predicted in 1889 that instead of insuring a Democratic victory at the polls in 1890, "the honest white Democrats of the West will repudiate

17. *Democracy vs. Radicalism,* 1884, p. 126.

18. Josephus Daniels, *Tar Heel Editor* (Chapel Hill: University of North Carolina Press, 1939), p. 328. See also the speech of the Negro state senator, Henry Eppes, on "The Repeal of the Present System of County Government," made before the Senate of North Carolina, 1877. Manuscript in hands of R. Faulkner Eppes.

19. See *Democracy vs. Radicalism,* 1888, p. 25; Raleigh *News and Observer,* July 17, 1888, September 10, 1890, October 13, 1892, October 11, 1894; Greensboro *Daily Record,* August 19, 1892; Daniels, *Tar Heel Editor,* p. 361.

20. Raleigh *News and Observer,* August 29, 1890. See also *Democracy vs. Radicalism,* 1882, pp. 6-8; 1884, pp. 5-6, 11.

the wrongs of the present Bourbon system of county government."[21] Although these and other pleas and admonitions were in vain, as the Democrats continued to win victories at the ballot box, the ever present fear that one day the West would turn against them must have been most disquieting.

In addition to the establishment of the county government system, the North Carolina legislature between 1877 and 1894 took even more drastic steps to decrease the voting power of the Negroes of the eastern part of the state. The legislative session of 1876-1877 fired the opening barrage when it passed a series of suffrage qualification laws. The most thorough and widesweeping of these enactments was the act to regulate elections. The wide, almost autocratic powers granted to the registrars and judges of elections, the residence requirements, and the right of one voter to challenge another—all of these pointed to the intent of the framers to disfranchise or reduce the number of Negro voters. The responsibilities and powers of the registrars, for example, illustrate this rather clearly:

It shall be the duty of the registrar and judges of elections to attend at the polling place of their township or precinct with the registration books, on the Saturday preceeding the election, from the hour of nine o'clock A.M. till the hour of five o'clock P.M., when and where said books shall be open to the inspection of the electors of the precinct or township, and any of said electors shall be allowed to object to the name of any person appearing on said books. In case of any such objection, the registrar shall enter upon his books, opposite to the name of the person so objected to, the word "challenge," and shall appoint a time and place on or before election day, when he, together with said judges of election shall hear and decide said objection, giving due notice to the voter so objected to.[22]

It will be noted that the registration books were open only two working days, Saturday and Monday, prior to election day. Obviously, then, in the case of a challenge little time was left in which the person challenged could prove his qualifications.

To further secure a strangle hold on the ballot box, the Democrats decreed that all election judges were to be appointed by the justices of the peace. The law on that point read: "The board of justices of the peace for each county, on or before the first Monday of the month next preceding the month in which each election is held, shall appoint four judges or inspectors of election, two of whom shall be of a

21. Winston *Union-Republican*, March 28, 1889.
22. *Laws and Resolutions, 1876-1877*, c. 275, sec. 8. Act of March 12, 1877.

different political party, where possible, from the registrars, at each place of holding election in their respective counties."[23]

It would seem that much of the Democratic control over local elections would be reduced by the above provision calling for four judges, two being of a different political party, which meant in eastern North Carolina, two Republicans and two Democrats, but as Mabry points out, "illiterate and gullible Negroes or corruptible whites were appointed to serve as Republican judges," and the Democrats, therefore, were able to dominate the situation notwithstanding.[24] As a further limitation on Negro voting, the act stated that "upon request of any elector, the registrar shall require the applicant to prove his identity, or age, and residence, by the testimony of at least one elector, under oath."

This, however, was not enough for the North Carolina legislators, and in a subsequent section they gave to the judges almost limitless power to determine the eligibility of voters: "The judges of election shall in no case receive the vote of any person unless they shall be satisfied that such person is in all respects qualified and entitled to vote; and for the purpose of satisfying themselves as to the right of any person who shall claim a right to vote, they shall have power to examine such person, and any other person or persons, under oath or affirmation, touching such right."[25]

The law, thus far, represented the most conclusive and thorough effort by the whites to restrict the use of the ballot by the Negroes of North Carolina since 1865. Nevertheless, the legislature of 1877 went one step further, and in another section it centered its attention directly on the question of residence requirement. Contrary to the state constitution that granted the franchise to "every male person who has been naturalized, twenty-one years old or upward," and who had lived in North Carolina for a year, and ninety days in the county, the General Assembly in the 1876-1877 session required that a voter "shall have resided for ninety days immediately preceding an election, within the limits of any ward of a city or town, and not otherwise, shall have the right to vote in such ward for mayor and other city or town officers."[26] Article VI, section 1, of the state

23. *Ibid.,* sec. 9.

24. William A. Mabry, "The Negro in North Carolina Politics Since Reconstruction," *Trinity College Historical Society Papers,* XII (1940), 21.

25. *Laws and Resolutions, 1876-1877,* c. 275, sec. 63. Act of March 12, 1877.

26. *North Carolina Constitution as Amended by the Constitutional Convention of 1875,* Article VI, sec. 1; *Laws and Resolutions, 1876-1877,* c. 275, sec. 66. Act of March 12, 1877.

constitution, as amended by the Constitutional Convention of 1875, upped the residence requirement in the county from thirty to ninety days in order to take advantage of the frequent tendency of the Negroes to move from county to county, and hence disfranchise a larger percentage of Negroes than whites; that section of the 1877 law which required a ninety-day residence in a particular ward of a city or town was calculated to disfranchise even a larger number of Negroes. This modification, incidentally, was completely constitutional, for the Convention of 1875 had distinctly given the legislature "full power . . . to modify, change, or abrogate any and all provisions" of Article VI excepting sections seven, nine, and thirteen."[27]

The election law of 1877 also enabled the Democrats of North Carolina to preserve for seventeen years what Helen Edmonds calls "monolithic solidarity" in the eastern counties when it set up a board to determine the final official vote for each county. A brief description of its organizational structure and function reveals how it could conceivably control election results, especially in the "Negro counties." The judges of election appointed one man from each precinct to act as county canvasser. He, in turn, carried a return of his precinct vote to the county canvassers' meeting, which was held on the second day after the election. In the presence of the sheriff and other interested electors who wished to be present, the county canvassers were required by law "to open and canvass the returns and make abstracts stating the number of votes cast in each precinct for each office, the name of each person voted for, and the number of votes given to each person for each different office, and sign the same." The returns of the county canvassers were then sent to the State Board of Canvassers at Raleigh, which, in turn, announced the final count.[28] It is interesting to note that the legislature did not specifically empower the county canvassers "to judicially determine" the votes cast until 1883.[29] That these wide, almost unbridled, powers were subject to abuse by county canvassers, in particular when counting returns in the "Negro counties," may be seen from an examination of the decisions of the North Carolina Supreme Court with respect to election procedures.[30]

The Republican journal, the Raleigh *Signal*, disgustedly editorialized that the election law of 1877 gave the Democrats "absolute con-

27. Mabry, *Negro in N.C. Politics*, p. 15; *North Carolina Constitution*, Article VI, sec. 4.

28. *Laws and Resolutions, 1876-1877*, c. 275, sections 20-28, pp. 53, 55. Act of March 12, 1877.

29. *Code of North Carolina, 1883*, Vol. II, sec. 2694.

30. See Chapter VII on the North Carolina Supreme Court.

trol of every registration book and polling place, and every returning board in the State."[31]   Moreover, the Republican state Executive Committee attempted to convince the "laboring class of the white population" that the suffrage laws harmed them also. It warned that the Democratic party cared "no more for the humbler whites than it does for the colored men; and in order to reduce the blacks to a degraded position, the members of the Democratic party are compelled to legislate also against their own race . . . in striking at the colored man, they are compelled to disfranchise the laboring white man."[32]   That such counsel failed to impress the majority of "the humbler whites" is shown by their support of the Democratic party between 1876 and 1894.

The election law of 1877 remained unchanged for twelve years. Then in 1889, the North Carolina legislature turned its sight once again on the question of suffrage qualifications. Apparently, many Negroes who registered to vote each election year were unable to give a satisfactory answer as to place of birth, place of residence, and full name.[33] At any rate, in 1889, the General Assembly passed an act that declared flatly that "No registration shall be valid unless it specifies as near as may be the age, occupation, place of birth and place of residence of the elector, as well as the township or county from whence the elector has removed—in the event of a removal—and the full name by which the voter is known."[34]

In a bitter denunciation of this section, the Raleigh *Signal* declared that "it must be apparent to every fair-minded man that this qualification cannot be met by a large number of white and colored, while the intelligent and honest registrar may know that the ignorant elector is fully qualified." The editor continued: "This is a simple and undeniable truth, and . . . that amendment was made for the very purpose of reducing the Republican vote . . . for how many illiterate whites, as well as colored, can give his age correctly, or the place of his birth?"[35]

The editor also said that section 3, which stipulated that age, occupation, and place of birth "as near as may be," would be used only for the Democratic electors, while section 6, which was identical to

31. Raleigh *Signal*, February 28, 1889.

32. "Address to the Voters of North Carolina," Republican State Executive Committee, March 7, 1889, p. 3.

33. See Helen G. Edmonds, *The Negro and Fusion Politics in North Carolina, 1895-1901* (Chapel Hill: University of North Carolina Press, 1951), p. 69.

34. *Laws and Resolutions, 1889,* c. 287, sections 3 and 6. Act of March 7, 1889.

35. Raleigh *Signal*, March 21, 1889.

section 3 but without the clause "as near as may be," would be employed in registering Republican voters.[36]

If the general spirit and intent of the act thus far was to restrict further Negro voters, one section, at least, seemed to be an improvement over the 1877 election law. According to section 8 of the earlier statute, registration books were to be open only two working days before an election, Saturday and Monday. The law of 1889 provided that the registration books were to be open from the Saturday preceding the election until the following Saturday; thus persons who were challenged were given at least seven days to prove qualifications.[37] This seemingly liberal portion of the law, however, was effectively poisoned and enfeebled by another section that placed greater power in the hands of the registrars to determine the eligibility of voters. Section 12 of the 1877 election law provided that, upon the request of any elector, the registrar could require the registrant to prove his identity or age and residence by "the testimony of at least one elector under oath." The 1889 law changed this statement to read "by such testimony, under oath, as may be satisfactory to the registrar."[38] In effect, then, the registrar could register or refuse whom he pleased, and there was no appeal from his decision. That this section of the law was subject to abuse by white registrars in the "Negro counties" of eastern North Carolina who desired to keep the Negro vote at a minimum is fairly obvious.

Section 8 of the new election law appeared the most novel. It provided that election officials could "rail off" a space of enclosure with an opening at one end or one side for the entrance of the voter, and an opening at the other side for his exit. Only one voter was allowed to enter at one time, and no one except the judges was allowed to speak to him. His ballot was to be put in the proper box by him or by judges at his request.[39] In protesting this section, the Raleigh *Signal* said that "requiring white men and black men who cannot read to put their ballots in the right boxes is to require an impossibility; and the further provision that every ballot put in the wrong box shall not be counted, is simply to establish an educational qualification, . . . without providing for this change in our law in so many words."[40]

The section, however, causing the greatest amount of agitation

36. *Ibid.*
37. *Laws and Resolutions, 1889,* c. 287, sec. 4.
38. *Ibid.,* sec. 6.
39. *Ibid.,* sec. 8.
40. Raleigh *Signal,* March 7, 1889.

and opposition, was number 9, which gave the canvassers the power and authority "to judicially pass" upon all the facts relative to the, election and "judicially determine and declare" the results. The clearest statement in opposition to this section was given by Richmond Pearson, a former chief justice of the North Carolina Supreme Court. He said that the county board of canvassers "instead of recording a historical fact . . . can make history to suit themselves. . . . So that instead of a 'government of the people, by the people and for the people,' we are to have a government by irresponsible commissioners, arbitrary registrars and infallible returning boards." He described the law as undemocratic and dangerous and predicted the disappearance of the Republican party in the state unless the law was repealed.[41] On March 11, 1889, the day of the passage of the election bill, Henry H. Faulkener, Negro state senator, in a short, moving protest, cut through the pretense that the law was intended to provide for fair elections. "I do most solemnly protest against the passage of the election law," he said, "because I believe it will operate against my race and deprive them of the God-given rights that are guaranteed them by the Constitution of the United States, and ought to be held sacred, and will deprive the Eastern Counties of their legal representation."[42]

The Raleigh *Signal* prophesied that "the amount of wrong, injustice and fraud that may be perpetrated under this law, not to say crime, cannot be told by the addition of figures."[43] Another Republican newspaper, attacking the bill several days before its passage, charged that "under pretense of disfranchising the 'nigger' in the East, his law places the ballots of the white men of the West at the disposal of a lot of ringsters and, under the cry of 'a white man's government,' saps the very foundation of liberty of all the people . . . such legislation is infamous."[44] A North Carolina Negro, Charles N. Hunter, writing in a national magazine about the election law of 1889, declared: "I am sorry that I cannot say the relations between the races in this State are improving. . . . There has not been such bitterness in North Carolina since emancipation barring the years immediately succeeding reconstruction. We feel keenly the hardships of our present situation, and are determined, under God, to find relief. We can no longer endure the oppression of the Southland than a magazine could stand the application of a torch."

41. From the Asheville *Citizen*, quoted in the Raleigh *Signal*, March 28, 1889.
42. *Senate Journal*, 1889, 916.
43. Raleigh *Signal*, March 7, 1889.
44. Winston *Union-Republican*, February 28, 1889.

Hunter then urged the periodical not to publish his name. Since he was a public school teacher, Hunter said that he was aware of the probable consequences to him were his identity known. "Free speech," he concluded, "is no more possible for colored people in the South than a free ballot."[45]

Typical of the editorial opinion of the Democratic papers was the retort of the New Bern *Daily Journal,* which, while admitting that the law was not perfect, said that it was "as nearly so as the present condition of affairs will permit." The Tarboro *Southerner* said: "There is nothing wrong about the law. It is plain, simple, to the point. An elector who knows whom he is voting for will equally know as well what box to deposit his ballot. If he doesn't know, it makes no difference if he votes not at all."[46]

At the same time the Republican press and Negro citizens of the state were protesting the "infamous" election law of 1889, and the white supremacists were congratulating themselves on a job well done, the United States Congress was debating a bill that guaranteed to insure fair elections. The Lodge or Force bill, in brief, was this: a petition signed by five hundred persons in a district, or fifty persons in a county, would permit federal officers to supervise federal elections.[47] Perhaps at first glance, one would not understand the sudden explosion in North Carolina in particular, and the South in general, against the bill, but upon a closer scrutiny, one could explain the wrath. Helen Edmonds correctly points out that the Lodge bill would have inevitably exerted an influence upon state politics, as federal and state elections were often held simultaneously and in the identical place.[48] This, of course, the white citizens could not possibly accept, because it would certainly have challenged, if not defeated, white supremacy. Therefore, the North Carolina General Assembly in 1891 drafted a resolution that requested that its representatives in the United States Congress oppose the Federal Election bill.[49]

Not only did the legislators of North Carolina enact laws curbing the power of the Negro vote in the "Negro counties" of the state, but they also attempted to reduce it in the "Negro towns" of the eastern sections. In some, such as New Bern, the legislature simply passed an

45. Quoted in the *Independent,* November 14, 1889. Charles N. Hunter Scrapbook, 1891-1911, Duke University Library, Durham.
46. New Bern *Daily Journal,* March 9, 1889; Tarboro *Southerner,* February 28, 1889.
47. For a discussion of this bill, see Ruth E. Byrd, "The History of the Force Bill of 1890 and its Effect upon State Constitutions" (Unpublished master's thesis, University of North Carolina, 1939).
48. Edmonds, *Fusion Politics,* p. 11.
49. *Laws and Resolutions, 1891,* p. 653.

act permitting a rearrangement of the city's voting wards in such a way as either to locate the Negroes in one ward, or to divide them among several wards in such a way that their votes would be impotent.[50] It was, however, the political power, real or fancied, of the Negroes of Wilmington, North Carolina's largest city during the period, that drew the special attention of the state legislators between 1877 and 1894. Accordingly, the General Assembly on March 6, 1877, passed the first of a series of laws designed to free this port city of "Negro domination and Negro rule." An eligible voter was required to be not only a resident of North Carolina for one year, but also a "bona fide resident in the particular ward in which he applies to be registered, ninety days next preceding any such election, and no other person shall be so entitled." This section of the law also carried the following provision:

Any elector may, and it shall be the duty of the registrar, to challenge the right to register of any person known or suspected not to be lawfully entitled to register; and when any such challenge shall be made, it shall be the duty of the registrar to inquire into and decide as to the right of the person so challenged to registration, and if it shall appear that such person is not so entitled, he shall be excluded from registration.[51]

Section 5 of the law is an interesting and illuminating provision that declared that voters were not only to be challenged by the judges of elections, as provided in section 4, but also that "no registration, in the first place, was to be considered valid, if the registration did not specify the name of the person applying for registration, and the number of the lot, the number of the block, and the number of the ward (and subdivision of the ward, if there be) in which he resides."[52]

Evidence is not available, but it would appear that the exacting provisions of section 5 of the 1877 law worked a hardship on both Negro and white voters of Wilmington, for six years later it was amended to read that the board of aldermen for the city were to have each block and lot "properly numbered at least thirty days" before an election, "the numbers of the block to be printed in large letters and placed on two posts of each block, and the number of each lot to be printed in large letters and put in each end of the lots in some convenient place and notice of the same to be published for one week thereafter in the city papers."[53] The next session of the General

50. *Ibid., 1876-1877*, c. 81. Act of February 7, 1877.
51. *Ibid.*, c. 192. Act of March 6, 1877.
52. *Ibid.*, sec. 5.
53. *Laws and Resolutions, 1883*, c. 308. Act of March 9, 1883.

Assembly made further changes in the registration law of Wilmington, for the 1877 act was again amended to provide that each voter was also required to give the number of the house in which he lived.[54] Thus, with the almost autocratic power given the registrars and judges of elections, in addition to the web-like intricacies involved in registration procedures, the illiterate Negro voters of Wilmington had little or no chance of realizing the opportunity to exercise the franchise.

Consequently, with the Negro's vote partially controlled by legislative enactments, there was no longer the fear of Negro domination on the city council by the election of Negro aldermen. However, the franchise, though weakened in certain respects, was still exercised by the Negroes of Wilmington; and the mayor was elected by city-wide popular vote. Therefore, in order to relieve the local citizenry of the responsibility of electing the local executive, the legislature, on February 20, 1891, passed an act that provided that the mayor of Wilmington was to be elected by the board of aldermen, either from one of its own members or from the city at large.[55]

The law permitting the aldermen of Wilmington to elect that city's mayor represents the culmination of suffrage restrictions and disabilities against the Negro group during the period. Only by a liberal interpretation of these laws by the North Carolina Supreme Court could the Negroes look forward to the retention of some of the suffrage privileges and rights they enjoyed between 1868 and 1876.

54. *Ibid., 1885,* c. 156, sec. 1. Act of February 26, 1885.
55. *Laws and Resolutions, 1891,* c. 429, sec. 1. Act of February 20, 1891.

7

"The Law Knows No Distinction"

The law knows no distinction among the people of the State in their civil and political rights and correspondent obligations.
    Justice Smith, *Capehart vs. Stewart*, 80 N.C. 101 (1879).

Between "the glorious" Democratic victory in 1876 and that party's defeat in 1894 by "a mongrel party," the Democratic-dominated General Assembly of North Carolina, as it has been shown, enacted a series of well-defined statutes spelling out the legal status of the Negroes of the state. The question at this point, then, may well be to what extent did the members of the North Carolina Supreme Court regard themselves as the policemen of these laws? The query is of special significance because Article IV, section 21, of the state constitution declared that the Supreme Court justices were to be elected "by the qualified voters of the State," for a term of eight years. Accordingly, if the masses of the white citizens of North Carolina, as reflected in the laws passed by the legislatures, were so far in favor of white supremacy as to demand the protection of their interests, would the judges hold opinions very different? A partial answer can be found in an examination of the various decisions they made which involved the rights and privileges of Negroes of North Carolina.

By far the largest number of "Negro cases," or cases that might eventually affect the Negro in one way or another, coming before the North Carolina Supreme Court, centered around the legality of the suffrage and public school laws passed by the legislators between 1877 and 1894. That the Negroes of the state, along with liberal-minded whites, would contest the constitutionality of these legislative enactments, as well as their local application and interpretation by local white public officials, should occasion no surprise.

One major group of suffrage cases argued before the State Supreme Court involved the "jurisdiction" of the state and county canvassers. Under the election act of 1877, the legislature had granted to them certain specified powers with respect to counting and certifying the results of county, state, and congressional elections.[1] Two years later the court received its first "power of county and state canvassers" case. It developed out of the elections held in Edgecombe County on November 5, 1878. On that day, James E. O'Hara, the Republican candidate from the Second Congressional District of North Carolina for a seat in the United States House of Representatives, received a large number of votes from the Negroes of Edgecombe County. The returns from the various voting places in the county, as prescribed by law, were made to the Board of County Canvassers at its meeting on November 7, 1878. The Board, during the process of counting the returns, rejected approximately 1,400 votes from the precincts in Edgecombe County—votes, incidentally, which would have made O'Hara the victor over his Democratic rival William H. Kitchin. In an effort to compel the members of the Edgecombe County Board of Canvassers to reassemble and recount the ballots, including the rejected ones, O'Hara instituted court action through mandamus proceedings.

The case, heard before the Rocky Mount Superior Court, received widespread publicity and attention. Negroes "from far and near" flocked into the courthouse chamber "to see the man of their color fight his way into the National Halls of Legislation." A reporter for the Tarboro *Southerner,* in describing the attentiveness of the Negroes present, wrote that "it was amusing to watch Sambo's countenance corrugated in 'rapt attention to legal discourse of which he did not comprehend the sound, sentiment, or seeming."[2] This reporter, perhaps, was correct about the inability of the Negroes to grasp the legal verbiage, but when the judge ruled in favor of O'Hara, they under-

1. *Public and Private Laws and Resolutions of the State of North Carolina, 1876-1877,* c. 275, sections 20, 25, 26, 27, 53, 55.
2. Tarboro *Southerner,* December 12, 1878.

stood quite clearly that a Negro had won an important victory in a white man's court.

The Edgecombe County canvassers, however, appealed to the Supreme Court of North Carolina, where the counsel for O'Hara requested that the lower court's ruling be upheld. But Chief Justice Smith, in reversing the judgment of the superior court, held that the matter had passed beyond the jurisdiction of the court and ruled that the preceding had to be dismissed. The court reasoned that, since the State Board of Canvassers had acted upon the returns transmitted to it and had issued a commission to Kitchin, O'Hara had no cause for action. Smith declared that had the State Board of Canvassers received the corrected returns "in time to be acted upon before its final adjournment," O'Hara's right "to the aid of the Court would seem to be clear and indisputable; but on account of the delays incident to judicial proceedings, the remedy by mandamus is practically useless." The court, however, having refused to issue the writ, suggested that O'Hara contest the election before the House of Representatives.[3] O'Hara followed the court's advice and carried the issue before the United States Congress on April 15, 1879. His opponent, Kitchin, nevertheless, retained the contested seat.[4] Thus, in its first test, the North Carolina Supreme Court was able to postpone a direct decision as to the extent of the authority of the county canvassers.

But the issue would not stay down, and a year later it reached the Supreme Court again in the case of *John H. Peebles vs. Commissioners of Davie County*.[5] Here, the court held that a board of county canvassers "had no authority to revise the registry or to examine into the qualifications of those who were refused permission to vote." Chief Justice Smith continued: "They may and must determine the authenticity and regularity of the returns themselves; but when received, they must be counted as imparting absolute verity, as far as the county canvassers are concerned, in determining the aggregate vote and its results."[6] This decision, in effect, said that the powers conferred upon the boards of county canvassers of elections did not extend to inquiries into any facts that could be claimed to have made the election invalid, such as fraud, threats, or intimidation.

That such a ruling encouraged greater abuses in the eastern

3. *O'Hara vs. Powell et al., County Canvassers*, 80 N.C. 104 (1879), at 106.
4. *Congressional Record*, Forty-sixth Congress, 1st session, 1879, p. 468. See also Samuel D. Smith, *The Negro in Congress, 1870-1901* (Chapel Hill: University of North Carolina Press, 1940), pp. 117-18.
5. 82 N.C. 385 (1880).
6. *Ibid.*, at 389.

counties by both electors and county canvassers is obvious and, no doubt, accounted for the Supreme Court's assertion in 1887 that although the declaration of the results of an election by the boards of county canvassers established a prima facie right in favor of the persons ascertained to have been elected, "it does not exclude jurisdiction of the proper courts to examine and determine the correctness and sufficiency of the returns and the true results of the election." Justice Merrimon, in concluding this opinion, remarked that

The registrar and judges of elections, within their several voting precincts, exercise judicial power and decide many important questions in respect to the election they hold and the rights of persons claiming the right to vote; but these decisions are not final, nor generally are they conclusive. . . . The purpose is to leave the matter so decided upon, to be contested by any parties interested regularly before the proper courts when need be.[7]

But long, drawn-out litigations cost money, and "the unfortunate thing about the system of justice is that only the wealthy can take every chance to secure what they regard as their right."[8] Since the majority of the Negro office-seekers were men of average or below-average means, many otherwise contested election cases were never heard "before the proper courts."

However, a series of cases arising out of the November, 1886, elections in Craven County illustrates the determination of the North Carolina Supreme Court to become the final arbiter in spelling out the judicial powers of the county canvassers. In the contests for register of deeds, sheriff, treasurer, and coroner of Craven County, the county canvassers rejected many of the returns and therefore certified that the candidates had been elected even though they had received a minority of the aggregate vote cast.[9] Interestingly, all the minority candidates were Democrats. The New Bern *Daily Journal* upheld the action of the board in "determining the results of the election . . . upon the ground of intimidation, fraud and corruption. . . ." It appeared that some Negro voters had desired to vote the Democratic ticket, but other Negroes had "persuaded" them not to do so.[10] However, when the cases came before the North Carolina Supreme Court in 1887, Justice Merrimon invoked the doctrine of *Gatling vs. Boone.*

7. *W. J. Gatling vs. Thomas D. Boone*, 98 N.C. 573 (1887).

8. Raleigh *News and Observer*, April 19, 1914.

9. *Hancock, Jr. vs. Hubbs*, 98 N.C. 589 (1887); *Hahn vs. Stinson*, 98 N.C. 591 (1887); *Kilburn vs. Patterson*, 98 N.C. 593 (1887); *Oden vs. Bates*, 98 N.C. 594 (1887).

10. New Bern *Daily Journal*, November 10, 1887.

Not only did the North Carolina Supreme Court challenge the finality of the decisions made by the boards of county canvassers in the predominantly "Negro counties" of the East but also it thwarted the attempt of the county commissioners in that region to refuse to induct Negroes who had been elected to local offices. Chief among these cases was *Hannon vs. Grizzard*.[11] It developed out of the election held in November, 1882, in Halifax County. John H. Hannon, a Negro, was elected register of deeds for that county and was subsequently declared duly elected by the county canvassers. However, when he applied for admission to the office, the board of county commissioners refused his application required by the state constitution in that he had not "resided in the state twelve months next preceding the election, and ninety days in the county."[12] Having declared the office vacant, the board appointed James M. Grizzard, one of its own members, as register of deeds. Hannon brought action before the Halifax Superior Court to oust Grizzard and to install himself as the register of deeds. The Negro testified that he had been born in Halifax County in 1850 and that, although he had accepted a job in Washington, D.C., as a night watchman in the Treasury Department in 1875, he had continued to pay his poll tax in Halifax County and to vote there. He further stated that he never had been absent from the county "for twelve months at one time . . ." and that he had always considered North Carolina as his home. Although requested to do so by Grizzard's counsel, the presiding judge refused to give instructions to the jury that Hannon "had not shown an actual *bona fide* residence in the State, and that being a single man, sleeping and boarding at Washington during his stay and while acting as a watchman, he was not meanwhile a resident of the State within the meaning of the constitution," and that the jury should thus bring in a verdict against him. Instead, the judge instructed the jury that if they believed that Hannon "was born in 1850 in Halifax County, and there had his fixed abode until 1875, when he accepted service under the department at Washington . . . returning once or twice a year on leave of absence, voted and paid taxes to the county and town authorities until January 1883 when he came back to the county; where he had since remained, with no intention of abandoning his home . . . ," then the issue should be found in his favor. The jury ruled in Hannon's favor, and Grizzard appealed to the North Carolina Supreme Court.[13]

11. 89 N.C. 115 (1883).
12. Article VI, sections 1 and 4.
13. *Hannon vs. Grizzard,* at 118.

Chief Justice Smith, upholding the decision of the lower court, said that the residence clause in the North Carolina constitution was not intended to deprive its own citizens of the right to vote "when they left the state and resided temporarily beyond its limits, with a constant purpose to retain their homes and return to them when the object, which called them away was attained." He pointed out that the residence clause referred "more especially" to individuals entering the state for the first time, that Hannon's constitutional residence remained unchanged, and that none of his political rights as a citizen of North Carolina had been lost by his employment and temporary residence in Washington, D.C.[14] Commenting on the court's decision, the Wilson *Advance* noted cryptically: "The [North Carolina] Supreme Court has decided that Hannon, colored, is entitled to the office of Register of Deeds in Halifax. J. M. Grizzard, democrat, elected by the Commissioners, steps down and out. He made a good officer."[15]

During the period under survey, the North Carolina Supreme Court was also called upon to decide the extent of the power granted to the registrars of elections by the legislature. Although the 1877 session had given them vast jurisdiction, the 1889 session of the General Assembly, in spite of strong protests, extended their authority even further. That the court would get a case challenging the validity of the 1889 election law was never doubted by its critics. The two big questions were: When would it be given such a case? And how would it decide? Three years after the passage of the 1889 law, the Supreme Court of North Carolina answered these two queries.

In the election of 1890 in Montgomery County, Travis N. Harris opposed George M. Scarborough for the office of register of deeds. The former was defeated, but upon learning that some of the ballots cast for him had been rejected by the registrar, he instituted court action against Scarborough for the office in a special term of the Superior Court in Montgomery County. The verdict was against Harris, and he appealed to the Supreme Court of the state. Testimony revealed that the registrar, acting under section 3 of the 1889 election law, had thrown out some of the ballots. That section declared that "no registration shall be valid unless it specifies, as near as may be, the age, occupation, place of birth, place of residence of the elector as well as the township or county from which the elector has removed. . . ." Evidence was introduced to show that some of the voters in Little River Township had given as their place of birth and residence

14. *Ibid.,* at 121.
15. Wilson *Advance,* November 16, 1883.

"Montgomery County." Further testimony showed that when the voters appeared for registration and registered, the registrar questioned them, and the voters' answers were as they had been written in the registration book. The Supreme Court was called upon to decide two questions: first, the constitutionality of the 1889 election law and, second, whether the registrar had carried out the duties of his office following his oral questioning of the voters, or had accepted the ambiguous answers with full knowledge that the registration would be invalidated. In answer to the constitutionality of the statute, Justice Avery said, "It is now well settled that legislatures acting under such grants of power, may enact registration laws for the purpose, both of preventing those not entitled to vote from enjoying the privilege, and of securing the right of suffrage to the qualified electors; though they have no power to add to their constitutional qualifications."[16]

On the question as to whether the registrar had performed his duty fully and completely, Justice Avery remarked that "In absence of proof to the contrary, it is always presumed that the officer has done his duty. Every citizen is presumed to know the law governing his relations with others. . . . In the absence of any definite information on the subject, the failure to enter upon the registration book such facts connected with the history of an elector . . . must be considered due to carelessness or inexcusable ignorance of such elector."[17]

Justice Clark, in a strong minority opinion, dissented, in part from the reasoning of Justice Avery in the majority opinion. His liberal thoughts are in sharp contrast to the conservative ones of Justice Avery.

When the voters in Little River Township and precinct, to the interrogatives of the registrar, gave simply "Montgomery County" as their place of birth and residence, such an answer, if truthful, and in the absence of a requirement in the statute that the voter should particularize further by giving the name of the town or township of birth and residence, was sufficient, and it was in error to hold that the votes of persons so registered should be thrown out. Most especially is this so, when the officer of the law receives such responses without objection or demand for further particularity or identification on the part of the voter.[18]

Justice Clark admitted that simply declaring "North Carolina" as a place of birth was indefinite, "but," he added, "it was error of the Court to hold, as a matter of law, that *per se,* this was the fault of the voter and invalidated the vote given by him. . . . If the registrar, when

16. *Harris vs. Scarborough,* 110 N.C. 232 (1890) at 263.
17. *Ibid.,* at 240.
18. *Ibid.,* at 243.

such response was given, had asked for a fuller and more definite response, and this had been refused or not given, then there would have been conduct on the part of the person offering to register which might be justly held as sufficient to deprive him of the right to vote."[19]

In spite of an occasional adverse decision, the Supreme Court of North Carolina was the single conspicuous protector of the suffrage rights of the Negroes of the state.

19. *Ibid.*

Part Two

Economics

8

"Your Work Is the Tilling of the Ground"

Each race has its appointed work before it. Your work is the tilling of the ground. You are an agricultural community. Address yourselves to the work, men and women alike. Become good farmers, get land, own your homes.

Address of Governor James S. Jarvis at the opening of the Colored Industrial Fair in Raleigh, 1883, quoted in the Chatham RECORD, November 22, 1883.

North Carolina in 1876 was predominantly a rural state, and continued to be so throughout the period in spite of the steady migrations of both whites and Negroes to the towns and cities. Since the large majority of the Negroes lived in the rural areas, most of this group derived a livelihood from the soil. White opposition restricted greatly their entrance into many of the skilled trades; and since the Negroes were forced to make a living or starve, they followed the line of least resistance and, incidentally, the traditional calling of that race since ante-bellum times, living from the soil. Of course, the other factor that wedded the Negroes of the state to the soil was that the bulk of them lacked adequate training in activities other than farming and hence could not compete successfully with the whites, assuming that there were no economic restrictions against them.

Specifically, 136,467, or 64.6 per cent of the total Negro population of North Carolina in 1890, were employed in agricultural pursuits, chiefly as agricultural laborers, tenants, and farmers. Indeed, 43.6 per cent of *all* Negroes employed in North Carolina in 1890 were agricultural laborers hired, in the majority of cases, by white farmers.[1] Agricultural or wage laborers appeared to be preferred over tenants, as the prevailing belief of a large portion of the white landlords was that the Negroes "worked better when working for wages."[2]

In the post-Reconstruction era, Negroes, however, whether tenants or wage laborers, shared some common problems. One was wage discrimination in favor of the white farm workers. Another was the practice of paying wages to farm hands and tenants in supplies. A third problem affecting Negro tenants was the operation of the mortgage and lien bond system.

With respect to wages, the weight of the evidence seems to support the view that Negro agricultural laborers were employed at wages lower than those paid to white agricultural laborers. A landlord in Caswell County (59.8 per cent Negro in 1880) was quick to admit that "there is some difference in the price paid to white and colored laborers."[3] This wage differential, however, was not restricted to the "Negro counties"[4] of eastern North Carolina. According to a white tenant in Davidson County (19.6 per cent Negro in 1880), Negro farm laborers received "about 40 cents per day," a sum somewhat lower than that paid to whites.[5] In Henderson, a mountain county in western North Carolina, with a Negro percentage of only 13.5 per cent in 1880, a white farm laborer pointed out that "white hands . . . received $1.50 to $2.00 per month more than colored."[6] Some Negro farm laborers, in consequence of the discriminatory wage scale, unilaterally dissolved an arrangement that they viewed as unfair and unjust. This practice of quitting the farm, sometimes in the midst of planting or harvesting crops, brought strong criticism from the North Carolina Commissioner of Labor, W. N. Jones. While ad-

1. Compiled by the writer from U.S. Bureau of the Census, *Eleventh Census of the United States: 1890. Population.* (Washington: Government Printing Office, 1897), Vol. I, Part II, p. 592.

2. See *First Annual Report of the North Carolina Bureau of Labor Statistics, 1887,* pp. 102-3, 111-12, 134, 136; *Second Annual Report, 1888,* p. 412; *Third Annual Report, 1889,* pp. 32, 36, 88, 132; *Fifth Annual Report, 1891,* pp. 38, 50.

3. *First Annual Report of the North Carolina Bureau of Labor Statistics, 1887,* p. 90.

4. Counties with 50 per cent or more Negro population.

5. *First Annual Report,* p. 127.

6. *Ibid.,* p. 129.

mitting that farms hands were "very" poorly paid, he declared that
low wages were "no excuse for abandoning a contract which has been
entered into and which can be performed." Although he recognized
one of the more disagreeable features of the farm-hand-landlord agreement, Jones observed, nevertheless, that "a bad bargain should be
adhered to as well as a good one." This should be done, he lamely
concluded, because "it dignifies and helps any one to do so. . . ."[7] The
State Chronicle, making no attempt to explain away the depressed
economic plight of the farmers, noted soberly: "it is a sad truth that
there is little profit in farming in North Carolina. . . . Farming pays
little profit and [Negro] laborers on the farm get small wages. . . ."[8]

There were two basic reasons for the lower wages paid to Negro
agricultural workers. In the first place, the bulk of the whites were
convinced that the Negroes would "live on less." In the second place,
they asserted that the Negroes demanded less wages. The following
three examples are cases in point. A landlord in Northampton County
(60.1 per cent Negro in 1880) said that he employed Negro farm laborers because it is not so expensive to feed them.[9] A white laborer in
Pitt County (50.9 per cent Negro in 1880), apparently much disgruntled and disgusted, ventured the opinion that since wages were so
low, "nobody but a lazy Negro can work at them and live."[10] Writing
in the *North Carolina University Magazine* Plato Collins, in two short
sentences, stated the principal reasons, real or fancied, which resulted
in lower wages for the Negroes of North Carolina. He wrote that, in
the first place, "the Negro is a cheap liver and demands less wages."
In the second place, "he can live on less, can dress well in our old
clothes."[11]

It seems, however, that no matter by what mode the whites justified
the low wages paid to the Negroes, the inescapable conclusion is that
the former, realizing the occupational restrictions placed upon the
Negroes, were well aware that the darker brother, in order to live,
would work at any price. Keenly aware of the economic obstacles
against them, as well as their lack of training in other pursuits, the
Negroes themselves accepted the low agricultural wages or migrated
to the towns and cities where a similar situation faced them. One
white newspaper editor, commenting on the "poverty of the town,"

7. *Ibid.,* 77-78.
8. Raleigh *State Chronicle,* April 27, 1888.
9. *Ibid.,* p. 103.
10. *Ibid.,* p. 42.
11. Plato Collins, "The Negro Must Remain in the South," *North Carolina University Magazine,* N. S., X (1890), 147.

failed to perceive this as one of the real motives behind the city-ward movement of the Negroes of North Carolina.

They [the Negroes] seem to imagine that there is degradation in agriculture, and honors in almost any employment in the crowded city. . . . The colored laborers, upon whom depend mainly the robust activities of the farm, congregate about the market places, whiskey shops, and grocery shops, and live upon a lean pittance, rather than remove to the corn and cotton fields, where they can obtain a good support for themselves and their families.[12]

Official wage statistics between 1876 and 1894 do not separate the two races. The following are averages for *all* farm laborers in 1889 without racial distinction: male "day hands" received from 35¢ to 65¢ a day; women "day hands" from 25¢ to 40¢. The average for the year for the men was 50¢ a day; for the women, 25¢. As to the monthly wage scale, men were paid from $6 to $10, with an average of $8. Women were paid from $4 to $5 monthly. The yearly wage was as follows: men, $75 to $120, with an average of $96: women, $36 to $70, with an average of $40.[13] Five years later (1894), the average wages for farm hands had changed very little from the 1889 figures.[14] It should be pointed out, however, that in many instances the low wages paid to the farmhands were counterbalanced by the practice of some landlords to furnish the families of the laborers with houses, garden patches, fuel, places to raise poultry and pigs, and "horses and wagons to go to church."[15]

The mortgage and lien bond system, according to one observer, proved "a worse curse . . . than droughts, floods, cyclones, storms, rust, caterpillars and every other evil that attends the farmer."[16] The general operation of the system is familiar to most. A description is, therefore, not necessary. Suffice it to say that the mortgage averaged about 40 per cent of the tenant's crop in the heavily Negro-populated eastern counties of North Carolina.[17] Frederick Douglass, one of the most militant and aggressive of the Negro leaders of the nineteenth century, described in some detail the workings of the mortgage and lien bond system as it affected the Negro.

12. Raleigh *Farmer and Mechanic*, November 8, 1877.
13. *Third Annual Report of the North Carolina Bureau of Labor Statistics, 1887,* pp. 25-141.
14. *Eighth Annual Report of the North Carolina Bureau of Labor Statistics, 1894,* p. 87.
15. *Ibid.*, p. 87.
16. *First Annual Report*, pp. 76-77.
17. *Ibid.*

The white landlords rent their land to the Negro at an exorbitant price per annum, and compel him to mortgage his crops in advance. The laws under which this is done are entirely in the interest of the landlord. He has a first claim upon everything produced on the land. The Negro can have nothing, can keep nothing, can sell nothing, without the consent of the landlord. As the Negro is at the start poor and empty handed, he has to draw on the landlord for meat and bread to feed himself and family while his crop is growing. The landlord keeps books; the Negro does not; hence no matter how hard he may work or how saving he may be, he is, in most cases, brought in debt at the end of the year, and once in debt, he is fastened to the land by hooks of steel. If he attempts to leave he may be arrested under the law.[18]

The tenancy laws, as Douglass pointed out, appeared to be concerned almost exclusively with protecting the interest of the landlord group. This may be seen from an examination of the North Carolina Code of 1883 relative to tenant-landlord relationships. Section 1754 declared that the landlord will have full possession of the crops "until the rents . . . and all stipulations contained in the lease or agreement are met by the tenant."[19] Section 1759 made it a misdeameanor for the tenant to remove the crop or parts without a five-day notice to the landlord.[20] Section 1701 made it unlawful for the tenant to "willfully and unlawfully demolish, destroy, deface, injure or damage any tenement house, uninhabited house or other outhouse," belonging to the landlord. For so doing he could be fined or imprisoned or both, "at the discretion of the courts."[21]

The punitive sections of the tenancy laws, notably the one concerned with the removal of crops, applied only to the tenant. The failure of North Carolina legislators to provide for criminal prosecution of landlords perhaps suggests a disinclination to guarantee fair and equal treatment for tenants. Furthermore, the courts of the state, in interpreting the removal statute, declared that a tenant could be found guilty if he removed cotton from the leased premises before the payment of rent and without the landlord's knowledge or consent, though it was with the intent of storing and preserving the crop for which purpose no adequate means existed on the leased premises.[22]

Although the tenancy laws were not aimed specifically at Negro

18. Frederick Douglass, "Lessons of the Hour" (Address delivered in the Metropolitan A.M.E. Church, Washington, D.C., January 9, 1894), pp. 28-29.

19. *The Code of North Carolina, 1883.* (New York, 1883), I, 666.

20. *Ibid.,* p. 668. See also "The Exodus into Indiana," *Leslie's Illustrated Newspaper,* XLIX (January 17, 1880), 362.

21. *The Code of North Carolina, 1883,* p. 669.

22. *State vs. Williams,* 106 N.C. 646 (1890).

tenants, their operation probably brought greater hardships upon them than upon whites. Thus, the Negro's already precarious existence as a non-propertied tiller of the soil was made even more so by the mortgage and lien bond system, mentioned above. This arrangement, which demanded approximately 40 per cent of the annual crop of the Negro and white tenant farmers in the eastern counties, led the North Carolina Bureau of Labor Statistics to declare that "the most profitable business . . . cannot pay such a per cent as that, much less farming. A farmer who pays it is carrying on a useless game, in which he must sooner or later lose all he has."[23]

There is considerable evidence that much of the unreliability of Negro tenants and farm hands can be attributed to the mortgage and lien bond system. A landlord in Bertie County (58.9 per cent Negro in 1890) admitted that the low moral status of farm labor in his area was caused by the malpractices of the system. "The poor Negro," he said, ". . . will steal his own cotton and sell it in seed to buy the necessaries of life under the belief and advice that it is no harm to steal [his] own mortgaged crop."[24] Partly in protest against the mortgage and lien bond system, a state group of "representative colored men" met in Raleigh in 1880 and drafted resolutions against the exorbitant rents exacted by white landlords for the use of their lands as well as "the nefarious law" known as the Landlord and Tenant Act.[25] The latter act was described as "opening a broad channel for the unscrupulous landlords to defraud their colored tenants out of their earnings."[26]

Negro members of the state legislature throughout the period were constant and bitter foes of the Landlord and Tenant Act. Most of their attempts, however, to modify or amend the law were unsuccessful. The effort of Edward Bridges in the legislature of 1889 is a case in point. Although the wording of his bill included both landlord and tenant, it is reasonably clear that Bridges was interested solely in the rights of the tenant. The bill, for example, required that all contracts and agreements entered into between landlord and tenant for a portion of the crop be made in writing and that a copy of the agreement be kept by each party; whenever any landlord agreed to furnish the tenant with supplies, each would keep then for "final

23. *First Annual Report*, pp. 77, 89, 99.
24. *Ibid.*, p. 87.
25. Raleigh *Signal*, January 21, 1880.
26. *Ibid.* The provisions of the Landlord and Tenant Act of 1877 were subsequently codified and are found in *The Code of North Carolina, 1883*.

settlement" a written itemized account of the supplies issued.[27] In the view of Bridges, the Landlord and Tenant Act, for the landlord, was a fruitful source of perjury and fraud. The bill would strengthen appreciably the position of the tenant in his relationship with the landlord. A Republican newspaper in Raleigh, commenting on the survival chances of the bill, pessimistically declared that inasmuch as similar bills introduced into every legislature since 1877 had been killed, Bridges' proposal would share the same fate.[28] The *Signal's* prediction was an accurate one. The proposal was rejected.

Another problem associated with the mortgage and lien bond system was the practice by the landlords of paying wages to farm hands and tenants in supplies or in orders upon the merchants. Since the average Negro farm hand or tenant was either illiterate or semi-illiterate, he knew very little about figures, and when paid in supplies he quickly ran ahead, or "ate up" his earnings. The result was that he received no money, became dissatisfied with the long hours of hard labor in the fields, and quit.[29]

There is some question as to whether the landlords or the town merchants (often one and the same person) were the greater exploiters of the Negro tenants and hired hands. Certainly, both were guilty of profiteering at the expense of the Negro agricultural workers of North Carolina. A Brunswick County landlord, for example, in 1887 attributed the plight of the farmers and tenants to "merchants who furnish them with supplies [and] charge such enormous prices that it is impossible for them [tenants and farmers] to pay it and live decently, or even above want.[30] A Chowan County laborer, on the other hand, said that a "great many" landlords "charge all they can" for the supplies they furnished to their tenants.[31]

As in the case of the operation of the tenancy laws, the practice of paying wages to farm hands and tenants was not restricted to the Negroes of North Carolina. White farm hands and tenants were also affected, but it may be safely presumed that the Negroes were the chief sufferers. In its first annual report, the North Carolina Bureau of Labor Statistics shows that the farm laborer and tenant usually had to take trade for his wages at high prices and concluded that between the merchant and the landlord, and the low wages paid, the agricultural laborers had little left at the end of the year.[32]

27. *House Journal, 1889*, p. 262; Raleigh *Signal*, March 7, 1889.
28. Raleigh *Signal*, March 7, 1889. See also *Senate Journal, 1877*, p. 125.
29. *First Annual Report*, pp. 79, 89.
30. *Ibid.*, p. 88.
31. *Ibid.*, pp. 124-37.
32. *Ibid.*, pp. 124-37.

Some of the whites were quick to admit that the wage scale, the mortgage and lien bond system, and the practice of paying a portion of the wages in supplies contributed to the inefficiency and unreliability of the Negro farm laborers and tenants of North Carolina. A Tyrrell County landlord, apparently answering critics of Negro agricultural workers, subscribed to such a view: "Tenants and wage-workers are generally reliable with those who deal justly with them. I am sure that much of the discontent and moving from place to place among tenants and laborers arises from the failure of the landlord to provide properly for their comfort."[33]

It is significant that the vast majority of imputations of the slovenliness of Negro farm workers and tenants came from the white landlords and white tenants in the predominantly "Negro counties" of eastern North Carolina where the malpractices of the mortgage and lien bond system and the payment of wages in supplies were most pronounced. Testimony from white landlords and white tenants in those counties where the Negro percentage of the total population was relatively small, on the other hand, emphasized the honesty, faithfulness, thriftiness, reliability of the Negro tenant and farm hand. A few examples are offered as cases in point. A landlord in Jackson County (5.4 per cent Negro in 1890) said that "the colored people of this section, as a rule, are . . . faithful workers."[34] A Johnston County (26.9 per cent Negro in 1890) landlord observed that the Negro laborers were "very reliable."[35] Testimony of whites in Rowan County (28.9 per cent Negro in 1890), Davie County (24.5 per cent Negro in 1890), and Burke County (17.1 per cent Negro in 1890) all alluded to the eagerness with which the Negro rural dwellers purchased land and homes, and a Randolph County (13.3 per cent Negro in 1890) tenant farmer voiced the sentiment of many whites in western North Carolina when he said, "I regret to say that the colored people of the laboring class are making more progress than the whites, they are much more interested in their mental and material improvement than the whites, and yet there are not many colored in this section."[36]

In the counties of eastern North Carolina where the Negro farm population predominated, cotton and tobacco continued as in the earlier periods to be the chief staples. Several factors made cotton of prime importance. In the first place, it was, along with tobacco, the best money crop. In the second place, not only did its cultivation de-

33. *Ibid.*, p. 110.
34. *Ibid.*, p. 99.
35. *Ibid.*
36. *Ibid.*, pp. 68, 108, 134.

mand little skill but also it provided employment for the entire family of a tenant farmer. In the third place, no costly agricultural implements were necessary in its culture. In the fourth place, the product was easily marketable.[37] Thus, in such "black counties" as Edgecombe, Bertie, Warren, Franklin, Lenoir, Pasquotank, Jones, and Pitt, cotton, as in the ante-bellum era, was the uncontested king. The 111 acres of cotton on the 236-acre farm of a Hertford County white planter represented the rule rather than the exception.[38] Little wonder, then, that one of its critics could say with vehemence that "the one-crop (cotton) system hangs like an incubus about [the] people and has well-nigh ruined them financially."[39] Despite these and similar protests, cotton continued to dominate the economy of the counties of eastern North Carolina.

Not all rural Negroes were hired hands or tenants, employed in most instances by white cotton and tobacco planters. In Piedmont and eastern North Carolina some possessed large farms. Thus, Negro rural dwellers appeared to have all the protection related to the acquisition, transfer, sale, device, and descent granted to any other rural citizen of the state, irrespective of race and color. And so, despite the low economic status of the masses of farm Negroes in North Carolina, numerous individuals of that group were able to accumulate a considerable amount of farm property. J. H. Johnson of Rockingham County owned 565 acres of land in 1886. In Vance County, Walter Bullock owned 760 acres; a Negro woman, Sally Henderson, of the same county, owned 440 acres.[40] The largest Negro landowner in Durham County in 1887 was A. B. Couth with 355 acres valued at $2,500.[41] Jesse Gossett, a Negro farmer in Davidson County, owned "about" 300 acres of land, and his farm products and stock were reported as "amongst the best . . . in the section." His farm used all "modern equipment."[42]

It would be misleading, however, to conclude that large landholding among the rural Negroes was a common practice. Obviously, such was not the case. The larger number of Negroes who owned farms were possessors of small estates worth several hundred dollars. There can be no question but that the bulk of this group in the

37. See Emory Q. Hawk, *Economic History of the South* (New York: Prentice-Hall, Inc., 1934), p. 235.
38. *Third Annual Report*, pp. 78-79, 107. See *Second Annual Report of the North Carolina Bureau of Labor Statistics, 1888*, p. 415.
39. *Third Annual Report*, p. 73.
40. *North Carolina Tobacco Belt Directory, 1886*, pp. 546, 591, 599.
41. *Durham City Directory, 1887*, p. 206.
42. Raleigh *North Carolina Gazette*, September 26, 1885.

post-Reconstruction era was propertyless. Although James E. O'Hara, in a speech at the annual fair of the North Carolina Industrial Association in 1879, cited with self-evident pride the 13,000 acres of land in Halifax, the 8,000 in Warren, and the "thousands" of acres in Edgecombe, Craven, and Northampton which "called the Negro master,"[43] he, in effect, was revealing the pitfully small amount of Negro-owned farm land. After the number of Negro urban dwellers is deducted, the figures of O'Hara betray the fact that in both Halifax and Warren counties the average holding was less than two acres.

Unlike the white farmers of the state, Negro farmers and agricultural workers were severely restricted in their efforts to discover an instrument or vehicle to give some uniform expression of their grievances. The constitution of the North Carolina Farmers' Alliance, first organized in the state in the spring of 1887, specifically excluded Negroes. And when the Negro farmers of the state announced plans to affiliate with the south-wide Colored Alliance in 1888, some white farmers became "somewhat excited." A white farmer in Wayne County, in an obvious attempt to discourage such a movement, advised the Negroes "not to confuse themselves over side issues." While admonishing them to "let the Alliance alone," the Wayne County farmer urged the Negroes of the state to turn to religion "and see the glory of the Lord. . . ."[44]

Apparently they did not heed these words, for in 1890 a white Raleigh newspaper carried the news of a session of the Colored State Alliance. If judged by the proceedings of this meeting, however, the main purpose of the Negro farm group was for social, economic, and moral improvement. Its 55,000 members pledged to provide for their families, live economically, and be good citizens. Although apparently of a political character in the past, the 1890 meeting also pledged to withdraw from partisan politics. "This last feature," gleefully stated the *Daily Journal* of New Bern, "is a very important one, [for] it means withdrawal from the Republican party."[45] The records are silent on the accuracy of this prediction.

This description of the Negro in agriculture prompts certain conclusions. The Negro tenants and hired hands who were allegedly most unreliable, dishonest, and inefficient lived in those counties in

43. *Journal of Industry* (Raleigh), November 19, 1879. Charles N. Hunter Scrapbook, 1879-1888, Duke University Library, Durham. See also Kinston *Journal,* January 29, 1880.

44. *Progressive Farmer* (Raleigh), December 18, 1888.

45. New Bern *Daily Journal,* August 28, 1890. See also the *Progressive Farmer* (Raleigh), December 23, 1890.

eastern North Carolina where there existed malpractices in the wage scale, the mortgage and lien bond system, and the partial payment of wages in supplies. Though conspicuously not owning the soil they tilled—even in the heavily Negro-populated eastern counties—some Negroes were able to accumulate a considerable amount of farm land.

9

"I Hope to See the Time When Workingmen Pull Together"

It has not been regarded as desirable . . . that the Negro worker should be considered as on the same plane as white men pursuing the same vocations in life. No matter what calling any white man may choose in the South . . . there is a wide and recognized gulf between him and the Negro workman.
Quotation from Raleigh NEWS AND OBSERVER, October 6, 1886.

There was in North Carolina a steady, if not spectacular, townward movement of both rural whites and Negroes throughout the period. A direct consequence of urban growth was an increasing labor element in the towns and cities of the state where industry was located. And if judged by the enthusiastic pronouncements of a Wilmington newspaper editor in 1887, industrialization was a state-wide phenomenon offering vast economic opportunities to the laboring classes. He wrote, "There is no doubt that there is now an era of remarkable prosperity in the state, such as it has seldom if ever witnessed. New villages are springing up in almost every direction. Capital in Durham, Goldsboro, Greensboro and Fayetteville is being invested in real estate and in industrial, mechanical and manufacturing enterprises, giving employment to hundreds of mechanics and artisans."[1] That North Carolina Negroes were not conspicuous among the "hundreds" of mechanics and artisans may be seen from an analysis of the United States census schedules of 1890. In that year, there were 217,086 Negroes employed in the state, but only 20,214, or 9.9 per cent were in trade and transportation, or manufacturing and mechanical industries.[2]

Next to agriculture, and this should occasion no surprise, the majority of the Negroes of North Carolina were found in domestic and personal service.[3] Thus in 1890, 51,584, or 24.5 per cent of all employed Negroes in North Carolina were so engaged. In Raleigh, in 1876, Negroes who were engaged in domestic and personal service comprised 56.6 per cent of the total Negro labor force of that city.[4] Twelve years later, the percentage had risen to 68.9.[5] In Greensboro, in 1880, the percentage of Negroes in this field was 50.0.[6] The New Bern directory of 1881, as well as those of Asheville (1887), Wilmington (1889), and Charlotte (1893), reveals a similar situation.[7] Moreover, it is interesting to note that a closer examination of the domestic and personal service field shows that the Negroes were largely confined to six occupations. There were barbers and hair-dressers, laborers, laundresses, nurses and mid-wives, restaurant and saloon keepers, and servants. Because Negroes were numerically superior in these six occupations, they can be properly labeled "Negro jobs." On the other hand, there were certain jobs in domestic and personal service in which their representation was comparatively small, such as engineers and firemen (not locomotive), boarding and lodging housekeepers, housekeepers and stewardesses, and hotel keepers.

1. Wilmington *Daily Review*, January 7, 1887.

2. Compiled by the writer from the U.S. Bureau of Census, *Eleventh Census of the United States: 1890. Population.* Vol. I, Part II (Washington: Government Printing Office, 1897), p. 592.

3. Domestic and personal service included the following occupations: barbers and hair dressers, boarding and lodging housekeepers, stationary engineers and firemen, hotel keepers, janitors, laborers (not specified), launderers and launderesses, nurses and mid-wives, restaurant and saloon keepers, servants (including housekeepers and stewards), sextons, watchmen, policemen, detectives, and waiters and waitresses. U.S. Bureau of Census, *Eleventh Census of the United States: 1890. Population.* Vol. I, Part II (Washington: Government Printing Office, 1897), pp. ci-ciii.

4. Chataigne's *Raleigh, N.C. Directory, 1875-76*, 41-130.

5. Compiled by the writer from the *Raleigh City Directory 1888*, pp. 2-119.

6. Compiled by the writer from Emerson's *Winston, Salem, and Greensboro, North Carolina Directory, 1879-80*, pp. 79-116.

7. New Bern, 48.0 per cent; Asheville, 77.0 per cent; Wilmington, 57.3 per cent; and Charlotte, 79.0 per cent.

That the 1890 census schedules, with respect to "Negro jobs" in the domestic and personal service field, reflected an occupational pattern that was present throughout the entire period may be seen from an examination of the occupations Negroes held in the cities and towns of the state between 1876 and 1894. In Raleigh, in 1876, out of 405 Negroes in domestic and personal service, 346, or 85.4 per cent were in the six "Negro jobs."[8] Twelve years later the percentage stood at 91.4.[9] In other major cities and towns of North Carolina, the concentration of Negroes in the "Negro jobs" was conspicuous throughout the period. In Greensboro in 1880, the percentage was 72.2; in New Bern in 1881, 79.2 per cent; in Asheville in 1887, 91.1 per cent; in Wilmington in 1889, it was also 91.1 per cent; and in Charlotte in 1893, the percentage stood at 93.4, the highest recorded for the period.[10] The Negroes of North Carolina, then, instead of escaping from the "Negro jobs," found themselves toward the close of the nineteenth century confined almost exclusively to these pursuits.

However, in spite of the employment of large numbers of Negroes of the state in domestic and personal service, it is interesting to note that frequent objections were voiced by the whites as to the honesty, reliability, availability, and efficiency of the "colored help," particularly with the performances of Negro servants. In 1892 a white lady in Edenton complained that it was "hard to get on with servants who have no honesty and no virtue."[11] A white man in a small North Carolina town bemoaned the fact that the only Negro servants available were "rough farm laborers, brought up in cabins off the plantations" because "all the well trained family Negroes, who had spent their lives in their masters' houses" had departed for the larger cities in North Carolina "to see something of the world."[12] The problem of securing cooks in Greensboro convinced the white housewives of that city that Negroes could not be employed "for love or money."[13] And in Charlotte, a white woman declared that it was becoming a serious problem for white households of that city to secure competent and reliable servants. "Negro domestics that are at all competent," she

8. *Raleigh City Directory, 1875-76*, pp. 41-130.

9. *Directory of the City of Raleigh, 1888*, pp. 2-119.

10. *Winston, Salem, and Greensboro Directory, 1879-80*, pp. 79-116; *New Bern City Directory, 1880-81*, pp. 41-106; *Asheville City Directory, 1887*, pp. 30-272; *Directory of the City of Wilmington, 1889*, pp. 17-193; *Directory of Charlotte, 1893-94*, pp. 148-93.

11. A. B. Hart, "Cross-Section Through North Carolina," *The Nation*, XLIV (March 17, 1892), 208.

12. A. L. Bassett, "Going to Housekeeping in North Carolina," *Lippincott's Magazine*, XXVIII (August, 1881), 206.

13. Greensboro *Daily Record*, February 11, 1891.

added, "are very few." She concluded her complaint with these observations: "The rising generation of Negresses is not taught domesticity. The girls grow up with big 'notions.' Very few care to cook, and those who consent to wait in the dining room are very apt to be disagreeably insolent.[14]

The question may well be asked, "If the Negro servant and laborer were inefficient, unreliable, and dishonest, how does one explain his monopoly of the domestic and personal service field?" The answer seems to be found in the belief of the North Carolina whites that it was economically and socially desirable that the Negroes perform the menial tasks. Aside from the belief held on the part of many white employers that Negroes were less arrogant and more controllable than the "poor but respected white man," there was the belief that nature had made the Negro inferior, debased, and degenerate. In addition, however, to the social inferiority of the Negro as a justification for his employment in the menial pursuits, there was the simple, elementary fact that Negro labor could be bought for less money. As an Iredell County manufacturer put it: "The colored laborers are less grasping, and are more disposed to accept wages that will leave some margin of profit. . . ."[15]

Not only was the work of the Negroes obtained on the cheapest possible terms, but, as in the case of the rural Negroes, part of this wage was paid in orders on the local stores. Thus, money was kept entirely, or partially, out of the hands of the Negroes. A white carpenter in Anson County wrote the North Carolina Bureau of Labor Statistics that "many hundred" of Negro laborers in his area "are paid in orders, and never see a cent of money, and are compelled to trade at one place."[16]

It would appear, then, that the complaints and protestations possibly would not have been necessary had the servants and laborers been adequately and fairly paid. Their wages, in spite of the absence of official wage statistics, were admittedly, "extremely low,"[17] and therefore may provide a partial explanation of the Negro's alleged dishonesty, or tendency, as one white man said, "to get a good deal in other ways."[18]

The next largest group of predominantly non-agricultural workers among the Negroes of North Carolina was to be found in the manu-

14. Charlotte *Chronicle*, January 4, 1889.
15. *First Annual Report*, p. 68.
16. *Second Annual Report*, p. 57.
17. Bassett, "Housekeeping in N.C.," *Lippincott's Magazine*, p. 206.
18. *Ibid*.

facturing and mechanical industries.[19]   Here, according to the census schedules of 1890, 12,518, or 5.5 per cent of the total working population were laboring at some occupation in this area.[20]   Although the group was made up of some thirty-eight occupations, the bulk of the Negroes, male and female, were employed in five.   These were tobacco and cigar factory operatives, saw and planing mill employees, carpenters and joiners, blacksmiths and wheelwrights, and marble and stone cutters.[21]   Although state-wide statistics before 1890 are lacking, an examination of the occupations of Negroes in individual cities and towns between 1876 and 1890 will reveal a comparable circumstance. In Raleigh, in 1876, for example, 124, or 73.8 per cent, of the workers in manufacturing and mechanical industries were employed as carpenters, blacksmiths, stone cutters, or saw and planing mill workers.[22] In Winston in 1880, 83.2 per cent of that city's working Negro population were tobacco workers, blacksmiths, and stone cutters.[23]   The Durham city directory of 1887 listed the above three occupations as comprising 84.1 per cent of all its employed Negro population.[24]

However, it would be erroneous to conclude from the above figures, especially those taken from the census of 1890, that these occupations were "Negro jobs."   For example, out of a total of 2,365 blacksmiths and wheelwrights in North Carolina in 1890, only 831, or 35.1 per cent, were Negroes.   The number and percentage of Negro carpenters and joiners were somewhat less; the total count in North Carolina for both races was 7,110, of whom 1,798, or 25.1 per cent were Negroes. However, the term "Negro jobs" would be a proper one for brickmaking and tobacco factory work.   In 1890, out of a total of 607 brickmakers, 443, or 72.9 per cent, were Negroes; out of a total of 5,719 tobacco and cigar factory operatives, 4,241, or 74.1 per cent, were Negroes.

19. This group was composed of the following occupations: bakers, blacksmiths, bleachers and dyers, boot and shoemakers, bottlers, box makers, brickmakers, builders and contractors, butchers, cabinet makers, carpenters and joiners, carriage makers, confectioners, coopers, distillers, gas work employees, harness makers, leather tanners, machinists, marble and stone cutters, brick and stone masons, mill and factory operatives, millers, molders, oil well employees, painters, photographers, plasterers, printers, newspaper publishers, saw and planing mill employees, seamstresses, tailors, tinners, tobacco and cigar workers, upholsterers, wheelwrights, and white-washers.   U.S. Census Bureau, *Eleventh Census of the United States: 1890. Population* (Washington: Government Printing Office, 1897), Vol. I, Part II, pp. ci-ciii.

20. Compiled by the writer from *ibid.,* p. 59.

21. Out of 12,518 employed Negroes in the mechanical and manufacturing industries, 9,680, or 77.3 per cent were to be found in these five occupations.

22. *Raleigh City Directory, 1875-76,* pp. 41-130.

23. *Winston, Salem and Greensboro Directory, 1879-80,* pp. 1-44.

24. *Durham City Directory, 1887,* pp. 21-138.

The question at this point may well be asked, "How are the predominance of Negroes in certain skills and the absence of that group in others to be explained?" In an effort to interpret the scarcity of Negro workers in the cotton and woolen mills of North Carolina, two opinions have been advanced. One holds that Negro workers in the textile mills of the state were either barred altogether or restricted to a small number engaged in some of the preparatory processes because of the large number of white women inside the plants. Thus, if Negroes were employed, they worked outside the mills as laborers, draymen, and firemen and were, therefore, removed from all close contact with the white females. No opportunity, then, was afforded which might encourage the slightest possible lessening of the Negro's deference toward white women.[25] The other view suggests that the Negroes were barred from work in the textile mills, or employed in the more menial and "hard labor jobs" in order to prevent them from competing with the large numbers of poor white laborers. The rise of the textile mills, cotton factories in particular, in effect, represented an economic victory for the poor whites over the Negroes.[26] However, it would seem that an embodiment of the two views would come closer to a definitive answer: the sentiment of most white North Carolinians was that to employ Negro labor extensively in the textile mills of North Carolina was both socially and economically undesirable.

On the other hand, there appears to be only one opinion concerning the reason for the wide use of Negroes in the tobacco industry of North Carolina. First, the work in the leaf factories was mainly a hand process, performed under very bad working conditions, extreme dust, and poor wages. The work itself was monotonous, offering little or no opportunity for advancement, and often was carried on in badly lighted factories under the worst unsanitary conditions.[27] Little wonder, then, that the Negroes monopolized this industry.

Sources, in addition to the census schedules of 1890, will verify the extensive employment of Negroes in the tobacco and cigar factories of North Carolina. As early as 1878, the sale and manufacture of tobacco made up the leading industry in Winston, with fifteen independent tobacco factories and four tobacco warehouses employing a

25. For a clear statement of this view, see Holland Thompson, *From the Cotton Field to the Cotton Mill: A Study of Industrial Transition in North Carolina* (New York: Macmillan Co., 1906), p. 249.

26. This interpretation is ably espoused by Liston Pope in his study, *Mill-hands and Preachers: A Study of Gastonia* (New Haven: Yale University Press, 1942), pp. 12-13.

27. John Donald Rice, "The Negro Tobacco Worker and His Union" (Unpublished master's thesis, University of North Carolina, 1941), pp. 11-13.

working force of "more than 1,000 hands, mostly Negroes."[28]   Eleven
years later, a Forsyth County manufacturer of chewing tobacco reported that 80 per cent of his employees were Negroes.[29]   In 1888 a
white painter in Winston stated that there were about "twenty-five to
thirty tobacco factories" in that city which employed "about eight or
ten hundred hands, the most of them being colored, and women and
children."[30]

Although the Negroes of North Carolina appeared to have monopolized the work in the tobacco factories of the state, there were
serious objections to their employment in this, as well as in many of
the other occupations in the manufacturing and mechanical industries.
A white laboring man in a town in Iredell County was not only opposed to Negroes working in the tobacco factories but also felt that if
they must be hired, it was unwise to pay them "good wages" because
they spent the money "as fast as they make it."   He said that the
"average darky" of his town was "content if he owns a good axe,
razor and 'possum dog."[31]   A white lawyer of Elizabeth City bitterly
criticized "the few contractors" in that town for hiring Negro carpenters in preference to white carpenters.[32]   A marble worker in Durham
County said that he had "never seen a Negro marble cutter," and that
he would "never learn one the trade."[33]   A white carpenter in Burke
County complained about the "unjust and unnatural discrimination
against white working-men by their own race," and declared that he
had personally witnessed many instances in which white men had been
turned down and Negroes employed.[34]

A great deal of this opposition to the employment of Negroes arose
over the fact that Negroes could be hired more cheaply than whites.
A bricklayer and plasterer in Lenoir County voiced a sentiment shared
by many white artisans when he said, "Wages are going down all
the time. Five years ago we got fifteen cents per yard to do plastering,
and now we only get eight or nine cents for the same work. The
botch of a Negro has put wages down. There are some of our wealth-
iest men who never employ a white man for anything."[35]

Significantly, the protests against the employment of Negroes in

28. Adelaide Fries, *Forsyth County* (Chapel Hill: University of North Carolina
Press, 1949), p. 81.
   29. *First Annual Report*, p. 66.
   30. *Second Annual Report*, p. 90.
   31. *Third Annual Report*, p. 281.
   32. *Second Annual Report*, pp. 117-18.
   33. *Ibid.*, p. 183.
   34. *Ibid.*, p. 63.
   35. *Second Annual Report*, p. 105. See also *ibid.*, p. 94.

the manufacturing and mechanical industries came mainly from the white workers, and not the white employers. The latter group's protests were negligible possibly because of its ability to exploit the cheapness of Negro labor for its own benefit. At any rate, the white employers were more apt to praise the Negro workers than to criticize them.[36]

An examination of the wage scales of the workers in the tobacco factories clearly shows the extent of the white employers' exploitation of the Negroes' labor. In the plug tobacco factories of North Carolina in 1880, for example, the selling price ran from $0.33 for common tobacco to $1.00 for "select fancy tobacco" per pound. Yet, the average labor cost per pound for all grades was only 5½ cents! It was estimated that an additional 1½ cents per pound covered all expenses such as wear and tear on the machinery, and taxes other than internal revenue, leaving the balance for cost of material and profit.[37] The average daily wages of workers in plug tobacco factories in North Carolina in 1880 were: sorter, $0.80; stripper, $0.48; caser, $1.12½; plug-maker, $2.00; pressman, $1.12½; packer, $1.00; laborer, $1.00; and twister, $2.25.[38]

Negro labor was cheaper in the factories manufacturing smoking tobacco. In 1880, the selling price was as high as $1.00 per pound; labor cost, on the other hand, was as low as a penny per pound! The wages per day in a typical smoking tobacco factory were: sorter, $0.40; stripper, $0.40; caser, $0.75; cutter, $0.75; packer, $0.50; and laborer, $0.25 to $0.50.[39]

The tobacco industry of North Carolina also utilized large numbers of Negro women, boys, and girls, obviously because their labor could be bought for less money than was paid to the adult Negro male. A chewing tobacco manufacturer in Forsyth County, with 80 per cent of his employees Negroes, paid children $.50 per day, women $.75 per day, and "as high as $1.25 for men. . . ."[40] That these wages continued to remain low throughout the period may be seen from the wage scale of a plug tobacco manufacturer in Iredell County in 1894. This factory, which employed all Negro help, paid skilled women workers $0.60 per day; unskilled were paid $0.40 per day. Children were paid $0.25 per day.[41]

36. *First Annual Report*, p. 71; *Second Annual Report*, p. 178.
37. U.S. Bureau of the Census. *Tenth Census of the United States: 1880. Statistics of Wages* (Washington: Government Printing Office, 1883), XX, 46.
38. *Ibid*.
39. *Ibid*.
40. *First Annual Report*, p. 66; *Second Annual Report*, p. 90.
41. *Eighth Annual Report of the Bureau of Labor Statistics of North Carolina, 1894*, p. 84.

In addition to the small wages, the working hours were long, averaging sixty-nine per week in 1885. At the end of the period, there was little change in the long work week of the laborers, for in 1894 it was sixty-six hours.[42] In the tobacco factories, Negro children of ten years of age worked eleven hours a day.[43]

Hence, the miserly compensation and long hours, coupled with the unhealthy, unsanitary conditions surrounding the work, accounted for the extensive use of Negroes in the tobacco industries of North Carolina between 1876 and 1894. Here, then, was at least one occupation in the manufacturing and mechanical pursuits in which the Negroes of the state were left relatively free to earn a livelihood.

Nonetheless, and despite the fact that Negro workers composed the work force in the tobacco industries, the large majority of that group were confined to agricultural and domestic and personal service jobs. This fact is further attested to by the small numbers found in trade and transportation. Comprising approximately fourteen occupations, the federal census schedules of 1890 show that of the total number of Negroes in the state in that year, only 4.4 per cent were in trade and transportation.[44] The bulk of these were railroad employees, followed by draymen, drivers, teamsters, and hackmen. Although no detailed breakdown of the railroad workers is given by the 1890 federal census schedules, it is reasonable to assume that the greater proportion of the Negro workers in trade and transportation were "hands" or common laborers, performing most of the out-of-door, laborious, and hazardous work. Thus, along with the railroad workers, the vast majority of the Negroes engaged in trade and transportation were found in the occupations requiring little or no skill, but a great deal of physical strength and stamina. It is noteworthy to observe, therefore, that of the 7,696 Negroes employed in trade and transportation, 5,522, or 70.4 per cent, were railroad employees, draymen, hackmen, teamsters, and drivers.[45]

On the other hand, certain pursuits in trade and transportation were almost exclusively white. Negroes were not listed in any appreciable numbers as salesmen or saleswomen, clerks, bookkeepers,

42. United States Department of Labor, *History of Wages in the United States from Colonial Times to 1928* (Washington: Government Printing Office, 1929), p. 426.

43. *Eighth Annual Report,* p. 84.

44. Compiled by the writer from *Eleventh Census of the U.S.: 1890. Population.* Vol. I, Part II, p. 592. The occupations in this area included the following: agents, auctioneers, boatmen, and canalmen, clerks, draymen, hackmen and teamsters, foremen, hostlers, hucksters and peddlers, livery stable keepers, messengers and office boys, porters and helpers in stores, sailors, steam railroad employees, and undertakers.

45. *Ibid.*

and agents. The few Negroes engaged in these occupations were there as a result of the establishment of Negro businesses; and since most of these enterprises were small, the number of positions available was also small. It appears safe to conclude, therefore, that an absence of Negro business establishments in North Carolina between 1876 and 1894 would have meant an absence of Negro clerical workers.

The inequality of economic opportunity among the urban non-professional class was extended to the wage scale. In 1887, for example, the Carolina Central Railroad employed five white brakemen at $0.96 a day and forty Negro brakekmen at $0.75 a day.[46] Differences in the wages paid to Negro and white railroad laborers were manifested on the Raleigh and Gaston and Raleigh and Augusta Air-Line Railroad, and the North Carolina Railroad. The former paid the whites $0.89 a day, the Negroes $0.80 a day; while white laborers on the latter railroad received $0.87 a day, the Negroes received $0.72 a day.[47]

Sometimes Negro workers went on strike in protest against either the low wages paid or a threatened reduction in the wages paid to them by their employers. On September 26, 1886, the stevedores of Wilmington used this method to oppose a wage reduction. The situation was brought about through the distrust by the stevedores of one of their number. William Howe, a boss stevedore, contracted to stow cotton on the steamer *Carbis Bay* at the rate of $0.30 per bale and agreed to pay the men he employed $4 or $5 per day—the head workman of each gang to receive the latter price. The stevedores claimed that Howe could not afford to pay the price agreed upon and notified him of their unwillingness to work any longer unless their pay was guaranteed by the captain of the *Carbis Bay* or consignees. Howe, faced with an emergency, sent to Norfolk and engaged thirty-five stevedores from that city.[48]

The Negro assemblies of the Knights of Labor held an emergency meeting on September 27. On the next day the thirty-five stevedores from Norfolk marched on board the *Carbis Bay* ready to go to work at loading the vessel with cotton. They were met by a delegation from the Negro stevedores of Wilmington who persuaded the Norfolk group to abandon the vessel. When twenty of the visiting stevedores promised to return to Norfolk, it signaled the end of the brief strike. On September 28, not only did the entire thirty-five return to Norfolk, but "boss" William Howe agreed that the wages of the striking

46. *First Annual Report*, pp. 163-64.
47. *Ibid.*, pp. 167, 169.
48. Wilmington *Morning Star*, September 26, 1886.

stevedores would be paid.[49] The strike of the stevedores led John Holloway, a Negro member of the legislature of 1887, to introduce a bill for the better protection of laborers. It required the owner of a vessel that was unloaded in the port of Wilmington to receive in writing from the "boss" stevedore a sworn statement that the laborers had been paid. It passed.[50]

Apparently the successful strike of the Wilmington stevedores caused "twenty-five or thirty" firemen of that coastal city to launch a strike on December 31, 1886, for an increase in wages from $0.90 to $1.25 per day. For three days, until January 3, 1887, they held out, but failed to get the increase.[51]

In April, 1887, there was a strike of Negro workers against the Raleigh City Waterworks for an increase in pay. In commenting on the situation, the *Carolina Watchman* of Salisbury predicted that the waterworks would hold no conference with the striking Negroes nor grant them any increase in pay.[52] Records are silent on the outcome of the strike. Harley E. Jolley, in a reference to this strike, concludes that it was probably a failure.[53]

49. *Ibid.*, September 28, 29, 1886: *Third Annual Report of the Commissioner of Labor, 1887*, pp. 436-37.

50. *House Journal, 1887*, 67; *Public Laws, 1887*, c. 145. Act of March 2, 1887.

51. *Third Annual Report of the Commissioner of Labor, 1887*, pp. 436-37. See also Wilmington *Morning Post*, January 2, 1887.

52. Salisbury *Carolina Watchman*, April 21, 1887.

53. Harley E. Jolley, "The Labor Movement in North Carolina, 1880-1922," *North Carolina Historical Review*, XXX (July, 1953), 361.

10

Organizations for Economic Betterment

The design of the North Carolina Industrial Association and the object of the Industrial Fair is to place before the world every evidence of our progress as a race which it is possible to secure. In this work we call upon our farmers, mechanics, artisans, and educators, to come forward and place on exhibition their best productions.

Clipping from the JOURNAL OF INDUSTRY (Raleigh) in the Charles N. Hunter Scrapbook, 1879-1888.

. . . our organization [the Knights of Labor] . . . recognizes no color or creed in the division of men.

From speech of Terrence V. Powderly before the Tenth Regular Session, Knights of Labor of America, Richmond, Virginia, October 24, 1886.

The economic status of the Negroes of North Carolina left much to be desired. That the more articulate Negroes of North Carolina were not satisfied with the comparatively low economic status of the group is attested to by their interest in economic-betterment organizations. Among the more important of these agencies promoting Negro welfare in North Carolina and the South in general after Reconstruction were Negro-sponsored local and

state-wide industrial and agricultural fairs, and the Noble Order of
the Knights of Labor.

Perhaps one of the more notable efforts on the part of the Negroes
of North Carolina to improve their economic well-being was the
organization in 1879 of the North Carolina Industrial Association.
The aims and purposes of the group were set forth in section 2 of an
act passed by the North Carolina legislature on March 14, 1879:

... the object and business of said association shall be this: to encourage
and promote the development of the industrial and educational resources
of the colored people of North Carolina, to gather statistics respecting
their progress in various pursuits and customs peculiar to civilized and
enlightened nations; to hold annually at such time and place as it may
elect an exibition of the products of their industry and education, and to
offer such premiums for articles so exhibited as the means of the association will allow.[1]

The following Negroes founded the association: Caesar Johnson,
L. B. Hinton, S. Ellison, W. H. Matthews, Osborn Hunter, Jr., J. A.
Long, C. N. Hunter, James H. Jones, C. J. Proctor, G. W. Hayes,
M. Lewis, Joseph Hill, Sylvester Dunston, H. Biggs, A. Sears, W. M.
Graves, Americus Hunter, Jr., Charles M. Hunter, Tony Burns, Frank
Johnson, Reuben Rhodes, and Thomas Bradford.[2]

In the fall of 1879, this association began its practice of sponsoring
an annual fair that was held at Raleigh.[3]

Great effort was expended by the organization to arouse enthusiasm
among the state's Negro population. Special trains were chartered at
reduced rates to transport Negroes from all sections of North Carolina. Negro speakers were employed to canvass the entire state urging
local delegations to send large crowds to Raleigh.[4] Letters were sent
to Negro merchants, tradesmen, farmers, and mechanics in and out
of the state requesting that they submit exhibits of their work.[5]

Thus, at the 1879 fair, the Negroes displayed everything from
"an oil painting to a pumpkin, from a goose to a knitted spread."[6]
In the 1888 fair, the following were exhibited: field crops and samples,

1. *Laws and Resolutions of the State of North Carolina, 1879* (Raleigh: The Observer Printing Co., 1879), p. 800.

2. *Ibid.*, pp. 799-800.

3. For an intimate description of the 1879 fair, see the article, "The Colored Fair
at Raleigh, N.C.," *Frank Leslie's Illustrated Newspaper*, XLIX (December 6, 1879),
242-43.

4. Such efforts were quite successful in 1880; the daily attendance averaged nearly
4,000 persons. (Raleigh *News and Observer*, October 2, 1880.)

5. Appleton's *Annual Cyclopedia*, N. S., IX (1884), 593.

6. "The Colored Fair," *Frank Leslie's Illustrated Newspaper*, p. 243.

horses, mules, cattle, sheep and swine, poultry, household supplies, bees and honey, horticulture and orchard products, wines, staple goods and ladies' work, painting, drawing, musical instruments, jewelry, silverware, machinery, agricultural implements, sample work shops, manufactures in leather, plows and plowing match, dairy and vegetable gardens.[7] Other popular features of the fairs were the co-operative drill contests and the brass band competitions. For example, at the 1885 fair, any company of the North Carolina State Guard winning first place would be awarded "twenty-five dollars in gold." The best performing brass band would be awarded fifty dollars in cash; second and third places were worth thirty and twenty dollars respectively.[8]

Not only were individuals invited to display the products of their work at these annual fairs, but the association also sought Negro Americans of national and international repute as speakers. In 1879, at the first annual fair, the North Carolina Industrial Association invited Robert Brown Elliot, the brilliant Negro lawyer and politician from South Carolina, to deliver the annual address. "Professional engagements" prevented him from accepting.[9] In 1888, William Still, author of the *Underground Railroad,* was unable to speak because of the "pressure of business."[10] However, the association was able to present such Negro notables as Frederick Douglass and Bishop James W. Hood, and P. S. B. Pinchback.[11]

In addition to the occasional difficulty of obtaining a speaker of prominence and affluence, and in spite of the careful planning and the untold amount of energy spent in organizing and arranging for the fairs, apathy was sometimes reflected in the activities of the "workers," those individuals who, in their respective communities, were given the responsibility of arousing local interest in the project each year. One such "worker," for example, wrote, "We have called three mass meetings, but have not had . . . a full attendance, though we are not discouraged. I think we shall be able to yet give Western No. C., Buncombe county especially, a full representation, if not in articles or fund I am almost sure a number of people."[12]

7. New York *Age,* September 15, 1888.

8. Raleigh *North Carolina Gazette,* September 26, 1885.

9. Letter from R. B. Elliot, Columbia, S.C., dated September 30, 1879, to Oliver Hunter. Charles N. Hunter Papers, Duke University Library, Durham.

10. Letter from William Still, Philadelphia, Penn., dated October 19, 1888, to Charles N. Hunter. Hunter Papers.

11. Raleigh *News and Observer,* October 2, 1880; Raleigh *Gazette,* November 7, 1891.

12. Letter from James L. Love, Asheville, N.C., dated September 19, 1886, to G. Wasson. Hunter Papers.

However, in spite of the many difficulties that confronted them, the fairs, if judged by the favorable reaction of both whites and Negroes inside and outside the state, were eminently successful. The remarks of Blanche K. Bruce, the only Negro ever to serve a full term in the United States Senate, commending the efforts of the North Carolina Industrial Association, are typical of the attitude held by most Negroes of the time: "The State Industrial Exposition of the colored race—especially those organized in North Carolina—have abundantly and satisfactorily attended the progress of our people, and at the same time have been auxiliaries to advance that progress. The fairs in your own state proved not only the hopeful growth of the race, but have supplied the opportunity and the evidence alike of our capacity to conduct such enterprises."[13]

These fairs also attracted the attention of the Negro newspapers outside the state. A reporter of the *Freedman's Friend,* a Negro newspaper of Philadelphia, covering the 1879 fair, declared that despite the inclement weather not only was the fair "a complete success" but that the white people appeared to be "much interested" in the welfare of the Negroes as evidenced by their large daily attendance and their contributions for the support of it.[14] According to an editorial in the Raleigh *News and Observer,* the fair of 1880 showed "considerable advancement over the exhibitions of a year ago, and is in every way creditable to the exhibitors. The entries are excellent; the stock is much better than last year; the cotton and agricultural products are superior, and other articles are in keeping."[15] Another white observer at the 1889 fair noted that the "exhibits were over the average."[16] Further favorable white sentiment toward the fairs is seen in a legislative grant of a thousand dollars following an appeal to that body by the association in 1887 for "some aid and encouragement" in order to "have an exposition which shall be open not only to the colored people" of North Carolina but to those of other states as well.[17]

Whites of the state were also quick to cite the success of these fairs as a refutation of the "outside-of-the-South" charges that the Negroes were maltreated. The *New Bernian* observed with some vehemence that the exhibitions at the 1879 fair, controlled and managed by

13. Blanche K. Bruce to Charles N. Hunter, October 14, 1886. Hunter Papers.
14. Philadelphia *Freedman's Friend,* February, 1880.
15. Raleigh *News and Observer,* October 2, 1880.
16. Turner's *North Carolina Almanac, 1891,* p. 35.
17. Message of Governor Alfred M. Scales to the Senate and the House, January 1, 1887. Alfred M. Scales Letter Book, 1885-1889, State Department of Archives and History, Raleigh, pp. 83-84. See also *Laws and Resolutions of the State of North Carolina, 1887,* pp. 772-73.

Negroes throughout, spoke volumes to the world at large, and contradicted emphatically "so far as the State of North Carolina is concerned, all the defamatory and false assertions that the Negro is oppressed, down-trodden and denied the rights and privileges of citizenship."[18] And the whites were especially pleased when one of these annual fairs was not graced with the presence of prominent state and national Negro political leaders. Commenting on the 1881 fair, one white paper of the state noted with obvious satisfaction the "absence of the old political schemers and demagogues who usually lead the Freedmen by the nose on all public occasions." It went on to say that "Stewart Ellison, Jim Harris and others were not prominent . . . even Bruce did not come."[19]

Representative of the locally sponsored Negro fairs was the Eastern North Carolina Industrial Stock and Fruit Fair. The 1890 fair, lasting four days, opened on August 26 in New Bern, and, according to the city's white weekly paper, the exhibits were "very creditable indeed." Displayed were squash, egg plant, pumpkins, pepper, beets, tomatoes, oil paintings, counterpanes, fancy embroidery and needlework. Some of the egg plants of E. R. Dudley measured two feet in circumference; some of his pumpkins were "over five feet," and his pepper stalks were four-and-a-half feet tall. Warren C. Coleman, of Concord, exhibited "a four-year-old cow that gave four gallons of milk, a watermelon that weighed fifty-seven pounds, and a cantaloupe that weighed thirty-five pounds."[20]

As in the case of the state-sponsored fair, the white community aided in making the New Bern fair a success. The Negroes were not only granted the privilege of using the fair grounds but in numerous other ways the whites co-operated with the Negroes. The Negro speakers for the occasion, George H. White and J. C. Price, were generously praised. "Instead of endeavoring to arouse malice, prejudice, and hatred," noted the *Daily Journal*, "they took the occasion to speak in high terms of the good feelings and peaceable relations existing between the races in Eastern North Carolina."[21]

Unquestionably, these annual fairs sponsored by the Negroes of North Carolina benefited both the Negro minority and the state at large. There is no question but that the exhibitions promoted a degree of harmony, co-operation, and mutual respect between the races. They stimulated the Negroes to improve their livestock, farm

18. New Bern *New Bernian,* November 29, 1879.
19. Raleigh *Farmer and Mechanic,* November 10, 1881.
20. New Bern *Daily Journal,* August 28, September 4, 1890.
21. *Ibid.*

products, and tools and machinery by offering prizes for superior articles. They advanced the material interests of North Carolina as a whole by encouraging the development of the educational, agricultural, and industrial resources of the Negro people of the state.

Another organization, national in scope and interracial in character, was looked upon by the Negroes of North Carolina as "a light to guide the sons and daughters of toil to higher and better things."[22] The Noble Order of the Knights of Labor, organized in 1869 by nine Philadelphia garment workers, established its first assembly in North Carolina in Raleigh on June 18, 1884.[23] From their inception, the local assemblies in the state did not prohibit Negro membership. On the contrary, they included positive provisions that provided that "the (outside) color of a candidate shall not debar him from admission: rather let the coloring of his mind and heart be the test."[24] Hence, that order attempted to organize all the "oppressed," male and female, white and Negro.

Some of the organizing methods among Negroes of the Knights of Labor met with occasional criticism. A white man residing in Washington County complained to Governor Alfred M. Scales that the Knights threatened to lynch anyone who attempted to work on terms other than what they suggested. "In this way," he wrote the Governor, "they have coerced a great many colored people to join them."[25]

Whatever the method employed, the Knights of Labor were successful in organizing the Negro workers of the state. Unfortunately, membership statistics are scanty. Therefore, the numerical picture is incomplete. According to the Greensboro *North State,* there were in 1888 over 1,600 Negro Knights in Edgecombe County.[26] The organization of Negro female servants in Wilmington by the Knights was reported in one of the newspapers of that city. The number of such

22. *Journal of Labor,* November 29, 1887, quoted in Sidney H. Kessler, "Organization of Negroes in the Knights of Labor," *Journal of Negro History,* XXXVII (July, 1952), 273-74.

23. H. M. Douty, "Early Labor Organization in North Carolina, 1880-1910," *South Atlantic Quarterly,* XXV (July, 1935), 261. The "assembly" was the unit organization. Assemblies were either composed of workers in one occupation or else were mixed, that is, composed of workers in various occupations. The assemblies in North Carolina were of the latter type.

24. See Philip S. Foner, *History of the Labor Movement in the United States* (New York: International Publishers, 1947), 510-11.

25. W. A. Alexander to Governor Alfred M. Scales, December 30, 1887. Governors' Papers, State Department of Archives and History, Raleigh.

26. Greensboro *North State,* July 26, 1888.

workers organized was not cited.[27]   George L. Tonoffeski, Secretary of
the Knights of Labor of North Carolina, declared in May, 1890, that
there were 275 assemblies in 50 counties of the state, with the membership being about equally divided between the two races.[28]   Although the local assemblies of the state did not prohibit Negro membership, it appears that separate white and Negro locals were the rule
across North Carolina.   For example, in Greensboro in 1890 there
were two separate lodges, each having its own officers, meeting place,
and date of meetings.   That the Negro laborers were organized into
separate assemblies is further attested to by the employment in 1886
of an assistant state organizer, presumably a Negro, to foster the
movement among Negroes.   Yet a white brick mason in Harnett
County, while admitting that trade unions were performing valuable
service for the working man, declared that he was not in favor of the
labor policy as pursued by the Knights of Labor because he did not
"believe in the association of the races."   Apparently, then, some of the
local assemblies in the state were integrated.

White employers of Negro labor viewed with dissatisfaction the
rise of Negro membership in the Knights of Labor for another
reason.   An Iredell County manufacturer admitted that he, as a
general rule, preferred Negro laborers over white because the former
were disposed to accept wages that would leave him a larger margin
of profit.   However, the organization of Negro workers by the Knights
of Labor had resulted in a "refractory element" that exacted prices
that were "out of proportion to the services rendered."   In other words,
organized Negro laborers received a larger share of the total profits
and for this reason were resented.

In many instances, Negro members of the order had to contend
with local white newspapers that were invariably hostile to them.
For example, Kessler says that in 1886, the editor of the Durham
Recorder attempted to spread a rumor that a Negro member of the
Knights of Labor had "knocked down and brutally kicked" a twelve-
year-old white child in the Duke tobacco factory.   Although the
rumor was ill-founded, it illustrates the extent to which local whites
would go in an effort to intimidate Negro members of the order.[29]
In April, 1887, the Knights of Labor were credited with fomenting
a strike of Negro laborers against the Raleigh City Waterworks.
The *Carolina Watchman* of Salisbury predicted that the waterworks

27. Wilmington *Star*, cited in the Charlotte *Home-Democrat*, June 25, 1886.
28. Wilson *Advance*, May 1, 1890.
29. Kessler, "Knights of Labor," *Journ. of Negro Hist.*, pp. 260-61.

would hold no conference with the strikers nor grant them the increase in pay they demanded. Instead, the paper continued, the Waterworks "will proceed to take in others who are not bound like slaves to obey the commands of official Knights."[30] White organizers of Negroes also came in for their share of local ill feeling. In Durham, John Ray, a white printer and one of North Carolina's most active organizers for the Knights, faced the threats of both the white employers and the local town newspaper.[31]

Therefore, in view of the opposition to the organization in the Knights of Labor by the local white communities of North Carolina, especially after 1886, there can be no doubt that the aspirations of that order to improve the living standards of the Negro workers, and to be "a light to guide the black sons and daughters of toil to higher and better things" gradually dimmed and eventually became ineffectual as an instrument on their behalf. Indeed, by 1894, the report of the Labor Commissioner for North Carolina stated that there were no Knights of Labor in the state.[32]

30. Salisbury, *Carolina Watchman*, April 21, 1887.
31. Kessler, "Knights of Labor," *Journ. of Negro Hist.*, p. 261; Douty, "Early Labor Organization," *South Atlantic Quart.*, p. 261.
32. *First Annual Report*, p. 262.

11

The Negro as Professional
and as Businessman

*I have a colored man for a foreman who is a
college graduate, and he is the only one of such I
ever knew to go back to a trade, or to work with his
hands after receiving a college education.*

ANNUAL REPORT OF THE NORTH CAROLINA BUREAU
OF LABOR STATISTICS, 1887, p. 71.

Although the country and town Negro worker
comprised the bulk of that group's employables, the ruling element in
Negro society of North Carolina in the post-Reconstruction era consisted chiefly of clergymen, professors, and teachers; government officials, both federal, state, and local; and physicians and surgeons.
According to the census schedules of 1890, of the 2,036 Negroes in
professional service, 1,940, or 95.2 per cent, were either clergymen or
teachers.[1] The reason for the large number of ministers and teachers
and the comparatively smaller number of physicians, lawyers, and
government officials is fairly obvious. As a result of segregation, the
Negro minister and school teacher enjoyed an almost complete
monopoly, being relatively free from white competition. Such was
not the case with the other professions.

1. United States Census Bureau, *Eleventh Census of the United States: 1890.
Population.* Vol. I, Part II (Washington: Government Printing Office, 1883), p. 592.
Professional service included clergymen, lawyers, government officials, physicians and
surgeons, teachers, and artists.

An examination of the Negro professional in individual towns and cities of North Carolina shows, as was the case over the entire state, that this group constituted only a very insignificant proportion of those employed. In Raleigh in 1876, Negro professionals (almost exclusively teachers and clergymen) made up only 1.6 per cent of the gainfully employed Negroes of that city.[2] By 1888 the percentage had reached a mere 3.8, with the overwhelming number continuing to be teachers and clergymen.[3] The percentage of Negro professional men and women in Greensboro increased from 2.1 in 1880 to 4.5 in 1887.[4] Asheville, Charlotte, New Bern, and Wilmington showed similar proportions.[5]

The high status of North Carolina Negro school teachers and clergymen dated from the end of the Civil War, but physicians and lawyers were now beginning to grow in number and influence. In 1890, according to the federal census schedules of that year, there were forty-six Negro physicians and surgeons in the state. Most of these lived in Raleigh and other eastern North Carolina towns possessing large Negro populations; very few lived in the country. In Asheville and other mountain towns, Negro medical practitioners were less numerous or nonexistent. The small number of Negro physicians in North Carolina as compared with teachers and clergymen led one Negro physician, Dr. L. A. Rutherford, to seek the advice of a North Carolina Negro educator in regard to the wisdom of the establishment of a North Carolina Negro medical association. One of the purposes of the proposed association was to bring to the attention of the mass of Negroes the presence of Negro physicians, for Rutherford declared that "hundreds of our people never met a colored physician."[6]

In order to remedy this situation four young Negro physicians, possibly with the encouragement of Rutherford, organized in 1887 the Old North State Medical, Dental, and Pharmaceutical Society. The founders, M. T. Pope, J. T. Williams, L. A. Scruggs, and A. M. Moore, were all graduates of the Leonard Medical School at Shaw University. Pope, Williams, and Scruggs were in the class of 1886;

2. *Raleigh City Directory, 1875-1876*, pp. 41-130.

3. *Ibid., 1888*, pp. 2-119.

4. *Winston, Salem, and Greensboro Directory, 1879-1880*, pp. 79-116.

5. *Asheville City Directory, 1887*, pp. 30-272; *Directory of Charlotte, North Carolina, 1893-1894*, pp. 149-193; *New Bern City Directory, 1880-1881*, pp. 41-106; *Directory of the City of Wilmington, 1889*, pp. 17-153.

6. Rutherford to Charles N. Hunter, n.d. Charles N. Hunter Papers, Duke University Library, Durham.

Moore was in the class of 1888 and joined the organization before he finished his medical training.[7]

Until the establishment of the Leonard Medical School at Shaw University in 1880, formal medical instruction for Negroes was lacking in North Carolina. Unfortunately, statistics are unavailable as to the number of young men who attended or graduated from the medical college during the period under study. The record, however, reveals that the first class was graduated in 1886 and consisted of M. S. Abbott of Pensacola, Florida, James H. Bugg of Savannah, Georgia, M. T. Pope of Raleigh, A. T. Prince of Beaufort, South Carolina, L. A. Scruggs of Southern Pines, and J. T. Williams of Charlotte.[8] Despite the small graduating class in 1886, the medical dormitory building could accommodate sixty boarding students.[9]

North Carolina's only school for the training of Negro physicians was apparently viewed with respect and admiration by the whites of Raleigh. A white newspaper of that city, although describing the institution as a "college for darky doctors," warmly declared that not only was it a good medical college, but was "one of the handsomest edifices in the South." Possessing a distinguished white faculty, the college had lecture rooms, dissecting rooms, "and all the appliances including a number of costly models of human anatomy, imported directly from Paris, France."[10] For its day and time it was apparently quite complete.

One serious handicap confronting the Negro physicians was the belief held by some whites *and* some Negroes that Negro doctors were incompetent and untrained. An example of this doubt as to the competency of the Negro physicians was expressed by a white school teacher of Tarboro. In a letter to his mother on September 20, 1882, he said that although a recently arrived Negro physician rode around Tarboro "with a very fast horse as if he was busy," the white teacher declared that he knew very little about his skill or charges. He therefore concluded that "the darkies had better employ the white doctors they have. . . ."[11] Unfortunately, there is no available information about the fees charged or the professional incomes of Negro physicians.

7. Souvenir program of the Old North State Medical, Dental and Pharmaceutical Society, Inc., Fifteenth Annual Session, June 1, 2, 3, 1937, Durham.

8. J. A. Whitted, *A History of the Negro Baptists of North Carolina* (Raleigh: Edwards, Broughton, and Company, 1908), p. 58.

9. Raleigh *Farmer and Mechanic*, January 30, 1884.

10. *Ibid.*

11. Letter dated September 20, 1888. Peter Evans Smith Papers, Duke University Library, Durham. This letter is incomplete and does not give the names of the sender or the recipient.

The legal profession, similar to the medical profession, made slow progress. According to the 1890 census schedules, there were in North Carolina only fourteen Negro lawyers. Most of these were located in the larger towns of eastern North Carolina, notably New Bern, Tarboro, Raleigh, and Charlotte. Since there was no established law school in the state for Negroes until the late 1880's when the Law Department of Shaw University was opened, legal training was acquired through apprenticeship, usually in the office of a white lawyer. George H. White read law under Walter Clark, judge of the Superior Court, and later judge and chief justice of the Supreme Court of North Carolina.[12] John S. Leary, an outstanding Negro lawyer of Fayetteville, also received an excellent apprenticeship under the careful eye of an able white lawyer.[13] As might be expected, some of the Negroes, like James E. O'Hara and George H. White, combined law and politics. As lawyer-politicians, both men served in the United States Congress as representatives from North Carolina. The law also offered other public service opportunities. White, for example, was elected solicitor of the Second Judicial District in 1886.[14]

Legal practice for the Negro, as was the case with medical practice, was fraught with economic insecurity. Not only were potential clients, in the main, comparatively poor, but too often the Negro mass failed to turn to Negro lawyers. This lack of support by the Negroes of Raleigh in 1893 prompted its two race lawyers, E. A. Johnson, an 1890 graduate of the law school at Shaw University, and J. H. Branch, to consider moving to another locality. The *Gazette,* a local Negro newspaper, aroused by their decision, declared: "Our people are proud of them, and will not have it said . . . that as many colored people as there are in the city of Raleigh, and as much legal business as they have on hand at all times for lawyers, that the only two lawyers of the race in the city will have to leave and go elsewhere to earn a living by their professions."[15] The records do not reveal whether the editorial was sufficiently effective in reversing the decision of the two Negro lawyers to quit Raleigh.

Similar to the *raison d'être* of all Negro newspaper editors in the United States, Negro newspaper editors of North Carolina were in-

12. D. F. Sinclair, *Biographical Sketches of the Members and Officers of the General Assembly, 1889* (Raleigh: Edwards, Broughton, and Co., 1889), p. 7.

13. W. H. Quick, *Negro Stars in All Ages of the World* (Richmond: S. B. Adkins and Co., 1898), p. 242.

14. In 1886 the Second Judicial District was composed of Warren, Halifax, Bertie, Northampton, Craven, and Edgecombe counties. Quick, *Negro Stars,* pp. 270, 314-15.

15. Raleigh *Gazette,* May 28, 1893.

spired by a desire "to uplift the race," and at all times "to take an un-compromising stand against those who outrage, oppress and malign the Negro." Negro newspapers of the state were published weekly, semi-monthly, and as monthly journals. By 1890 there were about eleven newspapers as compared to five in 1880. Some of the principal cities and towns of Piedmont and eastern North Carolina had Negro-edited newspapers. Among these were Raleigh, New Bern, Charlotte, Salisbury, Goldsboro, and Edenton. Circulation statistics for these and other Negro journals are meager. John H. Williamson's Raleigh *Banner* was reported to have a circulation "reaching two thousand or more" in the early 1880's. This was probably the exception, for as a general rule, the Negro newspapers did not survive long enough to build up a sizable subscriber group. As a matter of fact, between 1877 and 1894 at least twenty Negro newspapers were founded in the state, most of which failed to sustain two years of publication.[16] Thus the long lives of the *Star of Zion* of Salisbury, the Charlotte *Messenger,* and the Raleigh *Gazette* were unique among Negro journals of North Carolina. Actually, the average circulation of the Negro papers in the state probably did not exceed five hundred suscribers each.

The Negro newspaper was of a size similar to that of its white contemporary and usually comprised four pages devoid of headlines and pictures. A representative of the Negro papers of the state in terms of make-up was that of the Raleigh *Gazette* of December 16, 1893. At a yearly subscription rate of $1.50,[17] the seven columns on each of its four pages carried national and international dispatches. The paper devoted a respectable amount of space to items of local interest, such as those pertaining to social functions, religious and fraternal activities, schools, health, and business. The advertisements came largely from local white businessmen. Since the issues of the *Gazette* appeared once a week, it is reasonable to assume that its news was sometimes stale. Significantly, the paper's attitude towards the whites did not appear hateful or vengeful.

The publisher-editor of these Negro papers was sometimes a printer who learned the trade in the printing office of a white newspaper. John C. Dancy, the editor of the *Star of Zion* of Salisbury, for example, was taught the printer's trade in the office of the Tarboro *Southerner.* Sometimes the editor of a Negro newspaper was a college or university graduate, such as E. H. Lipscombe, the publisher of the Asheville

16. Garland I. Penn, *The Afro-American Press* (Springfield, Mass.: Willey and Co., 1892), pp. 111-14, 183.
17. Thomas Donaldson to Matthew Ransom, January 30, 1894. Ransom Papers. University of North Carolina Library, Chapel Hill.

Mountain Gleaner. All too frequently, he was a politician turned journalist as was the case of James H. Harris, editor-publisher of the *North Carolina Republican* of Raleigh in the early 1880's, and the Raleigh *Gazette* in the mid-1890's. North Carolina Negro newspaper men in the period from 1870 through 1890 were usually native-born slaves of the 1840's, the outstanding exception being John H. Williamson, who was born in Georgia.

Among the Negro papers of the state were those published by religious bodies, the weekly *Star of Zion* of the African Methodist Episcopal Zion Church, the weekly *Afro-American Presbyterian,* and the bi-weekly *Baptist Pilot.* Although their main preoccupation was with the religious and moral development of the Negroes of the state, occasionally they would speak strongly upon questions involving the rights of the race. The *Star of Zion,* for example, was most bitterly opposed to the school law of 1883, which provided that taxes collected from whites were to support white schools and that taxes collected from Negroes were to support Negro schools.

Of the non-religious newspapers, the most widely read were the *Journal of Industry,* the Charlotte *Messenger,* the Raleigh *Banner,* and the Raleigh *Gazette.* The *Journal of Industry,* the weekly organ of the North Carolina Industrial Association until 1881, was owned, edited, and published by Negroes and was "devoted to the moral, material and educational interests of the colored race." Its editors were Charles N. Hunter and his brother Oliver. A white newspaperman from the North, while on a visit to Raleigh in 1879, described it as "being a very creditably gotten up industrial journal."[18] The sometimes militant, outspoken editorials of these two men drew praise from such outstanding Negroes as Richard T. Greener, professor of the law school of Howard University, and Blanche K. Bruce, United States senator from Mississippi.[19] An example of this paper's aggressiveness may be gleaned in a compliance by the mayor of Durham, Isaac Link, to its demand for the facts relative to a Negro prisoner who had died while in the custody of the Durham police. The explanation by Link in showing that the death was not caused from injuries at the hands of the police "was a full one" and satisfied the editors that there was no foul play involved.[20]

18. "The Colored Fair at Raleigh, N.C.," *Frank Leslie's Illustrated Newspaper,* XLIX (December 6, 1879), 242.

19. Richard T. Greener to Charles N. Hunter, May 7, 1879; Blanche K. Bruce to Charles N. Hunter, April 30, 1879. Hunter Papers.

20. Isaac Link to the editors of the *Journal of Industry,* June 15, 1880. Hunter Papers.

In Charlotte, William C. Smith's *Messenger,* although not as aggressive or militant, was very popular with the middle and upper-class Negro. Vigorous opposition to intemperance and immorality probably contributed to its popularity with these two classes in Negro society. The pages were filled with the importance of improving the Negroes' morals, the education of their offspring, and the ownership of land. John H. Williamson's Raleigh *Banner,* founded in the spring of 1881, succeeded the *Journal of Industry* as the organ of the North Carolina Industrial Association. Although its main interest was in the advancement of the educational and industrial status of the Negroes of the state, it was concerned with all questions affecting the group. Williamson, in 1884, sold his interest in the *Banner* and founded the Raleigh *Gazette.* As in the case of his earlier paper, the *Gazette* was devoted to education and industry among the Negroes. It easily became one of the most influential Negro papers of the state. By 1893 the *Gazette,* now under the editorship of the able political leader, James H. Harris, was championing the political cause of the Negro. In explaining the philosophy of his paper to the Negroes of the state and, incidentally, the reasons that should cause them to support it, he wrote, "the *Gazette* represents the race; it is your paper; it defends you; it is your weapon. . . ."[21] The *Gazette's* discussion of political issues, although critical of the emphasis on white supremacy by the white press of the state, was generally conspicuous for its mildness.[22]

Despite its limitations the Negro press of North Carolina was instrumental in demonstrating the intellectual capacity of the race and represented one of the best means of informing the public at large of the Negroes' development, achievement, aspirations, and progress.

For magazines the literate North Carolina Negro relied largely on white periodicals. Indeed, it was not until 1890 that the Negroes of the state could point to a magazine that was considered by outlanders as a significant addition to the literary history of the race. The *Southland,* founded by the president of Livingstone College, J. C. Price, and edited by S. C. Atkins, was described by one Negro as "the fairest and finest publication yet." The first number was issued in February, 1890, and, apparently, was generally well received. A facsimile of the nationally known and widely read *Forum* in its typographical arrangement, its aim was to present the opinions of out-

21. Penn, *Afro-American Press,* pp. 182-83, 272-73; Raleigh *Gazette,* December 16, 1893.
22. See issues of the Raleigh *Gazette* for December, 1893.

standing Negro leaders on the racial situation in the South. Therefore, it is not surprising that the most outstanding feature of the
Southland was the space devoted to discussions of the race question.[23]

Perhaps the most important of the magazines published by a religious denomination in North Carolina was the *African Methodist
Episcopal Zion Church Quarterly,* edited by John C. Dancy. Despite
the attention given to religious topics, it exhibited a strong race
consciousness in such titles as "Alien Brothers," "Race Assimilation,"
"Slavery, Ancient and Modern," and in the editorial section were
featured such topics as "Race Educators." The issue for July, 1892,
also contained poetry. Typical of the magazines published by the
Negro colleges of the state was the Bennett Seminary *Visitor.* It was
described by a Greensboro paper as "a neat quarterly . . . edited with
ability by the Principal."[24]

Slow, steady, snail-like growth was evidenced in Negro industrial
and business enterprises. Many entered these fields, especially that of
business. The insistent urgings of white southerners such as Henry
W. Grady to build a "new South" based on industry and commerce
also fell upon the ears of the Negro men and women. And not being
ignorant of or indifferent to the successes of many white individuals,
they were tempted to invest their small savings in some business.
Another factor that contributed to the rise of Negro merchants, manufacturers, and traders was the refusal by the white businessman to
employ Negroes in other than menial jobs. Therefore some Negroes
felt that the only certain way to free themselves from the wage earning
class was to become their own employers.

Thus, in January of 1880, there were eighty Negro business establishments with an estimated worth of $79,500.[25] A more detailed
breakdown of the over-all worth will reveal that a vast majority of
the Negroes were decidedly men of small businesses, for sixty-one, or
76.25 per cent of the total value of the eighty enterprises were estimated to be worth five hundred dollars or less. Only three, or 3.75
per cent, were worth ten thousand dollars.[26] As small as these businesses were, however, they nevertheless afforded work to a small
number of Negro clerks, typists, bookkeepers, and the like—positions
that were not open to them in the white businesses of the state.

The eighty Negro business establishments in North Carolina in

23. Penn, *Afro-American Press,* pp. 125-26.
24. Greensboro, *Daily Bugle,* April 10, 1882.
25. Compiled by the writer from *The Mercantile Agency Reference Book,* January,
1880 (New York: Dun, Barlow and Co., 1879).
26. Compiled by the writer from *ibid.*

1880 were scattered almost evenly through thirty-eight cities and towns of the state. New Bern and Raleigh led in such enterprises with ten and seven respectively, but two smaller towns, Warrenton and Enfield, ranked first and second in terms of the estimated worth of Negro businesses.

Although the mercantile interests of the Negroes of North Carolina were varied, Dun and Barlow's report of January, 1880, shows that they were largely concentrated in the following businesses: general and grocery stores, liquor stores, bar-rooms and saloons, and blacksmith shops. As a matter of fact, these enterprises made up fifty-nine or 73.5 per cent of the eighty Negro establishments, with an estimated worth of fifty-five thousand dollars or 69.3 per cent of the total worth of all Negro businesses for 1879.

The status of Negro businesses in North Carolina, as reflected by the Dun and Barlow credit rating, was not a healthy one. According to this company's report of January, 1880, fifty-three, or 66.6 per cent, received no credit rating whatever because Dun and Barlow felt that the unsatisfactory state of those businesses and their investments did not meet the minimum accrediting standards. Moreover, only one Negro business, the livery stables of William S. Williams in the little town of Warrenton, was awarded a credit rating of "good."

What was the general picture of Negro enterprises nine years later? We learn that the reports of Dun and Barlow for January, 1889, listed 175 Negro merchants, manufacturers, and traders in North Carolina, an increase of ninety-five, or 54.2 per cent, over the 1880 figure. Their estimated worth was $129,000, an increase of forty-nine thousand dollars, or 38.3 per cent.[27] However, in spite of the growth, both in numbers and worth, Negroes continued to be small businessmen. In view of this, ninety-eight, or 56.0 per cent were estimated to be worth five hundred dollars or less, while only two, or 1.1 per cent, were worth ten thousand dollars.

The 175 Negro business enterprises were located in 57 North Carolina cities and towns. New Bern continued to lead in the number of such establishments with 17, but Wilmington, with 12, replaced Raleigh as the number two city. Raleigh, Tarboro, and Kinston followed with ten, eight, and seven respectively.

Although the Negroes entered a variety of businesses, Dun and Barlow's report of January, 1889, continues the trend shown in the 1880 report. Thus, taking in the four businesses of general stores,

27. Compiled by the writer from the *Mercantile Agency Reference Book*, January, 1889 (New York: Dun, Barlow and Co., 1888).

grocery stores, liquor dealers, and blacksmiths, there were 124, or 70.8 per cent, of the grand total that comprised $103,000 or 79.9 per cent, of the estimated worth of all Negro business establishments in North Carolina for the year 1888.

The credit rating of all of the Negro businesses in the January, 1889, report was lower than it was nine years earlier. Of the total, 124, or 70.8 per cent, received no rating whatever, and Dun and Barlow considered those businesses as not measuring up to the company's accrediting standards.

Although it is true that the vast majority of the Negro establishments were modest ones operating on small amounts of capital, with little or no credit rating, there were some prosperous individual businesses owned and operated by Negroes. A Negro, Thomas Hunter, owned a granite stone yard that employed "a great many hands." He declared that his business was "first class in every respect," and that he had just recently furnished "about thirteen hundred dollars worth of stone" in the construction of a white church in Charlotte.[28] In Kinston, L. H. Fisher and Wiley Lowrey were looked upon as two of that town's most successful businessmen. One newspaper stated that Fisher was "the largest colored merchant in the place, and he is doing business that many a one with much larger capital in larger and more reputed wealthier places might envy without being accused of malice."[29] Lowrey was described as "an energetic, wealth-earning, money-saving gentleman."[30] A reporter of the Wilmington *Morning Post,* on a visit to Tarboro on July 25, 1882, noted that "quite a number of colored men are engaged in business here of their own, and are doing prosperously." The businesses ranged from grocery, to dry goods, to drugs and medicines.[31] Dennis B. Yancey, one of the more successful businessmen of Greensboro, listed himself in that city's directory as a "dealer in choice fresh meats, poultry, vegetables, family groceries, country produce, notions, etc."[32]

In Concord, in 1889 a town with a population of 3,600, Warren C. Coleman owned the only general store. His business was estimated to be worth five thousand dollars, and was listed among the town's top ten concerns.[33] Perhaps the most successful Negro businessman in North Carolina, Coleman was born a slave in Cabarrus County

28. Thomas Hunter to Charles N. Hunter, August 25, 1886. Hunter Papers.
29. *North Carolina Republican,* quoted by the Kinston *Journal,* October 23, 1879.
30. *Ibid.*
31. Wilmington *Post,* August 6, 1882.
32. *Greensboro City Directory, 1887,* p. 89.
33. *Mercantile Association of the Carolinas Reference Book,* July, 1889, pp. 33-34.

on March 25, 1849. Following emancipation, he evinced a natural flair for business by establishing a barbershop in connection with a bakery, a novel combination to say the least. Later, he attended Howard University for one year. While there he maintained himself by selling jewelry. Returning to Concord in 1874, he entered the merchandizing field. On September 8, 1885, the seven thousand dollar loss incurred as a result of a disastrous fire revealed the extent of his business success.[34] Despite this heavy financial setback, Coleman, in less than four years had rebuilt a business establishment worth five thousand dollars.

In Oxford, B. Gee's general store was estimated to be worth ten thousand dollars. Of the thirty-three such stores in the town (thirty white and three Negro), only one, owned by a white man, D. A. Hunt and Son, carried an estimated value higher than Gee's.[35] It is, therefore, interesting to note that although Gee continued to prosper as a general store owner, four years later an item appeared in the Raleigh *Gazette,* which stated that he was considering the possibility "of making Chicago his future home."[36] The records do not reveal what may have prompted Gee to think about abandoning a successful business enterprise. The largest grocery business in Winston in 1889, estimated to be worth ten thousand dollars, was operated by two Negroes, Newsom and Jones.[37] Their store was the only one in the town, white or Negro, to carry a credit rating of "good" by the accrediting association of the two Carolinas.[38] In the same year several Negroes of Greenville and Warrenton were listed among the more prominent businessmen of their respective communities.[39]

Negro businesses in North Carolina were principally individual-istic. The few Negro "corporations" were usually organized for educational, religious, charitable, or mutual-benefit purposes. An example of the last type was the Real Estate Investment Company of Wilmington, incorporated in 1887. The stated purpose of this company was "to provide comfortable homes at a modest rent, and for buying and selling real estate."[40] An example of the charitable type was the in-

34. Quick, *Negro Stars,* pp. 264, 265, 266-267. Raleigh, *Carolina Gazette* September 26, 1885.
35. *Mercantile Association of the Carolinas Reference Book,* July, 1889, pp. 107-109.
36. Raleigh *Gazette,* December 16, 1893.
37. *Mercantile Association of the Carolinas Reference Book,* July, 1889, p. 131.
38. *Ibid.*
39. Dawson and King, general store owners; Allen F. Faulkener and L. Harris, blacksmiths; James M. Ransom, carriage-maker. *Ibid.,* pp. 204, 205, 267-268.
40. *Public and Private Laws and Resolutions of the State of North Carolina, 1887,* c. 41. Act of February 25, 1887.

corporation in 1887 of the St. Andrew's Home of Wilmington. The object was to supply a home for and alleviate the sufferings and necessities of the aged and indigent Negroes of that port city.[41] An example of the religious type was the Africo-American Presbyterian Publishing Company that was incorporated in 1889. Its chief object was to carry on in all its branches the general publishing and job printing business as well as to publish a religious newspaper. Capital stock of the corporation was $1,200 but the legislature authorized a maximum of $20,000.

Thus Negro business in the period between 1876 and 1894 was chiefly owned by Negroes who acted either independently or with one associate, very seldom with more associates.

41. *Ibid.*, c. 125. Act of March 7, 1887.

12

"You Can Better Conquer
Where You Are"

*I do believe that as a whole you can better conquer
where you are. . . . In due time you will get all
your rights or your children will—sooner there than
anywhere else.*
    United States Senator H. W. Blair to Charles N.
Hunter, April 13, 1889.

*My people are fully determined to better their con-
dition and be protected in all respects, and if this
cannot be done in the South, then the only remedy
is to emigrate. Either go West into that vast territory which is yet unoccupied, or go to Africa. . . .*
    Letter from a North Carolina Negro in the
SIXTY-THIRD ANNUAL REPORT OF THE AMERICAN COL-
ONIZATION SOCIETY, 1880.

The movement of Negroes from North Carolina
and other states in the South after Reconstruction to other areas of
the United States and outside the country was the result of unsettled
socio-economic and political conditions that had plagued that area
since 1865. The violent political campaigns between 1870 and 1876
which swept the Democrats into state offices were marked by open
racial conflict in South Carolina, Mississippi, and Louisiana. The
intimidation, whippings, and other forms of mob violence, coupled

with the enactment of state statutes designed to nullify the political, social, and economic gains made under the Reconstruction governments, resulted in widespread apprehension and a consequent interest on the part of southern Negroes in emigration. The great urge to migrate elsewhere was not confined to any one southern state. Some specific factors causing this Southwide movement were the general restriction of civil rights, the extravagant rumors of "good living and high wages" in the states outside the South, and the discontent brought on by the operation of the land-tenure and credit system.[1]

North Carolina in 1876 and in the years following was but a facet of this Southwide situation. Indeed, the determination of the whites "to redeem the state from ignorant Negro, carpet-bag and scalawag rule," as manifested in the almost frenzied white supremacy campaign of 1876 and its consequences, caused wholesale trepidation among the Negroes of the state. And this, coupled with the complete Democratic victory in the November elections, led a large portion of the Negro group to evince more than a fleeting inquisitiveness in the feasibility of emigration. As a matter of fact, the apprehension that "legislation under Democratic auspices would be inimical to their rights and interest" became so pronounced during the first months of 1877 that a Democratic member of the state legislature, Montford McGehee, of Person County, felt compelled to assure the Negroes that the duty of government was not only to protect all its citizens, "but," he added, "a wise government will use all the legal methods to impress its citizens with its readiness and willingness to protect."[2] The editor of a prominent Democratic newspaper in the "black city" of Tarboro underscored McGehee's words when he told the Negroes that the Democratic party of North Carolina was not only in a position to be the best friend "they ever had," but that it would be.[3]

The Negroes, however, demanded more than mere words; and when the members of the Democratic party early in 1877 introduced on the floor of the General Assembly bills to "rid the eastern counties of black domination," the Negro electorate nearly swamped its "tan" representation in the House with petitions on colonization and emigration.[4] Following the passage of the anti-Negro county government law on February 27, 1877, a group of Negro citizens of Burke County

1. See Carter G. Woodson, *A Century of Negro Migration* (Washington: Association for the Study of Negro Life and History, 1918), pp. 131-34.
2. Greensboro *Patriot*, January 10, 1877.
3. Tarboro *Southerner*, January 12, 1877.
4. The petitions came chiefly from Nash, Franklin, Halifax, and Granville counties. Raleigh *Observer*, February 6, 1877.

wrote Governor Vance a letter seeking his aid in assisting them to colonize. In reply, the Governor said, "Your note received in which you express your desire for my influence in aid of a plan for the colonization of your race, and your great fears of oppression. I cannot give aid to any such scheme. I think your fears are idle. So far as I am concerned, and the party with which I act, I know that there is no intention to oppose your people or deprive them of a single legal right."[5]

It appears that the Negroes of North Carolina were not reassured by the words of the Governor, and in the years between 1877 and 1880 an increasing number quit the state. The movement assumed such proportions that James H. Harris, a prominent Negro politician of North Carolina, felt it necessary to issue a call for a state meeting of "representative colored men" in Raleigh in January of 1880 for the expressed purpose "to investigate the causes contributing to the emigration of colored people from the state." With Harris as chairman, the meeting enumerated six grievances "of which the colored do justly complain":

1. Especially the rural districts, where the land owners exact exorbitant rents for their lands and necessary supplies, thereby sucking the life's blood from the colored sons of toil.

2. That the colored people have just cause for complaint of the nefarious law known as the Landlord and Tenant Act as amended by the legislature of 1876-77, thereby opening a broad channel for the unscrupulous landlords to defraud their colored tenants out of their earnings. . . .

3. That they complain of the justices of the peace being elected by the legislature, and from a class of citizens who too often have no sympathy with the colored laborer, and who are appointed against the will of the people, thereby taking from them their constitutional privileges of electing their own officers. . . .

4. That, in many of the counties, colored men are not permitted to act as jurors, notwithstanding that the bill of rights declares that every man shall have the right to be tried by a jury of his peers.

5. That in all the school districts, they are denied the right to select their own committeemen, and are thus deprived of the privilege to select and appoint their own school teachers.

6. That, in many counties of this State, under the operation of the present judiciary system, colored people do not get fair and impartial trials,

5. Greensboro *Patriot,* March 21, 1877. For a discussion of the county government law, see William A. Mabry, "The Negro in North Carolina Politics Since Reconstruction," *Trinity College Historical Society Papers,* XXII (1946), 17-22.

and that evidence that convicts a colored person fails to convict a white person charged with similar offences.[6]

These grievances, although formulated in 1880, had been long in existence and apparently explain why large numbers of Negroes rejected the advice of a Negro Baptist newspaper, the *National Monitor,* which had urged them "to work and pray" where they were and "to trust in God for the rest."[7]

Some North Carolina Negroes, particularly during the first ten years of Democratic rule after 1876, evidenced an interest in Liberia, and it was perhaps inevitable that they would turn to the fading American Colonization Society for aid and assistance. Founded in 1817, this organization, although receiving the support of public and private agencies, had been unable to carry out its purpose of colonizing American Negroes in Africa. Thus, by the 1850's, as a result of internal dissension, spirited opposition on the part of the free Negroes, and the cost of transporting and maintaining the emigrants, the American Colonization Society ceased to be a major factor in the efforts to solve the problem of what to do with American Negroes.[8] However, it continued, even after the Civil War, to urge and assist Negroes to emigrate to Liberia. In the 1870's, therefore, following the rise to power of the Democrats in all the southern states, a small number of Negroes showed some interest in Liberian emigration, and turned to the American Colonization Society for assistance.[9]

The extent of that interest with reference to the Negroes of North Carolina can be seen through an examination of the letters they wrote to the American Colonization Society during the period under consideration. Although not extensive, there were small groups, both in the rural and urban areas, who "talked up going to Liberia." In Charlotte in 1877, for example, the talk of a Liberian exodus from the city prompted the president of Johnson C. Smith (then Biddle) University, Dr. S. Mattoon, to submit a series of eight questions to the American Colonization Society, hoping "thereby to enable the Negroes to act understandingly or to abandon the agitation of the question." The questions covered such matters as the cost of transportation to Liberia, aid to individual Negroes by the Society and by the Liberian

6. Raleigh *Signal,* January 21, 1880.

7. Salisbury *Carolina Watchman,* May 1, 1879.

8. John Hope Franklin, *From Slavery to Freedom* (New York: Alfred A. Knopf, Inc., 1947), pp. 234-38.

9. See Woodson, *Negro Migration,* pp. 147-59, and George B. Tindall, *South Carolina Negroes, 1877-1900* (Columbia: University of South Carolina Press, 1952), pp. 153-68.

government, and conditions aboard ship. The president stated that he was deeply interested in the matter of colonization, but he thought it important that the Negroes "should know just what they can do, and not spend time on that which cannot be accomplished."[10]

Although the American Colonization Society's records do not reveal whether a reply was ever sent to Dr. Mattoon, some interest and agitation in the Liberian exodus continued.[11] Local mass meetings were held in such towns as Concord, Durham, and Raleigh, and at least one state-wide Liberian emigrant mass meeting was scheduled on August 15, 1877, in Greensboro.[12]

However, despite the meetings, the large masses of Negroes of the state manifested little interest in the movement to Liberia, for less than four hundred migrated. Actually, according to the records of the American Colonization Society, between 1876 and 1894 only 318 Negroes left North Carolina for that African country. For several reasons the movement of Negroes from North Carolina, as well as from other Southern and Northern states, the Liberia was inconsiderable. In the first place, Negro leadership was generally hostile to the scheme, and in the second place, many whites, especially those with agricultural interests, opposed the emigration of rural Negroes to Liberia.

From the outset, Negro leaders of North Carolina spoke against the Liberian movement. In 1877, Bishop James W. Hood, of the African Methodist Episcopal Zion Church, a bitter foe of the African exodus, apparently made a strong anti-emigration speech in Concord, for the white newspaper of that city observed that "the Bishop is certainly severe in his denunciation of colonization, and the vivid picture which he drew of black Liberia, with her thousand contagious diseases, the sweltering heat of a tropical sun, and her poor, half dead population, withering away like dew before the morning sun, was not calculated to inspire many sable bosoms with the desire to migrate."[13] Among other Negro leaders, James H. Harris and James E. O'Hara were equally as vociferous in opposing the Liberian emigration.[14]

10. Letter dated July 4, 1877. American Colonization Society Papers, hereafter cited as ACSP.

11. ACSP. Letters from C. Etheridge, Colerain, Bertie County, July 24, 1880; Dennis Thompson, New Bern, July 26, 1880; James A. Wright, Monroe, January 20, 1883; E. Gough, Charlotte, January 29, 1883; G. B. Breen, Forestville, July 1, 1885; A. Davidson, Huntersville, March 6, 1887.

12. ACSP. Letters from P. P. Erwin, Concord, April 7, 1877; Albert B. Williams, Raleigh, February 1, 1877; W. L. Kornegay, Durham, October 8, 1888. See also circular in ACSP, August, 1877.

13. Quoted in the Tarboro *Southerner*, February 3, 1877.

14. See Raleigh *Register*, November 1, 1877.

The hostility of the Negro leaders of the state, coupled with determined white opposition in the agricultural sections of eastern North Carolina, considerably reduced the number of potential emigrants to the African country. That the white attitude toward Liberian emigration was motivated largely by economic interest may be seen by the numerous editorials in the Democratic press of eastern North Carolina deploring the possible loss of "laborers just on the eve of pitching our crops."[15] The threatened reduction in the large surplus of cheap labor caused one paper to declare frankly that the whites ought not to sit idly by "and watch it [the surplus of Negro labor] destroyed."[16] Actually, the whites made efforts to discourage the "back to Africa" movement. As early as 1876, Charles H. Williams, a Negro from Seaboard, North Carolina, wrote the American Colonization Society that "demagogues and unprincipled white men" in his community were telling the Negroes that they were emigrating to a land where the practice of "inhuman barbarism" and the existence of slavery prevailed.[17] Another method, possibly more realistic and certainly equally as effective in preventing the Negroes from emigrating, was simply to prohibit them from selling their crops before harvest time. Even if the Negro tenants were permitted to sell "in the field," the whites would not pay them a just and fair price. Without a minimum of funds, the Negroes, the whites assumed, would easily realize the futility of quitting the farms of the state. In short, the whites felt it was not economically practical to allow the Negroes to go to Africa or anywhere else. There was much truth in the bitter complaint of one Negro: "The whites do not want us to go, and will not do anything to assist us that we might go."[18]

Although the above reasons partly explain the failure of Liberian colonization during the period under study, the major factor was simply that the bulk of the dissatisfied Negroes of North Carolina, as well as of the South as a whole, notwithstanding their approval of emigration, preferred to live elsewhere in the United States rather than in Africa. The first large interstate migration from the South after Reconstruction occurred in 1879. Thousands of Negroes left the southern states, particularly Louisiana, Mississippi, Alabama, and Georgia. Under the leadership of Moses Singleton, of Tennessee, and Henry Adams, of Louisiana, the movement was channeled largely

15. Warrenton *Gazette,* January 23, 1880. See also the Tarboro *Southerner* and the Kinston *Journal* for the months of December, 1879, and January, 1880.

16. Warrenton *Gazette,* January 23, 1880.

17. ACSP. Letters from Charles H. Williams, September 14, 1876.

18. ACSP. Letter from Charles W. Jones, Pasquotank County, July 28, 1876.

into Kansas. And although the exuberant claims by both relative to the number of Negroes they sent into the state may be open to question, there can be little doubt that they lured thousands from the South. The concern with which the white people of the South viewed this movement is further proof of its extent and scope.[19]

Although some of the Negroes migrating to Kansas were undoubtedly from North Carolina, it appears that the bulk of North Carolina Negroes moved into Indiana. Over a thirty-day period, Johnston and Wayne counties reportedly lost six thousand to this state! Little wonder, then, that the Indianapolis *Sentinel* was aghast over "the large number of Negroes" who poured daily into that city.[20] The Negro who has been credited with master-minding this early exodus from North Carolina, Sam L. Perry, was particularly active in Greene, Lenoir, Wayne, Wilson, Edgecombe, and Halifax counties. The white newspapers of the state were quick to brand the activities of this Negro as "politically inspired." They said that the Republicans were intent on carrying Indiana in the 1880 presidential elections, hence the effort to pack the state with Negro Republicans from North Carolina.[21] In answer to this charge, one out-of-state newspaper observed that "the colored emigrants know whether or not they have been deceived. . . . They know, too, whether the laws of North Carolina bear hard upon them or not, whether they receive pay for their labor and are treated humanely by their white employers."[22] Whatever the motives, political or otherwise, Perry's activities caused one paper to confess that "the exodus feeling is worked up to a fever heat, and in some sections nearly all are leaving."[23] With the aid of a Negro preacher named Williams, Perry "worked up" this "fever" by picturing Indiana as a paradise for Negro laborers and by depicting most graphically the wrongs heaped upon the Negro farmers of the state, particularly by the Landlord and Tenant Act. In support of Perry's denunciations of this law, a contemporary newspaper wrote that as a result of its passage, it was no secret why the Negroes were "eager to leave North Carolina for homes in the West." "If the

19. Woodson, *Negro Migration*, pp. 127-46; Vernon L. Wharton, *The Negro in Mississippi, 1865-1890* (Chapel Hill: University of North Carolina Press, 1947), pp. 106-16; Walter L. Fleming, " 'Pap' Singleton, the Moses of the Colored Exodus," *American Journal of Sociology*, XV (July, 1909), 61-83; John G. Van Deusen, "The Exodus of 1879," *Journal of Negro History*, XXI (April, 1936), 111-29.

20. Wilmington *Morning Star*, January 7, 1880.

21. Chatham *Record*, December 11, 18, 1879, February 19, 1880; Lenoir *Topic*, January 8, 1879; Kinston *Journal*, February 12, 1880.

22. "The Exodus into Indiana," *Frank Leslie's Illustrated Newspaper*, XLIX (January 17, 1880), 362.

23. Kinston *Journal*, December 4, 1879.

white owners of land in North Carolina had decided upon this method to get rid of their colored neighbors," it added, "they are in a fair way to accomplish it."[24] Perry, then, appeared to be attacking a real grievance.

The whites realized the wide following of Negroes that Perry was attracting and attempted to counter his charges by admitting that although some of what he said was true, he was greatly exaggerating the entire situation. Thus, the Kinston *Journal,* in reply to a charge by Perry that the whites cheated the Negroes out of their wages, declared that "we would pay no attention to such a statement, but for the fact that the mass of the crowd showed by their actions that they endorsed the sentiments, showing the deep prejudice existing in their minds against the white people. . . ." The paper admitted that perhaps a few whites were guilty of Perry's charges, but argued that it was demogogical to infer that this was a general practice.[25]

William H. Kitchin, who was the white United States representative from the Second Congressional District of North Carolina, the so-called "black second," and who, as I have already observed, had won a questionable victory over James E. O'Hara, a Negro, in the 1878 Congressional election, denied the assertion by Perry that the Negroes in North Carolina were given "the bad treatment." He said that "the very best relations existed between the whites and blacks, and there was never any complaint of ill treatment by the latter, as on the contrary, they said they were perfectly content."[26] Contemporary evidence, however, seems to refute this very optimistic picture of Negro-white relations in North Carolina in the early 1880's. The Warrenton *Gazette,* for example, disagreed with Kitchin when it declared that "the exodus . . . shows a bad state of affairs; it shows that they [the Negroes] are dissatisfied, and whenever this is the case the labor is unreliable."[27]

Although the 1878-1880 exodus fever in the Second Congressional District of North Carolina was the last that threatened to depopulate that portion of the state until 1889, the interstate movement of the Negroes was not halted. The continuing agricultural depression and economic exploitation of the Negro farm laborers served as a steady stimulant to either permanent or temporary migration. Thus, we learn from the white newspapers of eastern North Carolina of the

24. "Exodus into Indiana," *Leslie's Newspaper,* p. 362.

25. Kinston *Journal,* July 10, 1878.

26. Tarboro *Southerner,* January 15, 1880.

27. Warrenton *Gazette,* January 9, 1880. See also *ibid.,* January 23, 1880, and the Raleigh *Signal,* January 28, 1880.

persistent trickle of Negroes quitting the state, interestingly enough not for the West or the North, but for the deep South. On January 7, 1880, the Wilmington *Morning Star* reported that "five car loads of colored people passed through here yesterday morning en route to Georgia, where they are to work in the turpentine lands."[28] A year later 250 farm hands left Edgecombe County to work in the turpentine forests of South Carolina for two hundred dollars a year, "expenses paid and rations furnished."[29] The Raleigh *News and Observer* reported in 1883 "that there was considerable exodus of colored men from the eastern part of the state to the newly opened turpentine fields of Georgia and Alabama, and that this year these men are doing what they have never done before—taking the women with them—which course seems to indicate their purpose to remain."[30] These migrations from North Carolina to the deep South, it might be added, reinforce the theory that economics as well as a denial of civil rights prompted the withdrawal of Negroes from the state.

The second largest, if not the largest, exodus of Negroes from the state occurred in 1889. Similar to its predecessor, it was motivated by the "oppressive" mortgage and lien bond system, the agricultural depression (of 1888 in this instance), the generally lower wages paid to Negro agricultural workers, the county government law, and the enactment of harsh racial legislation by the General Assembly of North Carolina. The immediate cause of the 1889 exodus, however, was the passage of the 1889 election law by the General Assembly. That the statute would energize the exodus movement was voiced by the Raleigh *Signal* approximately a week before the bill's final reading. It warned the Democrats to "think twice before committing the State to a policy which may strip the land of its best, most reliable, most peaceable laborers." On the morning of the day the bill was enacted, the same paper again advised the General Assembly not to pass it, for "the Negroes of the State are alarmed and indignant at this proposition to disfranchise them, and if this bill becomes a law many thousands of colored people will leave the State during the next two years."[31]

On March 21, two weeks after the law was voted through the state legislature, the *Signal* once again spoke of an aroused Negro citizenry: "The colored people are becoming very much excited in regard to moving out of the State. The more intelligent class say an attempt has been made to disfranchise the poor and uneducated man, both white

28. Wilmington *Morning Star,* January 7, 1880.
29. Tarboro *Southerner,* January 27, 1881.
30. Raleigh *News and Observer,* January 30, 1883.
31. Raleigh *Signal,* February 28, March 7, 1889.

and colored. . . . Therefore they are advising every family to leave the State that can raise the means to do so. This is the fruit of the recent unconstitutional new election law."[32]

Mass Negro reaction to the election law of 1889 was not long in coming. On April 26 of that year, as a result of a call by a Negro minister, L. L. Ferrebee, Negroes assembled in Raleigh with "but one sentiment expressed and that was in favor of organizing and going to the Southwest." The intense interest of the Negroes in the convention was noted by the Raleigh *News and Observer* when it observed that on the morning of the opening session, "the colored populace was present in battalions . . . the old women and the children were there too." That journal also pointed out that the eastern part of the state was "heavily represented."[33]

Under the chairmanship of J. C. Price, an educator and one of the great Negro orators of the state, the convention organized, calling itself the North Carolina Emigration Association, and adopted resolutions that declared that the situation of the Negroes in the state

. . . was more precarious now than ever before; that they were subjected to legislative enactments which kept the Negro at the mercy of the landlord; that they were at a disadvantage in every contest; that when the judges were just, the juries were not; that the disposition to divide the educational fund in proportion to amounts paid in by the races was unjust and a direct attempt to keep the Negroes ignorant; that the county government system was impious and unjust and was especially designed to keep Negroes from participating in government; that in every campaign, the Democrats proclaimed that this was a white man's country and that the Negro must be kept down.[34]

The resolutions provided for the appointment of a state committee to visit a desirable section of the United States, "seek out a good place, lay claim to the lands, consult with the President of the United States" and report to the organization before they take any definite action in moving."[35]

Of these resolutions, the *News and Observer* caustically remarked that "from the character of some of the resolutions adopted, level-headed citizens, white and black, will conclude that it is high time for the members of the convention at least to emigrate and to the

32. *Ibid.*, March 21, 1889.
33. Raleigh *State Chronicle*, May 3, 1889, and the Raleigh *News and Observer*, April 27, 1889.
34. Proceedings of the [N.C.] *State Emigration Convention*, Raleigh, N.C., April 26 and 27, 1889. See also the Raleigh *State Chronicle*, May 3, 1889.
35. Raleigh *State Chronicle*, May 3, 1889.

greatest possible distance." Notwithstanding this effort to dismiss the convention as of no great importance, the whites of Raleigh were impressed by the determined seriousness of the Negroes. Again the *News and Observer*: "The Negroes to all appearance are preparing to sweep the whole population of their race from the State and land them in the far west." The newspaper then attempted to assure its readers that the Negroes were "moved by a dissatisfaction which we are very sure very few of them could explain and fewer still show to be based on any reasonable ground either of the undesirability of the present condition of affairs in North Carolina so far as they are concerned."[36] Another white newspaper, more removed from the area of disturbance, declared candidly that the movement of Negroes from North Carolina was attributable to the failure of the whites in the eastern part of the state to enable the Negroes to better their conditions: "He works from one end of the year to the other, and gets probably enough to eat and scantily clothe himself and family, that is all there is of life for him. If employers will take steps to make the colored people comfortable in the black belt and treat them as they should be treated, they will be as contented and prosperous as we find them in this [the Piedmont] region."[37]

It has been estimated that nearly fifty thousand Negroes migrated from North Carolina in 1889. The figure appears to be somewhat high. Nevertheless, it illustrates the extent of unrest. In most cases the destination was Kansas, Arkansas, Texas, or Oklahoma.[38] On November 14, 1889, the New Bern *Daily Journal* painted the following picture of a group of "exodusters" preparing to quit the state:

At Kinston yesterday the town was crowded with Negroes anxious to shake the North Carolina dust off their shoes and try their fortunes in some other state. It is said that there were about 1,500 enthusiastic "exodusters" in the town. At the depot an interesting spectacle presented itself in the huge mass of luggage piled on the platform. Old meat boxes, various other boxes, barrels, trunks of all shapes and sizes, were piled ten feet high on the platform. The train could not accommodate all who wanted to go. . . .[39]

Two weeks later when another 500 left Kinston, the Tarboro *Southerner* conceded that "the exodus fever seems to be very prevalent

36. Raleigh *News and Observer,* April 27, 1889.

37. Greensboro *North State,* January 14, 1886.

38. *Annual Cyclopedia,* N.S. (1889), XIV, 612; Lenoir *Topic,* January 22, 1890; Tarboro *Southerner,* December 11, 1890.

39. New Bern *Daily Journal,* November 14, 1889.

in that section."[40]   In the former, the white daily newspaper received a large number of complaints from the white citizens "about the large crowd of Negroes obstructing the sidewalks when talking with emigrant agents and their lieutenants." The movement from Tarboro continued into January of 1890, for on January 2, the *Southerner* reported that "another contingent for Texas left this morning . . . not many as before, but still too many."[41]   Indeed, the 1889-1890 movement of Negroes from the state so depopulated many of the eastern counties that the landlords "began to fear that help would entirely fail them. . . ."[42]

The opinion of the North Carolina whites on the exodus of Negroes from the state was divided. Josephus Daniels states that the large landlords in the eastern part of North Carolina were extremely alarmed over the movement because the Negroes were the main source of the labor supply for their "broad acres."[43]   It is, therefore, not surprising to observe that they employed various methods to halt the movement. One such method was the newspaper. Some of the white press in eastern North Carolina sought to dissuade the Negroes from quitting the state by picturing (in the worst possible manner) the plight of those already in other states who were originally from North Carolina. The Wilmington *Morning Star,* for example, wrote of the North Carolina Negroes who had migrated to Kansas: "Nine of the Negro 'exodusters' from North Carolina have died of scarlet fever, and many others are sick. The rascals who beguiled the ignorant and credulous Negroes to leave the Sunny South for the bleak winds and deep snows of Kansas, deserve to die of scarlet fever, or anything else that is bad."[44]   Terrible pictures were painted of Indiana. The Tarboro *Southerner* contended that "The most heartless atrocity ever perpetrated on an ignorant and deluded people was the exodus movement from the Second Congressional District to Indiana. Agents and missionaries were sent amongst them to fill their heads with delusive tales about the price of labor and improved living generally in Indiana—all false as hell in its blackness."[45]

The paper went on to say that "even Perry, the colored instrument, who seduced so many, is struck with the awe of the magnitude of his

40. Tarboro *Southerner,* November 28, December 12, 1889; Lenoir *Topic,* January 22, 1890.

41. Tarboro *Southerner,* December 19, 1889, January 2, 1890.

42. *Annual Cyclopedia,* N.S. (1889), XIV, 612.

43. Josephus Daniels, *Tar Heel Editor* (Chapel Hill: The University of North Carolina Press, 1939), p. 181.

44. Wilmington *Morning Star,* January 6, April 7, 1880.

45. Tarboro *Southerner,* March 4, 1880.

crime. . . . He told the Senate committee if he had two lots, the one in hell, and the other in Indiana, he'd sell out the latter and live 'in the former."[46] Under the title of "A Returned Exoduster," the Goldsboro *Messenger* quoted a Negro woman, Maria Bryant, as saying that the North Carolina Negroes in Indianapolis "were treated like dogs."[47]

The Wilmington *Star* quoted at length a letter written by "a Presbyterian colored preacher on the exodus" who described the migration as ". . . the saddest display of ignorance, indolence and improvidence" he had ever witnessed. In North Carolina "the colored people have a good chance and good climate and yet some want to go to Indiana and freeze to death for want of food, clothing and work."[48] Nine years later the *Star* was telling the Negroes that "their true home was among the Southern whites, who are the only people under Heaven who understand them and feel kindly for them."[49] Similar feelings were expressed by other white papers in the "black counties."[50]

The "Negro-stay-at-home" attitude voiced by a portion of the white press, however, was not shared by all the whites in the state. The following examples are cases in point. The *Progressive Farmer* declared that since the Negro "is, and will ever remain, so long as he stays, a running, festering sore on our body politic, we would hail with delight and rejoicing his peaceful departure, and would pray God's blessing to attend him."[51] Although realizing the labor problems created by the loss of the Negroes, the Gastonia *Gazette,* "after a good deal of thought on the subject," felt it was best for North Carolina if the Negroes did migrate. It listed two reasons: first, the friction between the races caused by "malicious men at the North and wicked designing men in the South might eventuate in explosions very much to be dreaded by whites, but more disastrous to the Negroes." Second, since the whites paid nearly all the school funds for the education of the Negro as well as the white children, and since in many eastern counties the Negroes received the larger portions, it would be definitely to the interests of the whites to let them go.[52]

The majority of the Negro leaders of the state appeared lukewarm

46. *Ibid.*

47. Quoted in the Chatham *Record,* January 29, 1880.

48. Wilmington *Morning Star,* January 13, 1880.

49. Quoted by the Raleigh *News and Observer,* May 1, 1889.

50. See the Tarboro *Southerner,* December 15, 1876, February 9, 1877, December 26, 1889, January 16, 1890; Warrenton *Gazette,* February 9, 1877; *Carolina Watchman* (Salisbury), January 7, 1886; New Bern *Weekly Journal,* September 4, 1890.

51. Quoted by the Raleigh *State Chronicle,* May 3, 1889.

52. Quoted by the Lenoir *Topic,* March 27, 1889. See also the *Carolina Watchman* (Salisbury), March 28, 1889.

toward *all* migration schemes. This was true in spite of the strenuous migration and colonization effort of John H. Williamson. On December 9, 1877, Williamson, a Negro member of the General Assembly in 1876-1877, introduced a resolution requesting and instructing North Carolina's senators and representatives in Washington to urge the passage of a law setting apart territory beyond the Missouri River "for the sole and exclusive use and occupation of the colored race." Williamson said that he introduced the resolution because he considered the legislation and policy of the whites hostile to the Negroes and because he believed that the members of his race could not hope for anything like justice in North Carolina. In addition, he declared that "the origins of the Negro race, his color, physical formation, ignorance and poverty formed the principal hobby for Democratic politicians to indulge in during political excitement."[53]

Two months after the initial introduction, Williamson's proposal was made the order of the day in the House. The lengthy period between its introduction and consideration, instead of dampening, appeared to have whetted the curiosity of the Negroes of Raleigh, for "when the hour arrived the galleries and a portion of the lobbies were packed by a dense crowd of colored people of both sexes."[54] During the debate, Williamson apparently made a brilliant speech in support of his resolution, for a white correspondent who covered the debate on the resolution wrote that the Negro "made a tearing political speech, in which he dwelt upon the wrongs of his race in not receiving their share of political rights and honors, waxing eloquent on the shot gun policy." J. C. Hill, another Negro member of the House of 1876-1877 and representing New Hanover County, vigorously opposed any policy "of sending the Negroes away from their homes and churches and school houses, to go among the uncivilized Indians and grizzly bears beyond the Missouri." He considered North Carolina "a good place for the development of the Negro into the good and valuable citizen." The white correspondent described Hill's speech as "abounding in practical sense, and clothed in strong if not very polished language." He also reported that Hill was "frequently applauded, and sat down amidst a round of applause from the whole House." Although Williamson's resolution was defeated sixty-eight to twenty-four, the entire affair was described "as a big day, in the House, for our American citizens of African descent."[55]

53. *House Journal, 1876-1877,* 115. See also Greensboro *Patriot,* February 14, 1877, and the Tarboro *Southerner,* February 16, 1877.

54. Greensboro *Patriot,* February 14, 1877.

55. Greensboro *Patriot,* February 14, 1877. See also the Tarboro *Southerner,* February 16, 1877.

Williamson's stand on the movement of Negroes from the state was atypical rather than typical of the Negro politicians. Since their position, to a large extent, depended upon Negro votes, they naturally took a conservative attitude toward the exodus of Negroes from North Carolina. In keeping with this sentiment, on September 17, 1877, James H. Harris, "in conjunction with other leading colored men" of the state, issued a call for a state convention "to consider the educational, moral and national interest" of the Negro group, "and to devise some plan for his advancement in these respects." The meeting was held in Raleigh on October 18 and 19, with 40 counties represented, and 130 representatives. Among the more prominent Negro leaders present were James H. Harris, J. T. Reynolds, James E. O'Hara, John H. Williamson, and W. P. Mabson. Under the chairmanship of James H. Harris, the convention passed a resolution opposing colonizing because "all colonizing schemes [are] impracticable and should be discouraged."[56] In 1880, before another group of "representative colored men" who met in the Senate chambers in Raleigh on January 15 and 16, James H. Harris again said that "in view of the fact that large numbers of our laboring population are leaving our State, migrating to the Northwest, seeking homes among strangers and in an incongenial clime, we deem it a matter of most serious consideration to the people of North Carolina to arrest this gigantic evil. . . ."[57] Henry P. Cheatham, the Negro Congressman from North Carolina discussed above, in a speech before a large gathering of Negroes in Halifax County in January, 1890, urged them not to leave eastern North Carolina to go away to Kansas.[58]

In addition to the active opposition to Negro migration by the Negro politicians, the Negro church and press of the state also sought to discourage it. The organ of the colored Baptists, the *National Monitor,* urged the Negroes "to stand their ground against the exodus," and to work and pray where they were "and trust in God for the rest."[59] The Baptist Educational and Missionary Convention of North Carolina, in its meeting from October 22 through 27, 1889, criticized "agents of sub-agents, who are doubtless prompted to agitate this movement solely for the fee that is in it." The delegates attending the convention felt that the methods employed to entice Negroes from the state were "impracticable, untimely, and injurious to our people." And then this significant statement from one of the speakers of the

56. Raleigh *Register,* November 1, 1877.
57. Raleigh *Signal,* January 21, 1880.
58. Wilson *Advance,* January 23, 1890.
59. Quoted in the Salisbury *Carolina Watchman,* May 1, 1879.

convention: "We do not condemn emigration in a general sense; we believe in it. We commend it, when we can go as free people and upon our own accord, especially when we find a place where our condition can be bettered."[60]

Speaking on the movement of Negroes from North Carolina to Arkansas, the New York *Age,* a Negro newspaper of that city, failed "to see the desirableness of Arkansas over North Carolina for the reception of any large number of colored men." It pointed out that "The civil, political and industrial conditions of that state are identical with those of North Carolina and other Southern States where the evils complained of and sought to be overcome are present. It appears to us just like jumping out of the frying pan into the fire."[61]

In an attempt at a class analysis of Negro reaction to colonization and migration, it appears that the Negroes who were generally dependent on other Negroes and not upon the whites to any comparable degree for economic security tended to oppose such schemes. Thus Negro politicians, ministers, bishops, merchants, and businessmen adopted a conservative, if not a hostile view, toward any movement designed to remove the Negroes from North Carolina. It was no mere accident that an astute politician like James H. Harris and an A.M.E. Zion bishop like J. W. Hood were in the vanguard of those who did not favor migration. On the other hand, the Negroes who were economically dependent on the whites were outspoken advocates of migration and colonization. The illiterate and semi-literate tenant farmers and day laborers—the recipients of unfair and, in many instances, cruel treatment at the hands of landlords and merchants and courts, underpaid and overworked, and lacking in material goods —these comprised the larger percentage of Negroes who wanted "to shake the dust of North Carolina from their shoes."

The General Assembly also adopted legislative methods to stem the movement. Significantly most of these measures were designed to curb the activities of emigrant agents operating within the state. Thus, on January 26, 1881, the state Senate attempted to check the exertions of this group by passing a bill that imposed a tax of five hundred dollars on persons engaged in hiring or employing laborers "going beyond the limits of the State."[62] The bill failed to get through the House. On March 11 of the same year, however, the legislature passed an act that prohibited under heavy fines all individuals from

60. Raleigh *Signal,* November 14, 1889.
61. New York *Age,* March 30, 1889.
62. *Senate Journal* (1881), p. 130.

inducing Negroes to quit the state. The penalty extended also to Negroes who, by allowing themselves to be enticed away by the out-of-state agents, violated their contracts.[63]

Notwithstanding this limited success, the opponents of the Negro exodus continued to agitate for additional restrictive legislation as Negroes continued to leave the state. "Stay the tide of emigration," the Tarboro *Southerner* demanded, "by making the dissension sewers and trouble breeders shut their mouths and cease their lying."[64] On April 3, 1890, the *Southerner* directly accused the emigrant agents of fomenting the exodus fever:

... short crops, bad treatment, politically or otherwise, had nothing to do with the movement. The glowing accounts of other localities and the seductive promises of the agents who received many dollars per head did the work.

As long as the Negroes can be persuaded to leave in paying quantities, the agents will come for them. If the people do not want them to leave, the agents must be kept away.

In the meantime, the radicals at the North will continue to assert and proclaim that the darkeys leave because of ill-treatment.[65]

A year later, a landlord in an eastern county continued the complaint against the unceasing activity of the emigrant agents, and urged the legislature to curb them. "We are bothered by people from other states persuading away our laborers, which ought to be a criminal offense. A good many never get back, and those who do return tend to demoralize those who did not go away."[66]

Urged by such proddings, the opponents of "the Negro departure movement" in the legislature of 1891 were able to push through both houses a bill that, as a result of its harsh provisions, was guaranteed "to keep emigrant agents away." The law declared:

That the term "emigrant agent," as contemplated in this act, shall be construed to mean any person engaged in hiring laborers in this state to be employed beyond the limits of the same.

That any person shall be entitled to a license which shall be good for one year upon payment into the state treasurer for the use of the state, of one thousand dollars, in each county in which he operates or solicits emigrants, for each year engaged.

63. *Public and Private Laws and Resolutions of the State of North Carolina, 1881,* c. 303. Act of March 11, 1881.

64. Tarboro *Southerner,* January 16, 1890.

65. *Ibid.,* April 3, 1890.

66. *Fifth Annual Report of the North Carolina Bureau of Labor Statistics, 1891,* p. 81.

That any person doing the business of an emigrant agent without first having obtained such a license shall be guilty of a misdemeanor, and upon conviction shall be punished by fine not less than five hundred dollars and not more than five thousand dollars, or may be imprisoned in the county jail not less than four months, or confined in the state prison at hard labor not exceeding two years for each and every offense within the discretion of the court.[67]

This law applied only to those counties with large Negro populations.[68]

Perhaps in anticipation of the deleterious effect the law would have on the activities of emigrant agents in the state, groups of Negroes made last-minute departures. On January 8, 1891, for example, a month before the law went into operation, the Greensboro *Patriot* reported "a large immigration of Negroes . . . into Oklahoma . . . where they expect to have freedom, social and political."[69]

However, if the supporters of the emigrant agent law viewed it as a "stopper" on the activities of the agents within the state, they were, apparently, destined to be disappointed. A year after its ratification, a Greensboro newspaper deplored the seeming indifference of the state in enforcing its provisions. The paper declared that "at least two thousand Negroes have left the state in the past six days and are being hired by hundreds by agents from Georgia and South Carolina. Though this is in defiance of law not a single arrest has been made." Movements of Negroes into Oklahoma were also reported as late as a year after the law became operative.[70]

The emigrant statute remained on the books for two years; then in September of 1893 the North Carolina Supreme Court declared it unconstitutional and void. With Chief Justice Shepherd delivering the opinion, the court held that since the law applied to certain counties in the state, it violated article 3 of the North Carolina Constitution, which, although authorizing the legislature to tax "trades, professions and franchises," provided that such taxes had to be uniform in their application. "The act under consideration," said the Chief Justice, "if intended to impose a tax in the legal significance of the term, very plainly falls within the inhibition of the organic law as interpreted . . . by this Court, for it cannot, with the least show of reason, be contended that the principle of uniformity is not violated when the same occupation is heavily taxed in one county; while in

67. *Laws and Resolutions, 1891*, c. 75. Act of February 6, 1891.
68. *Ibid.*
69. Greensboro *Patriot*, January 8, 1891.
70. Greensboro *Daily Record*, January 11 and February 1, 1892.

an adjoining county it is entirely free and untrammeled."[71] The court also declared the act void "for the unreasonableness of the license fee."[72] Once again the state's highest tribunal had demonstrated its racial liberalism. However, whether the Supreme Court's ruling would have materially stimulated the exodus movement during the period under consideration will never be known, coming as it did, approximately a year before the overthrow of "Bourbon democracy" in North Carolina.

One fact is clear: during the long, uninterrupted rule of the Democratic party in North Carolina from 1876 to 1894, the movement of Negroes from the state was a constantly recurring phenomenon. While census data on natives of the state do not tell the whole exodus story, the figures are nevertheless revealing. In 1890 there were 116,400 Negroes native to North Carolina living in other parts of the United States as compared to 93,390 in 1880.[73] Subtract from the first figure 17,885 Negroes who had migrated into the state between the 1880 and 1890 decade, and there was a net loss of 98,515. Comparing these statistics with the statistics on emigrations of white people, we find that in 1890 there were 172,585 whites native to North Carolina living in other parts of the United States as compared with 200,115 in 1880. Subtract from the first figure 34,324 whites who had migrated into the state between the 1880 and 1890 decade, and it will be seen that there was a net loss of 138,261.[74] The above findings seem to suggest that the economic factor was an important motivation in influencing both Negro and white migration from the state, though it is obvious that the socio-political disabilities that faced the former group should not be minimized as a cause.

71. *State vs. Moore,* 133 N.C. 697 (1893) at 700-1.

72. *Ibid.,* at 710.

73. U.S. Bureau of the Census, *Eleventh Census of the United States: 1890. Population.* Vol. I, Part I, p. 577; *Tenth Census of the United States: 1880. Population.* Vol. I, p. 490.

74. Joseph F. Steelman, "The Immigration Movement in North Carolina, 1865-1890" (Unpublished master's thesis, University of North Carolina, 1947), pp. 120-21.

Part Three

Social Environment

13

"A Big Stick
in Their Hands"

*The future is fraught with danger. The Negroes are
being rapidly educated, and the whites not in proportion. If Anglo-Saxon supremacy is to be maintained in North Carolina, we are pursuing a very
suicidal course.*

F. P. Venable before the second annual meeting
of the North Carolina History Society, November
29, 1888.

Article IX, section 2, of the constitution of
North Carolina as amended by the Constitutional Convention of
1875 provided for the establishment and maintenance of separate but
equal educational facilities for the Negro and white children of the
state.[1] In 1876 there were 529 Negro male and 288 Negro female
public school teachers in the state, teaching 152,998 Negro pupils in
all-Negro schools. At the same time, 1,294 white males and 783 females taught a total of 248,510 white children in all-white schools.[2]
There was no question, then, of the separation of the races in the
public schools. The question of equal educational facilities, on the
other hand, was another matter. Despite spirited opposition by a

1. *Constitution of North Carolina, as Amended by the Constitutional Convention
of 1875.*
2. Office of the Superintendent of Public Instruction, November 14, 1876. Legislative Papers, 1876-1877, State Department of Archives and History, Raleigh.

large majority of the whites of the state, however, this constitutional guarantee until 1885 at least was more nearly realized in North Carolina than in most of the former states of the Confederacy. However, after 1885, North Carolina was beginning to manifest a tendency already well established by that date in the other southern states—a capitulation to popular white feeling against Negro education.

The disposition of the whites of North Carolina to resist efforts toward equal educational opportunities for the Negroes of the state sprang from a variety of motives. Albert Bushnell Hart, the Harvard educator and historian, while on a trip through North Carolina in February of 1892, quoted a "public man of great intelligence" as saying that the white people of the state "don't want the Negroes to get educated, or to get rich, the more educated they are and the richer they are, the worse it is for us. . . . It is a big stick in their hands."[3] Sidney M. Finger, the state's Superintendent of Public Instruction in 1888, declared that "there is more or less prevalent among the white people of North Carolina the feeling that education spoils the colored people as laborers, to their own damage, and the damage of the white people, who own almost all the lands."[4] Charles S. Mangum suggests that the fear on the part of the whites of increased economic competition from the better trained Negroes may have been a factor in the opposition to Negro education in North Carolina.[5]

No matter what their motives, the Negro schools by 1890 evidenced signs of slow-emerging vitality. The decrease of Negro illiteracy from 75.2 per cent in 1880 to 60.1 per cent in 1890 showed that progress had been made.[6] Nevertheless, to the least discerning, it was apparent that much was yet to be done to remove the many educational deficiencies confronting the Negroes of the state.

It would appear that the school officials who controlled the school funds before 1885 manifested a genuine desire to be impartial. An inspection of the records will reveal that inequalities between the Negro and white schools in North Carolina were comparatively slight compared to other Southern states. In 1880, for example, North Carolina spent $1.47 per white pupil and $1.38 per Negro pupil.[7] Fourteen

3. Albert Bushnell Hart, "Cross Section Through North Carolina," *Nation,* LIV (March 17, 1892), 208.

4. *Biennial Report of the Superintendent of Instruction, 1887,* p. xlii. Hereafter cited as *Biennial Report.*

5. Charles S. Mangum, *The Legal Status of the Negro* (Chapel Hill: University of North Carolina Press, 1940), p. 133.

6. U.S. Bureau of the Census, *Tenth Census of the United States: 1880. Delinquent Classes.* Vol. I, p. 924; *ibid.* (1890), I, 202.

7. Compiled by the writer from the *Biennial Report of the Superintendent of Instruction, 1879-1880,* pp. 4-5, 73.

years later, the state was spending $1.93 per white child and $1.72 per Negro child.[8] The apportionment of the county school funds in New Hanover County in 1881 and Edgecombe County in 1883 reflects the over-all state pattern that persisted until 1885. The Board of County Commissioners for New Hanover County, resolving itself into a Board of Education on January 3, 1881, distributed the $11,147.50 school fund in the following manner: the 2,360 white children received $4,130.00, while the 4,010 Negro children received $7,017.50; the per capita expenditure was $1.75.[9] In 1883 the predominantly "Negro county" of Edgecombe distributed its school money as follows: $1,487.05 for white children and $3,512.89 for Negro children.[10] On a state-wide comparison, Negro teachers of North Carolina, like Negro pupils, received slightly less money per capita than white teachers. In 1883 the average salary paid to Negro teachers was $20.00 a month, for white teachers, $24.00 a month. Craven County in 1886 paid its white teachers $25.00 a month, its Negro teachers $20.00 a month.[11]

Public school teachers of the state were faced with an excessively heavy pupil load. The Raleigh *Gazette,* while rejoicing in the crowded condition of the Negro schools of that city inasmuch as that indicated "considerable awakening in educational matters," noted soberly that teachers were considerably overburdened. Declaring that a teacher could not properly teach more than forty pupils in a class, it said that the good work done by the Negro teachers of sixty or eighty pupils "only goes to show how much more efficient the work would be with a reasonable number."[12]

Inequalities between the races were also shown in the types of schoolhouses provided for the white and Negro children. In 1880, there were 3,779 schoolhouses for the white children, of which 1,034, or 20.7 per cent, were of logs; of the 1,766 for Negroes, 575, or 32.5 per cent, were of logs.[13] Five years later, the total number of schoolhouses for whites had increased to 4,271, of which 1,001, or 23.4 per cent, were of log construction; for Negroes, 1,942 schoolhouses, of which 552, or 33.4 per cent were of log construction.[14] Although the bulk of the public school buildings of·both races were frame constructions, of the brick schools in the state in 1880, the whites had

8. *Ibid., 1893-1894,* pp. 38-40.
9. Wilmington *Daily Review,* January 4, 1881.
10. Tarboro *Southerner,* September 20, 1883.
11. Appleton's *Annual Cyclopedia,* N.S. (1883), VIII, 584; New Bern *Daily Journal,* January 6, 1887.
12. Raleigh *Gazette,* October 24, 1891.
13. *Biennial Report, 1887-1888,* p. 157.
14 *Ibid., 1892-1893,* p. 92.

eighteen, the Negroes, one; in 1893, the numbers were twenty-three and two respectively.[15]

However, in spite of the inadequate, overcrowded facilities, lower pay to Negro teachers, and other educational limitations, contemporary testimony by the whites throughout North Carolina reflected a great deal of concern about the rising educational status of the Negroes. A Northampton County white man said that "the Negroes are improving in education faster than the whites, which is a sad state of things." "The whites," declared a white man from Pamlico County, "do not improve in intelligence, and but few are interested sufficiently to send their children to school. . . . The colored manifest much interest in education . . . and improve fast in intelligence. . . ." A white stone cutter in Rowan County complained that since the Negroes were getting "more schooling than the whites," he felt that "the system needs revising altogether."[16]

The desire on the part of the Negroes of North Carolina to acquire an education is understandable. Whether rightly or wrongly, they were convinced that education meant freedom from forced labor. Since such was their lot during slavery, the faith of the Negroes in the efficacy of knowledge to relieve them from the curse of manual labor was almost child-like. Indeed, it was very naïve, for as Sidney Finger said in 1890, "The colored people must not lose sight of the fact that manual labor . . . will be their lot to a larger degree than white people, because of the peculiar conditions and circumstances that surround them."[17] Employment figures for the period offer mute testimony to the truth of Finger's statement.

Education beyond the elementary level for the Negroes of the state was available. Private Negro secondary schools, though not extensive, were to be found in the state. Elizabeth City High School, for example, was founded in 1877 by a Negro who had neither land nor building. Five years later the school had a "comfortable two-story building and three acres of land valued at $2,000. The school term averaged nine months, and in 1884, eighty pupils were taught by a faculty of three.[18] Perhaps the best known and most respected of the private Negro secondary schools was the Howard Graded School in Fayetteville. This institution was organized in 1868 by A. W. Whitfield, Hettie McNeil, M. E. Pearce, Susan Cain, and Robert

15. *Ibid.*, *1887-1888.*, p. 157; *Ibid, 1892-1893,* p. 92.
16. *Second Annual Report of the North Carolina Bureau of Labor Statistics, 1888,* pp. 127, 195, 196.
17. *Biennial Report, 1889-1890,* pp. xl-xli.
18. Raleigh *Register,* June 4, 1884.

Harris. By 1883, it was credited as being responsible for "the general tone of intelligence and morality which prevades [the Negro community of] Fayetteville."[19] Other private secondary schools included the Dudley School in Wayne County and the Gray High School in Hillsboro.

John T. Reynolds, a Negro member of the 1876-1877 legislature, introduced a resolution for the creation of a committee to report a bill to establish a normal school for the education of colored teachers.[20] A resultant law authorized the 1876-1877 General Assembly to establish the state's first normal school for Negroes "at any place for the teaching and training of young men of the colored race for teachers in the common schools of the state for the colored race." The legislature appropriated two thousand dollars to defray the expenses of such a school. During the summer of 1877 Fayetteville was selected as the site for the proposed school.[21] The decision to locate the school in Fayetteville was probably influenced by the action of the Negroes of that city in offering to the state free of charge a school building belonging to that race and sufficient to accommodate more than two hundred students. Bishop James W. Hood, of the African Methodist Episcopal Zion Church, commenting on the selection of Fayetteville as the site for the first state supported normal school for Negroes, declared that since "the amount appropriated is small, . . . it is doubtful whether at any other place much good could have been accomplished with that sum. . . ."[22]

Despite such expressions of disappointment at the small appropriation, Negroes of the state viewed the establishment of the normal school at Fayetteville as "an advanced step" by North Carolina in providing for a more thorough system of public instruction for its Negroes. It was plain to the least discerning of the Negro group that the absence in the past of an institution dedicated to the training of Negro teachers hampered the educational progress of the race. Thus, Bishop Hood and other influential Negro leaders of the state urged all Negroes to support the school and to encourage all Negro youth to avail themselves of its facilities.[23]

19. Charlotte *Messenger,* June 30, 1883.

20. Legislative Papers, 1876-1877. State Department of Archives and History, Raleigh.

21. New Bern *New Bernian,* July 7, 1877.

22. *Minutes* of the Fourteenth Session of the North Carolina Annual Conference of the A.M.E. Zion Church in America, Salisbury, North Carolina, November 28—December 4, 1877, 6.

23. Bishop J. W. Hood to Robert Harris, "Report of the Principal, 1878-1879."

In the first year of the school's existence, however, some Negroes of the state were not inclined to heed the advice of leaders like Bishop Hood. On May 30, 1879, Robert Harris, the normal school's principal, charged that "enemies" of the school had been actively poisoning the minds of the Negroes against the institution by asserting that it was a "Democratic School" established by Democrats for the sole purpose of educating Negro Democrats. Apparently, the circulation of these charges had their effect because Harris admitted that such had prevented or discouraged many students from attending the school during the 1878-1879 school year.[24] However, those opposing the normal school must have had a change of heart, for no more was heard from them after the first year of the school's life.

Four years after the establishment of the school in Fayetteville, North Carolina established four additional state-supported normal schools for its Negro population. Since the greater portion of the Negroes lived in the eastern section, the State Board of Education considered it advisable to locate three of the schools in that area, specifically at New Bern, Plymouth, and Franklinton. The fourth school was established at Salisbury.[25] These schools continued in operation, and their locations, with one exception, remained fixed throughout the period. In 1887, the North Carolina State Board of Education removed the normal school from New Bern to Goldsboro, "believing that better results would be attained there.[26] In the same year, continued Negro dissatisfaction with the two thousand dollar annual appropriation to each of the Negro normal schools moved John H. Williamson, colored member in the legislature of 1887, to seek a four thousand dollar yearly increase. He was successful.[27] The Negro normal schools by the end of the eighties, then, were beginning to emerge from a ten-year financial quagmire.

Generally, these schools had a three-year course of study that qualified students to teach in the Negro public schools of the state. Of eight months' duration, they were divided into two terms of four months. There was no charge for tuition or books, and "an appropriate part" of the student's traveling expenses was refunded. Admission requirements were relatively mild. Any Negro youth

Annual Report of the Superintendent of Public Instruction of North Carolina, 1879, p. 36.

24. *Ibid.*, p. 36.
25. *Biennial Report, 1881-1882*, p. 15.
26. *Ibid.*, *1887-1888*, p. 67.
27. *House Journal, 1887*, pp. 57, 365. *Laws and Resolutions*, c. 408. Act of March 7, 1887.

between fifteen and twenty-five who was able "to pass a good examination in easy reading, spelling, writing, and the fundamental rules of arithmetic" would be permitted to enroll for training.[28] Divided into three classes—junior, middle, and senior—the students enrolled in the normal schools were passed from one class to the next higher one by "approved examinations" of the studies surveyed.[29] The subjects included spelling, reading, writing, arithmetic, grammar, composition, geography, United States history, North Carolina history, algebra, physiology, philosophy, elementary chemistry, botany, and bookkeeping.[30]

The problem of student discipline, though not a major preoccupation, did concern the normal school principals. At the Fayetteville Normal School in 1880, Charles W. Chestnutt was obviously pleased to report that during the entire course of the school year "the general deportment of the students . . . was good." As a consequence there was no occasion for suspending or expelling anyone.[31] A leaf from the diary of Chestnutt, dated March 18, 1881, however, tells us that as a principal-teacher, he was not free from "student distractions": [I] had a rough time in school today. I had to keep my men in and lecture them about "wenching." Then the girls got to fighting this afternoon. The young folks seem to have spring fever. I suppose this weather affects them somewhat like other young animals."[32]

The reports of the Negro principals are valuable in giving glimpses of other phases of normal school life. Chestnutt, for example, wrote in 1880: "A large proportion of our students are self-supporting. They teach in the country and work on the farm or in the workshops, and come to school for one, two, or three terms a year, as their means will permit. The presence of so many grown men, who are spending their time and scanty savings in striving to get an education, imparts a tone of earnestness to the school."[33]

The Negro principal of Franklinton Normal School was not as enthusiastic or optimistic in his report of 1882. He lamented the fact that out of the sixty-five students enrolled, only eight were teachers. He accounted for their absences in the following manner: "(1) Many were too poor to attend. (2) Many were too proud to show their

28. For a more detailed statement, see the New Bern *New Bernian*, July 7, 1877.
29. *Biennial Report, 1881-1882*, pp. 14-15.
30. *Ibid., 1883-1884*, p. 87.
31. *Ibid., 1879-1880*, p. 40.
32. Helen M. Chestnutt, *Charles Waddell Chestnutt* (Chapel Hill: University of North Carolina Press, 1952), p. 28.
33. *Biennial Report, 1879-1880*, p. 40.

ignorance. (3) Many were too wise in their conceit to attend. But while these did not appreciate the efforts of the state, those preparing to teach can soon take their places in the school room."[34]

The belief that North Carolina was squandering money in any effort to train the Negro teachers of the state was voiced by the whites also. The words of a Beaufort County landlord typify the general feeling of that group when he wrote that "money spent in educating the Negro does not pay . . . because of the inferior teachers. . . . I have lived here fourteen years, and I have never known a Negro teacher who could read intelligently or spell correctly half the common names in everyday use."[35]   Competency of Negro public school teachers was also questioned by some northern whites teaching in the colored schools. One such teacher held considerable doubt as to the wisdom of entrusting the instruction of Negro children to Negro teachers. "I hope the time will come when they may be so trusted," wrote Louise L. Dorr to Governor Zebulon B. Vance in 1877, "but I do not think it has come yet."[36]

In meeting the problem of efficient teachers, as it has been indicated, some northern white teachers were employed in the Negro schools. Significantly, these outlanders faced severe ostracism from the white community. Louise L. Dorr, who taught in a Negro graded school in Raleigh, observed sadly in 1877 that socially she had been a recluse since her arrival in that city five years earlier. "It may be that there is still sectional bitterness," she mildly wrote.[37]   Occasionally, Negroes, too, evidenced resentment towards the white teachers from the North. In Raleigh in 1877, for example, the Negroes attempted "to throw out" all the northern teachers from one of the Negro graded schools. The trustees, however, prevented it.

Perhaps the qualifications of Charles N. Hunter were the exception, rather than the rule, but his certificate, which evidences a high grade of scholarship, illustrates the fact that some Negro teachers of North Carolina were eminently fitted to meet the demands of the teaching profession. Hunter's grades for one year follow:[38] "Spelling (including sounds of letters), 100; defining, 100; reading, 100; writing, 98; arithmetic (mental and written), 98; English grammar, 100;

34. *Biennial Report, 1881-1882*, p. 110.
35. *First Annual Report of the North Carolina Bureau of Labor Statistics, 1887*, p. 87.
36. Louise L. Dorr to Governor Zebulon B. Vance, August 17, 1877. Governors' Papers, State Department of Archives and History, Raleigh.
37. *Ibid.*
38. Teacher's First Grade Certificate of Charles N. Hunter, October 16, 1886. Charles N. Hunter Papers, Duke University Library, Durham.

geography, 96; history of North Carolina, 96; and physiology and hygiene, 96."

In addition to participating in the annual teacher institutes sponsored by the state for each race which were designed to improve teaching and teaching methods, the Negro public school teachers of North Carolina organized the North Carolina Teacher's Association. The special object of the association was the promotion of educational progress among the Negroes of the state. The annual meetings, held at one of the state's private Negro colleges, usually lasted one week and presented a varied program. The 1886 meeting at the Kittrell Institute, for example, discussed such topics as "How to Teach," "Industrial Education," "School Discipline and Its Aims," "A Uniform Standard of Examinations and a Fixed Rate of Salary."[39]

To further aid the cause of "progressive education in North Carolina to the elevation and culture of the colored race in America," *Progressive Education,* a monthly journal, was founded in the 1880's as the official organ of the North Carolina State Teacher's Association. Through its pages, features, and articles like "Questions and Answers in the School Room" went out to its thousand or more members in 1888.[40] In addition, the North Carolina Teacher's Association established in 1886 a "reading circle" among the Negro teachers of the state.[41] The aim was "to do much among our people," wrote one of the founders of the organization to Governor Alfred M. Scales in 1886. A committee appointed by the parent body proposed a list of books that should be read before the next session of the association in June, 1887. Among them were Swett's *Methods,* McCarthy's *Short History of Our Times,* Guizot's *History of Civilization,* and Gow's *Morals and Manners.*[42]

Instruction beyond the public school level for the Negroes of North Carolina in other than the four state-supported normal schools was provided for by seven denominational institutions. These were Shaw University, Bennett Seminary, Zion Wesley Institute (later Livingstone College), Scotia Seminary, Biddle University (now Johnson C. Smith University), Kittrell Industrial School, and St. Augustine Normal School. Perhaps the largest and best known of these institu-

39. From the "Appeal," April and May, 1886. Charles N. Hunter Scrapbook, 1871-1928, Duke University Library, Durham.

40. Richard A. Lewis to Charles N. Hunter, October 15, 1888. Charles N. Hunter Papers, Duke University Library, Durham. See also the Raleigh *Visitor,* June 13, 1888.

41. S. G. Atkins to Governor Alfred M. Scales, September 13, 1886. Governors' Papers, State Department of Archives and History, Raleigh.

42. *Ibid.*

tions was Shaw University; located in Raleigh, the school was under the auspices of the Baptists. Between 1866, the year of its establishment, and 1884, more than 2,500 students received instruction within its walls. Of that number it was reliably reported, 1,500 eventually became teachers and preachers. In 1884 Shaw included five brick buildings and a teacher's mansion. The entire school property was valued at $125,000. Instruction to the 425 students enrolled in 1884 was offered in five general areas: normal, scientific, classical, theological, medical, and mechanical.[43]

Bennett Seminary (now Bennett College) of Greensboro was founded by the Freedmen's Aid Society of the Methodist Episcopal Church in 1873. Eleven years later it had a faculty of six and offered "the elements of a good education to all the needy of moral character, mental powers, suitable attainments and years who will obey the rules and pay their bills promptly." The enrollment in 1884 was 164, and more than 1,000 had been admitted since its establishment. The property in 1884 was valued at $10,000.[44] A reporter for one of that city's newspapers, after attending the ceremonies ending the 1888 school year, remarked, "The writer can say without hesitation, that the speaking, oratory, diction, and a general appreciation of good English words, were almost surprising, but quite gratifying to all who heard them. . . . Bennett's work is second to none.[45]

Although information on the distribution of its graduates during the period is sketchy, there is sufficient evidence to warrant the conclusion that a large proportion of the alumni of the Greensboro institution either remained or settled in North Carolina.[46]

The leading institution of the African Methodist Episcopal Zion Church in North Carolina was Zion Wesley Institute of Salisbury. Incorporated by the legislature of North Carolina in 1879, it offered instruction designed for training young Negro men and women for religious and educational work both in the United States and in Africa. Providing instruction in three courses of study—normal, theological, and classical—Zion Wesley Institute had in 1884 an enrollment of 149. Its forty acres of buildings and grounds were valued at $10,000.[47] By 1888, with the name now changed to Livingstone College, the Salisbury institution had expanded its course of study by adding a grammar school and an industrial department. Expenses, which included board,

43. Raleigh Register, June 4, 1884.
44. Ibid., June 4, 1884.
45. Greensboro North State, June 21, 1888.
46. Annual Catalog of Bennett College (1900).
47. Raleigh Register, June 4, 1884.

washing, tuition, room, and fuel, were $6.00 per month. The children of ministers were charged five dollars a month. The 210 full-time students in attendance in 1888 came from 75 towns in North Carolina and 12 states; among the latter were Rhode Island, Pennsylvania, and Massachusetts.[48]

The Presbyterian Board of Missions for Freedmen founded after the Civil War two schools for the education of the Negroes in North Carolina. Scotia Seminary, located in Concord, was chartered in 1870. In 1884 it had an enrollment of 242 and a teaching staff of twelve. The institution was called the "Mount Holyoke of the South" by its admirers. Its all-female student body, according to a Negro newspaper, were "from the best families throughout the country."[49] Although the statement by the editor of the Charlotte *Messenger* was basically true, a close examination of the catalog of Scotia Seminary reveals the fact the bulk of its students were drawn from North and South Carolina. For example, the 1893-1894 catalog listed a total enrollment of 286 Negro women, with 252 coming from the two Carolinas. Other states represented were Georgia, Virginia, New Jersey, Alabama, New York, Florida, Pennsylvania, and Tennessee. Liberia was represented in its student body by Sarah J. Lomax of Monrovia. Of its alumnae, roughly seven-eights entered the teaching profession. It is highly significant that at least three-quarters of the graduates of Scotia Seminary married professional and businessmen.[50] Between 1870 and 1884 over 1,800 women students of the Negro group received instruction at the school. Scotia Seminary must have had an excellent reputation, for in 1884 it was forced to refuse admission to "scores" for want of space.[51]

Biddle University (now Johnson C. Smith University) was founded in 1868 by the Presbyterian Board of Missions for Freedmen. With a faculty of thirteen and a student body of 187 in 1888, the object of the institution was the education of Negro teachers and ministers. Indeed, nearly one-third of its total enrollment in 1888 was preparing for the ministry. It is of interest to note that tuition was free in all departments.[52]

St. Augustine Normal School of Raleigh was founded in 1867

48. Report of J. C. Price, President of Livingstone College, before the eighteenth quadrennial session of the general conference of the A.M.E. Church, New Bern, N.C., May 2-23, 1888, quoted in the New Bern *Daily Journal,* May 11, 1888.

49. Charlotte *Messenger,* June 30, 1883.

50. *Annual Catalog* (1893-1894), p. 13. See *Annual Catalog* (1887-1888, 1889-1890, 1890-1891, 1891-1892); *Scotia Seminary* (1870-1905), pp. 4-17.

51. Raleigh *Register,* June 4, 1884.

52. Raleigh *Register,* June 4, 1884.

under the auspices of the Episcopal Church. Its three-fold object was "to afford young men and women superior advantages for obtaining a thorough academic education, to train and equip teachers for efficient service, and to prepare young men for the Holy Ministry." In 1884 the institution's 8 faculty members taught 131 students.[53] The African Methodist Episcopal Church in the United States incorporated Kittrell Industrial School in 1887.[54]

This survey of the non-state-supported institutions of higher education for Negroes of North Carolina prompts one significant observation: These seven institutions placed little stress on industrial and agricultural education. Only three, Kittrell, Livingstone, and Shaw, provided limited industrial training in such subjects as cabinet-making, printing, shoe repair, tailoring, and for the women, dress-making, needle work, and cooking. Interestingly enough, it was the industrial department at Livingstone which evoked special commendation from one of the prominent white newspapers of eastern North Carolina. On the other hand, these institutions emphasized religious and classical education. Since employment opportunities for the mass of Negroes of the state were best in the industrial and agricultural fields, the lack of emphasis on the part of private institutions for formal training in these areas is arresting.[55]

This fact becomes all the more significant when it is observed that the state throughout most of the period under study showed little or no interest in the establishment of an industrial and agricultural college for the Negro group. The establishment in 1887 of the North Carolina College of Agricultural and Mechanic Arts at Raleigh for the white youth of the state, however, prompted Negro members of the North Carolina legislature to seek legislative approval of a similar institution for Negro youth. Henry Eppes, representing the Fourth Senatorial District in the Senate of 1887, sought to establish an industrial school for the Negroes of North Carolina with an appropriation of $100,000 the first year, and $1,000 every year thereafter.[56] It was soundly rejected 37 to 1, the vote of Eppes being the only affirmative one.[57] Before the bill of Eppes came to a vote, Robert S. Taylor, another Negro member of the 1887 Senate and who represented

53. *Ibid.*
54. *Laws and Resolutions*, c. 107. Act of March 7, 1887. See also *Laws and Resolutions*, c. 18. Act of 1889.
55. New Bern *Daily Journal*, May 11, 1888; Edgar W. Knight, *Public School Education in North Carolina* (New York: Houghton Mifflin Co., 1916), p. 353.
56. *Senate Journal, 1887*, p. 38.
57. *Ibid.*, pp. 364-65.

the Fifth Senatorial District of Edgecombe County, sought to amend his colleague's bill by striking out $1,000 and inserting $10,000 as the school's annual appropriation. It, too, was decisively defeated.[58]

Not only was there solid legislative opposition to the bill of Eppes and the amendment of Taylor in the Senate, but the editor of the Chatham *Record* probably voiced the sentiments of a majority of the whites of North Carolina when he described the effort of Eppes as "one of the cheekiest propositions yet introduced on the Senate floor."[59] It would appear, then, that the whites of the state were not ready to make such "expensive appropriations" on behalf of Negro education. Further effort on the part of Eppes to impress upon the legislators in the 1887 session the widespread interest of the Negro citizens of eastern North Carolina in the setting up of an agricultural and mechanical college for Negroes can be seen in his presentation of a petition from the Negro citizens of Halifax County requesting the establishment of such an institution.[60] In the 1889 legislature, the voices of Negro representatives continued to be heard proposing that the state establish an institution to provide for the industrial and agricultural training of the Negroes of the state, but to no avail.[61]

Despite these disappointments and setbacks, events occurring in the United States Congress in 1890 were to turn these failures into success. The passage of Senator Justin Morrill's Agricultural and Mechanical Bill proved to be the most decisive. The object of that bill, as is commonly known, was the encouragement and instruction in the science of practical agriculture and mechanics. For this purpose an appropriation of $15,000 for each state was made, which was to be increased yearly by $1,000 until at the expiration of ten years the appropriation reached a limit of $25,000, at which point it was to remain. These annual appropriations were to be equitably divided between the two races in states where separate schools were maintained. Correspondence between the governor of North Carolina, Daniel G. Fowle, and the Secretary of the Interior, John W. Noble, established the fact that North Carolina could not share in the $15,000 appropriation until the state legislature provided for the Negroes an institution similar to the one already established for the whites.[62] Faced with the possible loss of the total appropriation, Governor Fowle on January 8, 1891, recommended the establishment of an agricultural and

58. Raleigh *Signal*, February 24, 1887.
59. Chatham *Record*, February 24, 1887.
60. *Senate Journal, 1887*, p. 319.
61. *House Journal, 1889*, pp. 2, 113.
62. See Daniel G. Fowle Letter Book, 1889-1891, pp. 124, 126-27.

mechanical college for Negroes, "for only this," he warned the legislators, "will entitle our State to her portion of the appropriation." Eleven days later, on January 19, 1891, Isaac Alston, a Negro representing the Nineteenth Senatorial District of Warren County, offered a bill to provide for the establishing of an industrial school for the Negroes of North Carolina. It was rejected.[63]

Nearly a month and a half was to pass before a similar bill was to be introduced. On March 5, 1891, John D. Bellamy, a white senator from Wilmington brought forward a bill that resulted in the act establishing the Agricultural and Mechanical College for Negroes. Ratified by the General Assembly of North Carolina on March 9, 1891, sections 3, 10, and 11 are of sufficient importance to merit their quotation. Section 3 stated that the primary object of the institution was to teach practical agriculture and the mechanic arts "and such branches of learning as relate thereto, not excluding academical and classical instruction." Section 10 provided that a sum of $2,500 be annually appropriated to sustain the college. Section 11 stipulated that until the site and buildings were furnished for the location of the college, the trustee board of nine members was to make temporary provisions for the college at some established institution within the state.[64]

Since Shaw University was one of the three institutions of higher education for the Negroes in the state offering mechanical and industrial training, the trustees decided to house the college there. That Shaw had the largest student enrollment, the most valuable physical plant, and a central location, probably, were reasons leading to its selection. At any rate in the college's first year as an annex to Shaw University ending May 18, 1892, four professors, two serving part time from North Carolina College of Agriculture and Mechanic Arts at Raleigh, taught more than two hundred students in horticulture, agriculture, mechanic industries, and shop work, including care and use of various carpenter tools, furniture-making, staining, shellacking, varnishing, polishing, and tracing, blue-printing, lettering, and geometric drawing, which were essential elements of the course in mechanical drawing.[65]

63. *Public Documents of the State of North Carolina, 1891,* Document No. 1. Biennial Message of Daniel G. Fowle, Governor of North Carolina, to the Legislature of North Carolina, January 8, 1891, pp. 14-16; *Senate Journal, 1891,* p. 126.

64. *Senate Journal, 1891,* pp. 800, 856-57; *House Journal, 1891,* pp. 971, 1001. See also *Laws and Resolutions, 1891,* c. 549. Act of March 9, 1891.

65. *Public Documents, 1893,* No. 1. Biennial Message of Thomas Holt, Governor of North Carolina, January 4, 1893. See also *Public Documents, 1893,* No. 27. Report of H. M. Tupper, President, Shaw University.

It is of interest to note that Negro sentiment across the state did not prefer the establishment of a state-supported liberal arts college for the race to the founding of a state-supported agricultural and mechanical arts college. In an address before the thirteenth annual North Carolina Industrial Fair in 1891, for example, James H. Young emphasized the need of a mechanical arts institution inasmuch as he was convinced that the future of the race depended "in a great measure upon its disposition to pursue the mechanical trades."[66] James H. Harris, politician and editor of the Negro weekly the *Gazette,* appears to have recognized the fact that this tardy effort on the part of the state to offer an industrial education to its Negro population may have come too late. Yet in a direct appeal to the young Negro males of the state to take advantage of this opportunity to get an industrial and agricultural education, he said, "For years, we held uncontestedly to the mechanical trades, but white boys are now turning their attention to those pursuits, and if we would win in the race, we must be equal to the emergency."[67]

Despite its comparatively late birth, the Agricultural and Mechanical College (now the Agricultural and Technical College of North Carolina) has continued to this day to educate a large proportion of the Negroes of the state.

66. Raleigh *Gazette,* November 7, 1891.   Charles N. Hunter Scrapbook, 1871-1928.
67. Raleigh *Gazette,* November 7, 1891.

14

To Deal Justly with All School Children

*God speed the day when Carolina shall be free from
... Negro haters. ... I have never spoken in this
chamber unless aroused by flings at the Negro race.
The sooner the whites of this state learn to respect
the rights of my people, then will come the joyful
day for us all.*

From speech of Henry Eppes before the Senate
of North Carolina, 1887.

As in the case of the suffrage laws enacted by
the North Carolina legislature between 1876 and 1891, we can also
see in that body a decided reflection of the attitude of the white
citizens of the state by the legislation relating to public school education for Negroes during the same period. In his message before the
General Assembly in January, 1877, the newly elected Democratic
governor, Zebulon B. Vance, urged the members to "make no discrimination in the matter of public school education," but to deal
justly and equitably with all school children of the state "with a
thorough North Carolina spirit."[1]

The record reveals that for the first three years following the 1876
Democratic victory, North Carolina made serious efforts to equalize
the schools of the two races. But by 1880 the promises and pledges of

1. Greensboro *Patriot*, January 17, 1877.

1876-1877 were cast aside. On March 29 of that year the legislature authorized the establishment of graded schools in the town of Goldsboro by an act that declared that "the taxes raised from the property and polls of white persons shall be appropriated exclusively to a grade school for white persons, and the taxes raised from the property and polls of colored persons shall be appropriated exclusively to a graded school for colored persons."[2] Charles L. Coon says that this was the first time a North Carolina law permitting the division of school taxes on a race basis was enacted.[3] This history-making law, however, got no further than its passage through the General Assembly; for when the question was put to a popular vote in early May of 1880, the poor whites and "ignorant" Negroes of Goldsboro united to defeat it.[4]

Refusing to accept this setback, the "good white people" of Goldsboro were successful on March 5, 1881, in obtaining from the legislature permission to hold another election in that city on May 2, 1881, upon the same question, taxation for a graded school. The act was similar to the previous one, containing also a provision that money raised by taxes paid by whites should be devoted exclusively to the education of white children, and that money raised by taxes paid by Negroes should be devoted exclusively to the education of Negro children. This time, through the strenuous efforts of Julius A. Bonitz, the editor of the Goldsboro *Messenger,* the act passed.[5] The town of Durham, apparently heartened by the success of the whites of Goldsboro, secured permissive legislation and also established graded schools with money collected from whites supporting white schools and money collected from the Negroes supporting Negro schools.[6] Commenting on the widespread feeling among the whites of the state in favor of the distribution of the school fund to the races in proportion each paid to the fund, a white newspaper, the Wilson *Advance,* cautioned that "the education of the Negro is a delicate question to handle and we think it would be unwise at this juncture to withdraw all aid from this class of our citizens and throw them on their own resources."[7]

On March 8, 1883, the legislature of North Carolina, however,

2. *Public and Private Laws and Resolutions of the State of North Carolina, 1880,* c. 27, sec. 8. Act of March 29, 1880.

3. Charles L. Coon, "The Beginnings of the North Carolina City Schools, 1867-1887," *South Atlantic Quarterly,* XII (July, 1913), 244.

4. *Ibid.*

5. *Laws and Resolutions,* c. 189, sec. 3. Act of March 5, 1881; Coon, "N.C. City Schools," *South Atlantic Quart.,* p. 244.

6. *Ibid.,* c. 231, sec. 3. Act of March 9, 1881.

7. Wilson *Advance,* February 16, 1883.

bowing to public demands, recognized the division of local taxes and authorized, by a general statute, any school district in the state to vote taxes on that basis. The procedure was that a written petition signed by ten white voters would entitle the county commissioners to order an election to be held. Likewise, a petition signed by ten colored voters would bring about a similar effect. In either case, the taxes collected were to support separate schools: from the whites, in support of white schools; from the Negroes, in support of Negro schools.[8] Describing the law as a "monstrous enactment—a disgrace to the State," a Negro newspaper of the state, the *Star of Zion* of Salisbury predicted that it would destroy the Negro schools.[9]

The passage of this general statute was due, unquestionably, to the insistent urgings of papers like the Clinton *Caucasian,* the Goldsboro *Messenger,* and the Raleigh *News and Observer.* The former was one of the first publications in the state to advocate the doctrine that each race should be held responsible for the education of its children. It argued that such a system would benefit both races:

It will unify the whites in favor of a more liberal system of public schools for their race, which they would cheerfully and willingly sustain; and, as the blacks are imitative creatures, they would be induced to do their best in the same direction. Thrown upon their own resources, and seeing that they will have to depend on themselves, all of them would pay their poll tax; whereas now, many thousands of them evade payment.[10]

In addition to passing the general statute, the legislature of 1883 enacted a series of laws authorizing specific cities of the state to divide school taxes along race lines through a popular vote. The Negro members of the legislature opposed all such proposals. The General Assembly debates over the Tarboro Graded School bill in February, 1883, is a case in point. E. H. Sutton, in an opposition speech, stressed again and again the impossibility of the Negroes to educate their children from taxes derived from Negro property holders "when they had nothing to tax." He concluded with the poignant observation that if his child had to be educated in that way, "he would be, like his father, an ignorant man."[11] Another Negro, James H. Harris, declared that the proposed bill was "wrong and unjust." In a moving but

8. *Code of North Carolina, 1883,* Vol. II, sections 2593 and 2595.
9. See the New York *Age,* March 3, 1883. Whether this forecast would have been borne out will never be known, for three years later the North Carolina Supreme Court declared the statute unconstitutional. See Chapter 15, pp. 160-63.
10. Quoted in the Wilmington *Daily Review,* March 14, 1883.
11. Raleigh *News and Observer,* February 9, 1883.

conciliatory plea, he expressed the hope that the whites would re-member that the Negroes served them "for 200 years. . . ."[12]

Robert R. Gray, one of the three Negro members of the North Carolina Senate in 1883, sought to amend the Tarboro Graded School bill in a most novel way. He asked that "in all cases where the father of any child shall be white, the tax levied on such father shall go to the white schools," and if such a father had children of both races, the tax "shall be divided between the white and colored schools *pro rata* according to the number of each." The amendment was sum-marily rejected.[13] On April 2, 1883, the legislature authorized an election upon the question of taxation for graded schools in that predominantly Negro city.[14]

The editor of the Tarboro *Southerner,* obviously pessimistic about the outcome of the voting, warned the whites of the city as early as April 12, 1883, almost a month before the election, that the "combina-tion of a few large taxpayers with the mass of the Negro vote" might possibly defeat the project.[15] When we note the amount of money which would have been applied to the graded schools for each race, as over against the number of Negroes and whites in the city's school population, we can understand the white editor's pessimism. There were 884 Negro school children in Tarboro, but only 374 whites; yet if the election results favored the graded school, the amount of money spent on the white school would be $5,950, but only $1,942 would be allocated to the Negro schools.[16]

When the final vote was counted and the results, 301 against and 154 for the graded school bill, were announced, the *Southerner* prompt-ly accused the Negroes of bringing about the defeat, saying that "the whites as a general thing voted for it, and the colored people against it." In a decidedly bitter editorial, the editor wrote in part:

The vote against it [the election for a graded school] was cast, with the exception of a few property owners, by Negroes who had for their reason that not enough of the money was given to them. On them rests the blame of a failure, and they have shown a degree of ingratitude that should instill disgust and contempt in the breast of those who have been paying so much to their support and education.

Race prejudice defeated the bill and the color line was drawn by the black ingrate. Two-thirds of the money that is collected annually in this county

12. *Ibid.*
13. *Senate Journal, 1883,* pp. 22, 514-15.   *House Journal, 1883,* p. 32.
14. *Laws and Resolutions,* c. 249, sec. 3.   Act of April 2, 1883.
15. Tarboro *Southerner,* April 12, 1883.
16. *Ibid.*

for schools is expended for the benefit of the colored schools, and three-fourths of it is paid by white property owners.[17]

As a result of the decisive defeat of the Tarboro school bill by the Negro voters of that city, the white citizens of another heavily Negro populated city, New Bern, looked forward to their graded school election with grave misgivings.[18] On May 6, the day preceding the election, these doubts gave way to entreaties. The Negroes were asked to "remember that when they want to build churches . . . they call upon their white friends to help them." Now, the whites asked, "Is it asking too much of our colored friends to help us adopt our school bill?"[19] At least one segment of the city's Negro population, the Negro teachers of New Bern and Craven County, heeded these pleas, for they promised unqualified support of the bill. In a hastily called meeting in New Bern on May 5, they drew up the following resolutions that are interesting for the phraseology as well as the point of view expressed:

. . . That we are in favor of the bill as passed by the wise law-makers of North Carolina, because it places education in reach of the poor children.

2. Politicians and enemies of colored education tell the colored voters not to vote for the Graded School bill because it is class legislation; this is not true, the bill simply provides that each race educate their children.

3. This bill is the wisest school bill the legislature has passed in years; it teaches us the simple and useful lesson—a lesson that is worth more to us as a race than thousands of gold dollars; that lesson may be stated thus: To become a powerful race we must depend on ourselves; this is the royal road to honor, wealth and virtue.

4. We shall be greatly surprised if the colored voters of New Bern fail to vote for this bill (for education). We feel sure that every Negro who possesses pride of race will vote for this measure.[20]

Apparently the Negro teachers of Craven County were "greatly surprised" following the May 7 elections; for although the school bill carried 376 to 296, all but "thirty or forty" of the ballots against it were reportedly cast by Negroes.[21]

In order to meet the growing discontent of the whites living in the densely populated eastern cities and towns—discontent caused by their inability, in some instances, to pass those bills designed to divide the school taxes along racial lines because the Negro vote was

17. Tarboro *Southerner,* May 10, 1883.
18. See *Laws and Resolutions,* c. 117. Act of February 13, 1883.
19. New Bern *Daily Journal,* May 6, 1883.
20. *Ibid.*
21. *Ibid.,* May 8, 1883.

sufficiently large enough to defeat it—the legislature on March 11, 1885, passed an act that gave to the justices of the peace and the county commissioners the right to elect the members of the county board of education. The board itself was "to consist of three residents of their county, who shall be men of good moral character, and who shall be qualified by education and experience and interest to specially further the public educational interests of their county." The county board of education, under section 6 of the new act, was authorized to apportion two-thirds of the school fund "in proportion to the whole number of children between the ages of six and twenty-one years." The remaining one-third was to be apportioned "in such manner as to equalize school facilities to all the districts ... without discrimination in favor of or to the prejudice of either race."[22]

The law, in effect, eliminated many Negroes from the county boards of education. It was hardly conceivable that the Democrats, who controlled the legislature, would appoint an appreciable number of Negro Republican justices of the peace, or that the justices of the peace, in turn, would appoint Negro Republicans as county commissioners. Since these men elected the county school board, it is therefore safe to assume that they selected Democrats of "good moral character," sound education, and the proper experience and wisdom "to further the public educational interest" of the white children of their respective counties.

Apparently convinced that great injury would come to the colored people through its operation, the three Negro members of the Senate of 1885, George H. White, Robert S. Taylor, and J. H. Montgomery, vigorously fought against its passage. When it became obvious to them, however, that the proposal would be enacted into law, they lodged a senatorial protest, directed specifically against section 6. "While it [section 6] says that nothing therein shall work a discrimination in favor of or to the prejudice of either race [it] is in itself proscriptive," wrote the trio, "and works in favor of one race and discriminates against the other." Notwithstanding the protest, the bill was overwhelmingly approved.

The passage of the 1885 school law marked the high point of educational limitations imposed upon the Negroes of North Carolina between 1877 and 1894. Only by a liberal interpretation of these laws by the North Carolina Supreme Court could the Negroes look forward to the retention of some of the educational privileges and rights they had enjoyed between 1868 and 1876.

22. *Laws and Resolutions*, c. 174, sections 1 and 6. Act of March 11, 1885.

15

The Educational Needs
of the Negro Are Great"

> Nor can the color line be recognized in the adminis-
> tration . . . [of] justice.
> Chief Justice Smith, *State vs. Sloan,* 97 N.C. 499
> (1887).

The Supreme Court of North Carolina, as in the case of suffrage laws, was committed to safeguard the Negro's privilege to acquire a public school education at the expense of all tax-paying citizens. This can be seen by the decisions it made in numerous and significant cases.

However, if the decision it handed down in its first "education case" was any criterion as to its attitude with respect to the education of Negro children, that group could expect little by way of equal justice.[1] The background to this case follows. In 1883, as I have already noted, the legislature authorized an election to be held in New Bern for the purpose of determining whether that city would establish a graded school. Section 3 provided that the tax raised from the polls and property of white persons was to be devoted to "sustaining" a school for the white children and that taxes raised from the polls and property of Negroes were to be used for supporting their school.[2] Following the election of May 7, 1883, J. W. Smallwood and other taxpayers of New Bern instituted proceedings against the mayor

1. *Smallwood and others vs. City of New Bern,* 90 N.C. 36 (1884).
2. *Public and Private Laws and Resolutions of the State of North Carolina, 1883,* p. 117, sec. 3. Act of February 13, 1883.

and the city council before the Superior Court of Craven County to prevent them from collecting taxes for the proposed graded school on the ground that the tax had not been approved by a majority of the qualified voters of New Bern. The lower court held for the city, and the plaintiffs appealed to the Supreme Court of North Carolina. There, the court held, on a legal technicality, that even though there was some question as to whether a majority of the qualified registered voters of New Bern had voted for the establishment of a graded school system, the fact that the mayor and the city council, who had been authorized and required by the legislature to submit the question to the voters of the city, "having ascertained that a majority of the qualified voters voted 'for schools,' their finding and decision in that respect . . . is final and conclusive."[3] The following remarks of Justice Merrimon, made in connection with the case, are most significant in that they suggest that the court was not yet ready to decide the constitutionality of the laws dividing the school monies along race lines: "It is hinted in the plaintiff's affidavit that the act is not valid, but so grave a question ought to be raised by proper pleadings, and generally with the avowed purpose. And such a question ought always to be argued by council. It is a matter of most serious moment to declare an act of the legislature unconstitutional and void."[4]

Yet, two years later, in 1886, this same court, in a series of decisions, flatly and unequivocally declared that such laws were unconstitutional and void. In the first of the series, *Puitt vs. Commissioners of Gaston County,* the North Carolina Supreme Court decided that "a law which allows a tax on polls of one color and on property owned by persons of the same color, to be applied exclusively to the education of children of that color, is unconstitutional" in that it violated the last clause of Article IX, section 2, of the constitution of North Carolina which states that "there shall be no discrimination in favor of or to the prejudice of either race." In the opinion, conspicuous for its spirit of liberalism, Chief Justice Smith said: "Nor can we shut our eyes to the fact that the vast bulk of property yielding the fruits of taxation belongs to the white people of the State, and very little is held by the emancipated race; and yet the needs of the latter for free tuition, in proportion to its numbers are as great, or greater than the needs of the former."[5]

As expected, the Democratic newspapers of the state did not concur in the decision, but perhaps the most bitter criticism came from the

3. *Smallwood et al. vs. City of New Bern,* at 41.
4. *Ibid.*
5. *Puitt vs. Commissioners,* 94 N.C. 709 (1886) at 715-16.

New Bern *Daily Journal.* The constitution, however, and not the Supreme Court, was attacked:

A constitution that will not allow the white people to tax themselves for the benefit of their own schools, after they have contributed liberally to Negro schools, is not the constitution that the white people of North Carolina want. The schools have been made separate and distinct; the constitution and the laws direct that the public school fund shall be divided *per capita* between the races. This is all right. But after the schools have been separated, and each receives its proportionate share of the public school funds, these schools ought to have the right to supplement their funds with additional taxes if they see fit, and a constitution that denies them this right should be speedily abolished.[6]

The Lenoir *Topic,* on the other hand, was not as deferential toward the justices. Speaking of the three, Chief Justice Smith and associate justices Ashe and Merrimon, it, not too enthusiastically, wrote that "we suppose that these gentlemen will desire re-election . . . certain it is that the nomination of each of them will be contested."[7]

The following year, in 1887, the North Carolina Supreme Court not only reaffirmed the principle as set forth in *Puitt vs. Commissioners* and *Riggsbee vs. Durham,* but in *Duke vs. Brown* it overruled the *Smallwood* doctrine. The case developed out of the passage of an act by the legislative session of 1885 which authorized, upon an approving popular vote of a majority of those who could vote, the issue of bonds in the aggregate of fifteen thousand dollars to enable the school commissioners of Durham to secure a loan to be expended "in the purchase and erection of suitable grounds for the Durham graded or public school for white children."[8] The lower court held to the letter of the act, and declared against Duke, who had argued that the bill failed to receive a majority of the votes of the qualified voters of the city. The case was appealed to the Supreme Court of North Carolina. Chief Justice Smith, in reversing the decision of the lower court, held that a majority of the qualified voters, and not merely of those voting, was necessary to enable a city or town to contract a debt. The reasoning of the Chief Justice was that "Indifference is not the test; *an active and expressed approval is necessary* [italics Smith's], and this is ascertained by a majority of those entitled to vote. However forcible may be the reasoning, and however nu-

6. New Bern *Daily Journal,* May 16, 1886.

7. Lenoir *Topic,* May 5, 1886. This paper's forecast was incorrect, for not only were the three Democratic justices renominated, but they were easily re-elected. *Annual Cyclopedia,* N.S. (1886), XI, 656-57.

8. *Duke vs. Brown,* 96 N.C. 127 (1887); *Laws and Resolutions,* c. 87, sections 2 and 3. Act of March 7, 1885.

merous the rulings in other states, which construe a failure to vote as an acquiescence in what is done by those who do vote, we cannot put such an interpretation upon our organic law."[9]

As a result of these unexpected decisions by the North Carolina Supreme Court in 1886 and 1887, Wilson, Goldsboro, Kinston, and other towns and cities in the state abandoned their white graded school system rather than support schools for their Negro children. However, it did not take these local whites long to see the absurdity of denying a public school education to their children in order to deny such an education to the Negro children, and, consequently, they re-established their schools, making provisions for the Negro children at the same time.[10] The whites, although complying to the letter of the law, still continued to complain about "the unjust division of the school money." Although dissatisfaction was most vigorously ex-pressed by whites in Franklin, Lenoir, Columbus, and Currituck counties, criticism was general throughout the eastern section of the state.[11] A disgruntled Sampson farmer, for example, summed up the sentiments of many North Carolina whites when he said: "We have two distinct races here in North America—the white and colored. I think it would be a good plan to have the free school funds divided in proportion to the tax paid by each race. I am sure it would render general satisfaction throughout the South among the white race, for it is fair and just to all."[12]

It can be readily seen that the non-liberal spirit of a large majority of the white citizens of North Carolina and the apparent severe and intolerant laws enacted by the General Assembly of the state were frequently assuaged by the rulings handed down by the state Supreme Court. It cannot be said, however, that the somewhat liberal interpre-tations of the Supreme Court of North Carolina won the commenda-tion of the white people throughout the state. But, by and large, the judges who sat on the Supreme Court bench between 1876 and 1894 were earnest, conscientious men who rarely catered to the interest of the white supremacy shouters and who were usually ready to grant protection to the unfortunate Negroes to the very limit of the law. Without Supreme Court justices like Smith, Merrimon, and Clark, the lot of the Negroes of North Carolina between 1876 and 1894 would have been even more precarious than it was.

9. *Duke vs. Brown*, 96 N.C. 127 (1887) at 131.
10. Charles L. Coon, "The Beginnings of the North Carolina City Schools, 1867-1887, *South Atlantic Quarterly*, XII (July, 1913), 246.
11. *First Annual Report of the North Carolina Bureau of Labor Statistics, 1887*, pp. 92, 93, 127, 130.
12. *Second Annual Report of the North Carolina Bureau of Labor Statistics, 1888*, p. 130.

16

"The Pulpit Is Demanding Prepared Men"

The pulpit is demanding prepared men for its occupancy. The pew demands talent that can lead and instruct it in the truths of the Gospel. Thought, well presented, must take the place of sound and noise, and senseless harangue and twaddle. These will not do in this enlightened time. We must study; we must arouse . . . but we must do so by reason, and not merely by exciting fear and dismay.
AME Zion Church QUARTERLY, II (July, 1892), 418.

In the post-Reconstruction period, religion, like education, continued to play an important part in the life of the Negroes in North Carolina. A few of this group who had been members of white churches when they had been slaves still retained their membership. In most cases, however, the Negroes by 1876 had established their own houses of worship and controlled them in accordance with the creed of the denominations to which they were affiliated.

In North Carolina as well as throughout the South the Baptists held the bulk of the Negro church membership. In 1882 the number of Negro Baptists in the state was estimated at 91,132.[1] Six years later

1. *North Carolina Baptist Almanac, 1882* (Raleigh: Edwards, Broughton and Co., 1882), p. 41.

the number had increased to 123,000.[2] Although Negro Baptists were found throughout the width and breadth of North Carolina, they were especially strong in the heavily Negro-populated eastern counties. The popularity of the Baptists, notably among the "plain Negroes," can be attributed to several factors. In the first place, its uncompounded mode of administration and control which granted to all members an equal voice in congregational matters appealed to the simple democratic convictions of the Negroes. In the second place, the ministers, although generally lacking in formal education and possessing a brand of originality that would more than satisfy the wildest apostle of the unconventional, nevertheless, with earnestness, passion, and eloquence, delivered discourses that went straight to the hearts of their hearers.

The Methodists were almost as successful as the Baptists in winning converts among the Negroes of the state. In 1882 an estimate put membership of this denomination at 47,200.[3] This figure, of course, included the African Methodist Episcopal Church, the African Methodist Episcopal Zion Church, and the Colored Methodist Episcopal Church, the latter a creation for the Negroes by the white Methodist Episcopal Church, South. Statistics are extremely sketchy on membership in each of the three Methodist bodies. At its fifteenth annual session in 1878, the North Carolina Conference of the African Methodist Episcopal Zion Church claimed 22,076 members, with 289 local preachers and 247 churches.[4] Unlike the Baptists, the Methodists had their most extensive following among urban Negroes. The main strength of the African Methodist Episcopal Church in the 1880's, according to one Methodist bishop, was in the vicinity of Wilmington and Raleigh.[5] The African Methodist Episcopal Zion Church in Fayetteville, Evans Chapel, had in 1880 a membership of 1,459.[6] Similar to the Baptists, many of the Methodist ministers were often uneducated but were endowed with a natural eloquence that fired the hearer with glowing, tumultuous, and almost uncontrollable fervor.

2. New Bern *Daily Journal,* October 18, 1888.

3. *Baptist Almanac, 1882,* p. 41.

4. *Minutes of the Fifteenth Session of the North Carolina Annual Conference of the A.M.E. Zion Church in America,* held in Goldsboro, N.C., November 27—December 4, 1878. Hereafter cited as *Minutes, Fifteenth Session of the N.C. Annual Conference of the A.M.E. Zion Church.*

5. James W. Hood, *One Hundred Years of the African Methodist Episcopal Zion Church* (New York: A.M.E. Zion Book Concern, 1895), p. 401.

6. *Minutes of the First Session of the Central North Carolina Conference of the A.M.E. Zion Church in America,* held in Fayetteville, N.C., November 10-18, 1880. Hereafter cited as *Minutes, First Session of the Central N.C. Conference of the A.M.E. Zion Church.*

In 1880, the church membership among Negro Presbyterians was 4,865. Moreover, two years later, there were no ordained Presbyterian ministers, and there were only two Negro churches connected with the North Carolina Synod of the Presbyterian Church. The "occasional preaching to the colored people" was performed by white ministers.[7] Negro Episcopal churches were found only in the larger towns and cities of North Carolina. Even here, scarcity of numbers may be seen in the fact that most of the white Episcopal churches had galleries set apart for the Negroes which were, however, mostly "unused, or sparsely occupied."[8] Apparently, there were a small number of Moravian Negroes in the state, for the Winston *Union Republican* carried an article that said that the "Colored Moravian Church in Salem sponsored an organ recital," and spoke encouragingly of the "intellectual capacity of the rising colored generation. . . ."[9] The Lutheran Church was also active among the Negroes of the state. In Concord a church of that denomination had a membership of thirty-two members.[10]

The distribution of Negro church membership in Raleigh was typical of the over-all state pattern. In that city in 1887 the 3,590 Negro church membership, according to figures furnished by the pastors themselves, was as follows: the Baptists listed a total of 2,005 converts; the Methodists, including A.M.E., A.M.E. Zion, and M.E., numbered 1,305; the Congregationalists, the Episcopalians, and the Presbyterians followed with memberships of 130, 75, and 25 respectively.[11]

The vast majority of southern white churches, as has already been observed, were unable to retain their Negro members after 1865 because the Negroes demanded separate church organizations and congregations and ministers and other church officials of their own race and choosing. There were, however, instances in which Negroes continued, after 1865, to be active members of predominantly white churches. Coffie Eborn, for example, son of a free Negro, was carried on the roster as a member of the North Creek Primitive Baptist Church of Beaufort County on September 14, 1877.[12] In New Bern

7. Turner's *North Carolina Almanac, 1880*, p. 29. See also *Presbyterian Church, North Carolina Synod Minutes, 1882* (Wilmington: Jackson and Bell, Printers, 1882), 371-72.

8. O. W. Blacknall, "New Departures in Negro Life" (1883) n.p.

9. Winston *Union Republican*, April 8, 1880.

10. Concord *Times* (no month and day listed), 1888.

11. Raleigh *State Chronicle*, May 26, 1887.

12. *Baptist Association, Minutes and Records, North Creek Primitive Baptist Minutes of Conference, 1877*.

in the same year that city's white leadership noted that "ample provision is made in the churches of the white population for all colored people who may desire to attend."[13] Whether the "ample provision" meant giving the Negroes a special section in which to sit at regular services, or providing them with special services at the end of the regular service, or permitting them complete freedom to participate in the services along with the whites is not clear. At any rate by the eighties and nineties even these isolated instances of Negro membership in white churches had disappeared.

The responsibility of the Negro churches of North Carolina for establishing a better trained and educated ministry had been long recognized by leading Negro clergymen of all denominations. While admitting that many uneducated ministers had had success in disseminating the gospel, C. R. Harris, a minister of the A.M.E. Zion Church of Charlotte, declared in 1875 that the need was for "superior ministers." In the first place, he reasoned, education was necessary for the correct interpretation of the Scriptures, and in the second place, the lack of education lessened the influence of the ministry upon those who were becoming educated. Since the minister must lead his flock, Harris concluded that he must be well informed on all topics, especially those which he professed to teach. "Our young people are learning the just use of the language. They read the Bible for themselves and compare what they read with what they hear. If they do not agree, they learn to disregard the instructions of the minister."[14]

A. W. Pegues, a Baptist minister, reminded those who contemplated a career in the clergy that "mere sound" would no longer satisfy the spiritual soul, and that the man who began his ministerial career with no other evidence of "a call to preach than loud vociferations accompanied with a peculiar tone" soon failed.[15] The Bishop of the Episcopal Church in North Carolina, T. B. Lyman, in 1885, remonstrated against what he considered as "the sweeping condemnation" of the "ignorant and superstitious colored Episcopal clergy." Bishop Lyman declared that in North Carolina he found the "experiment of admitting colored men to the ministry a very encouraging one, and that most of them were active, zealous and efficient church workers."

13. L. C. Vass *et al.,* to the North Carolina Board of Education, April 7, 1877. Governors' Papers, State Department of Archives and History, Raleigh.

14. *Minutes of the Twelfth Session of the North Carolina Conference of the A.M.E. Zion Church,* held in Concord, N.C., November 24—December 1, 1875, pp. 31-32.

15. A. W. Pegues, *Our Baptist Ministers and Schools* (Springfield: Willey and Co., 1892), pp. 18-19. See also the Wilson *Advance,* October 26, 1883.

"It is a fearful reflection upon the race," he added, "to intimate that they cannot be trained and qualified for the gospel ministry."[16]

The Negroes charged with the administration and control of the race's churches of North Carolina did not rest their case for an educated ministry on exhortations, but took concrete steps to remedy the defect. In spite of the large number of non-college Negro clergymen in North Carolina, it should be stressed that some of them were college graduates. And it was this small group of articulate, dedicated men which provided not only church leadership in general but also the stimulus for a better trained clergy. The Baptists consistently emphasized the need for an educated ministry and in this connection were the first to establish in the state an institution of higher learning, Shaw University in 1866, as primarily, though not exclusively, a Baptist institution. The Episcopalians also stressed the necessity of an adequately trained ministry and founded in 1868 St. Augustine Normal School (now St. Augustine University). The Presbyterian Board of Missions for Freedmen, convinced that the church would wither away in the absence of a continual flow of youthful educated ministers, founded in 1868 Biddle University (now Johnson C. Smith University). The African Methodist Episcopal Zion Church, although its organizing activities commenced in North Carolina shortly before the end of the Civil War, did not establish an institution in the state until 1879, the Zion Wesley Institute (later Livingstone College). Notwithstanding the fact that these institutions were founded chiefly to advance learning, a basic aim was to prepare young men for the "Holy Ministry." Biddle University, for example, in 1884 claimed 57 theological students out of an enrollment of 187 students.[17]

Although the Negroes were fewer than three decades removed from slavery, the constant emphasis on a better prepared ministry was yielding results. At the fourteenth session of the North Carolina Conference of the A.M.E Zion Church in 1877, fraternal greetings were brought to that body from the conference of the white Methodist Episcopal Church, South, which was also in session in Salisbury. The two white ministers who brought the greetings "expressed themselves happy to meet so intelligent a body of colored ministers."[18] Commenting on the eighteenth General Conference of the A.M.E. Zion Church of America, which met in New Bern, May 2-22, 1888, the editor of the daily white paper of that city described the body as

16. Raleigh *Register,* February 11, 1885.
17. Raleigh *Register,* June 4, 1884.
18. *Minutes of the Fourteenth Session of the North Carolina Annual Conference of the A.M.E. Zion Church in America,* pp. 9-10.

representing "the higher cultured people of the colored race . . . and a very gratifying exhibition of the advancement in learning and progress in religion they are making."[19]

However, despite the growing number of young, educated ministers in the state between 1876 and 1894, it was the large number of uneducated preachers who held complete power over the masses of Negro church-goers. Many of these preachers were none too well prepared for their offices. Dowd tells a tale about the reading difficulties of one "unlarnt" Negro clergyman. This Negro preacher is reported to have told him that "Now we niggers, you understand, ain't got much larnin. I sorter picked up some educashun and I darts along through the Scriptures and preaches the best I kin. Sometimes I come across things that I can't make out, but I just does like an old nigger preacher once told me to do. When I sees a word I can't make out, I just calls it Peter and pass on."[20]

The story is a plausible one. The problem of the uneducated clergyman was one with which the Negro church had had to wrestle since the Civil War. As noted above the Negroes had set up their own churches and in many instances had to develop their own ministers. An absence of institutions to train ministers was a chief drawback. Meanwhile ignorant men of limited backgrounds, men who had never seen a college or university and were unfitted to preach, were entering the profession. Blacknall gives us a description of what he considered to be a "typical unlarnt" Negro pastor of the period: "Neither in point of rite or doctrine is he fettered, scarce even guided by rule or precedent. He manufactures theology with the nonchalance of a Jesuit, and coins words with the facility of a Carlyle. He may just be able to flounder through a chapter of Scripture, uncouth in gesture, barbarous in diction . . . yet the salient points of his discourse are sound."[21]

Though recognizing his educational shortcomings, the uneducated Negro minister was not deterred from his primary object of saving obdurate souls. And notwithstanding the uncouth gesture, the barbarous diction, and a general air of extreme unconventionalism, the earnestness and passion of the untrained Negro minister gave dignity to his manner and eloquence to his jargon.

A practice that prominently featured the "unlarnt" preacher was

19. New Bern *Daily Journal,* May 22, 1888. See also the Greenville *Reflector,* December 6, 1893.

20. Jerome Dowd, "Rev. Moses Hester: Sketch of a Quaint Negro Preacher in North Carolina," *Trinity Archives,* IX (February, 1896), 295.

21. Blacknall, "New Departures," n.p.

the annual camp meetings. In rural North Carolina these mass religious gatherings, usually sponsored by the Baptists and Methodists, were special events and attracted people from many counties. For weeks preceding the opening day of the revival, the neighboring area would be seized with a religious mania "little short of absolute insanity." The camp meeting as a discussion topic overshadowed everything else. Pennies and nickels were husbanded to buy cloth to make new dresses, and chickens and pigs were fattened in anticipation of the great event.[22]

In a natural physical setting with twigs and branches acting as a roof against the force of the sun's rays or the dews of the evenings, the opening day and night activities foreshadowed the intensity of the fervor yet to come in the usually week-long revival.

To say that the preaching, singing, or praying was artistic would not be true, and to say it was earnest would be less than true, for it was something more; it was violent, it was emotional, it was comical. The sermon was a strange mixture of eloquence and humor, and some of the observations made by the preacher were absolutely startling in their nature. In referring to the expulsion of the money-changers and those that sold doves from the Temple . . . he represented the Savior as "going in" with his sleeves rolled up; and again, in accounting for the ascension of the Savior into Heaven after the resurrection, he swept away all theories and speculation with a single motion of the hand, and in his imagination pictured a windlass in heaven with a golden cord attached thereto, to one end of which, being lowered, the Savior was clinging, while beautiful angels, robed in white, labored at cranks to wind him up.[23]

The emotional effect upon the illiterate hearers must have been electrifying.

Opposition to the Negro camp meetings came from white employers of Negro farm labor and the more intelligent city and town Negroes. Many a white employer shared the feeling of a white coachmaker in Gates County who complained that his Negro workers "lose at least two months each year going as they say to 'meeting.' Can't a law be passed regulating this 'meeting' business?"[24] The whites who hired Negro help, then, were opposed to camp meetings chiefly for economic reasons. The Negroes, on the other hand, who were educated and cultured, protested the camp meetings be-

22. *Recollections of the Inhabitants, Localities, Superstitions and Ku Klux Outrages in the Carolinas* (*1880*), pp. 124-25.

23. *Ibid.,* p. 125.

24. I. Garland Penn, *The Afro-American Press* (Springfield, Mass.: Willey and Co., 1891), p. 273.

cause they considered them coarse, vulgar, and lowered people's opinion of their race. One of the most outspoken foes among the Negroes was W. C. Smith, editor of the Charlotte *Messenger*.[25]

However, if the white employers and the more articulate Negroes were opposed to the camp meetings, the white merchants of the locality where the meetings were held welcomed them. A white man noted that a camp meeting of the African Methodist Church was a "god-send to merchants, giving them the liveliest trade they have had in some time. . . . How many yards of calico and ribbon, how many yards of flour, sugar and candy, especially the last, and how many plugs of tobacco and cheap cigars they have sold, have not yet been recorded at the village exchange."[26] In addition to the economic benefits accruing to the local white merchants, it is undeniable that the camp meetings, despite the frequent "coarse, ignorant and senseless" sermons that excited sensibilities and aroused passions, had the effect of instilling the fear of God in the participants and thus causing them, if only temporarily, to forsake the ways of sin.

The Negro churches of North Carolina, while evidencing little or no interest in interchurch organization, frequently exhibited deep-seated interchurch animosities.[27] Because of the threat posed by membership defection to the Colored Methodist Episcopal Church, Bishop James W. Hood, at the thirteenth conference of the A.M.E. Zion Church of North Carolina in 1876, reiterated his promise to treat with justice and fairness every church member. "The Methodist Episcopal Church, South," he said, "with its millions of money [was] ready to buy every dissatisfied man, be his character what it may . . . and turn [him] over to the little body of colored members it has organized." Bishop Hood, therefore, reasoned that sound policy dictated that his church be precise and sensible in dealing with its members.[28] Apparently there was little love lost between some of the leaders of the African Episcopal Zion Church and the African Episcopal Church, for Bishop Hood spoke heatedly of a fellow minister who, after having been "fed, clothed and educated" at the expense

25. Raleigh *News and Observer*, August 27, 1888.

26. *Ibid.*, August 27, 1888.

27. There was some discussion concerning a union of the A.M.E. Zion Church and the Colored M.E. Church at the fourteenth conference of the former body in 1877, but nothing came of it. See *Minutes, Fourteenth Session of the N.C. Annual Conference of the A.M.E. Zion Church*, pp. 8-9.

28. *Minutes of the Thirteenth Session of the North Carolina Conference of the A.M.E. Zion Church in America*, Washington, N.C., November 22-29, 1876.

of the A.M.E. Zion Church, had, "viper-like," affiliated with "our worst enemies."[29]

Similar to the white churches, Negro churches assumed the responsibility of disciplining wayward ministers. Infractions included embezzlement of funds, insubordination, and "gross immorality." Bishop Hood, at the thirteenth annual conference in 1876, warned the ministers of the A.M.E. Zion Church that the wrongdoer, irrespective of the nature of the violation, would be ferreted out and punished. Stressing the need of a pure ministry, Hood declared that "neither talent, education, energy or anything else will make up for the want of purity." He, therefore, urged that clergymen should not only be free from "scandalous crimes," but should be free from the appearance of misdoings. In home visitations, he tactfully advised ministers "not to stay too long in one place, [for] I have heard rumors, respecting some among us, that are unpleasant."[30] As if to illustrate that this was no idle threat, at its annual conference the following year several ministers were expelled for "gross immorality."[31]

As regards the consumption of alcoholic beverages, the Negro church was a consistent but tolerant enemy. The A.M.E. Zion Church at its fourteenth session in Salisbury in 1877 urged each minister to preach a sermon on temperance in his church and to make an earnest effort to solicit temperance pledges from his members.[32] At the first conference of the Central North Carolina Conference of the A.M.E. Zion Church in 1880, all "good Christians" were urged to refrain from frequenting the barroom and "indulging in the customs and practices of known inebriates."[33] Negro ministers, in other ways, attempted to improve the moral tone of their congregations. Garland H. White, a Baptist preacher in Weldon, wrote Senator Matt Ransom in 1875 that he had "commenced reform among the colored people by turning off every man in my church who has been accused of stealing cotton, chickens, and pigs."[34]

29. *Minutes of the Sixteenth Session of the North Carolina Annual Conference of the A.M.E. Zion Church in America*, Lincolnton, N.C., November 26—December 3, 1879, pp. 4-5.

30. *Minutes, Thirteenth Session of the N.C. Annual Conference of the A.M.E. Zion Church*, p. 7. See also *Minutes, Sixteenth Session*, p. 3.

31. *Minutes, the Fourteenth Session of the N.C. Annual Conference of the A.M.E. Zion Church*, pp. 11-12. See also *Minutes, First Session of the Central N.C. Conference of the A.M.E. Zion Church*, p. 20.

32. *Minutes, Fourteenth Session of the N.C. Annual Conference of the A.M.E. Zion Church*, pp. 19-20.

33. *Minutes, First Session of the Central N.C. Conference of the A.M.E. Zion Church*, p. 35.

34. Garland H. White to Matt Ransom, December 10, 1875. Ransom Papers, University of North Carolina Library, Chapel Hill.

The Sunday School, fostered by all of the Negro denominations, acted among other things as an agency to propagate temperance ideals. Its primary function, however, was to give instruction in the Holy Scripture.

Membership statistics are extremely sketchy, but if judged by the 9,195 members of the Sunday Schools sponsored by the A.M.E. Zion Church in 1877, total membership in all the Negro churches in the state was probably in excess of 40,000. There can be no question that these schools served a useful purpose. Through them many young and adult Negroes attained a degree of literacy and self-respect not otherwise possible.

17

Social Relationship

Between the Races

You may call it foolish pride, you may call it groundless prejudice, but the God who made us both placed it there, our subsequent education nurtured it, and all our nature, all our associations have implanted in us the principle that it is not right, proper or just that the Anglo-Saxon and African races should mingle together on terms of social equality.

From a speech of W. B. Glenn, Republican, quoted in the Raleigh DAILY NEWS, February 9, 1875.

Any man who favors either mixed schools or mixed marriages is to be suspected at once as to his honesty, his virtue and his decency. Any party that will advocate the mingling of white girls and Negro boys in the same school is corrupt, rotten, utterly depraved. Any politician who will favor or countenance the intermarrying of a Caucasian woman with an African is a low, mean fellow that does not deserve the salutation of a dog.

Wilmington MORNING STAR, October 29, 1876.

The relationship between the Negroes and whites of North Carolina was governed by both legal and extra-legal practices. However, the most effective limitations on the relationship between whites and Negroes were unwritten agreements among the white group that any approach to social equality must be resisted at all costs. This "social equality" phobia so conditioned and governed every facet of the Negro-white relationship that a northern visitor, after "much friendly and agreeable conversation," concluded that "the Southern whites misapprehend and make a scarecrow" out of it. He agreed with the views of a North Carolina Negro who told him that "social equality is humbug. We do not expect it, we do not want it. It does not exist among the blacks themselves. We have our own social degrees, and choose our own associates. We simply want the ordinary civil rights, under which we can live and make our way in peace, and amity. This is necessary to our self-respect, and if we have not self-respect, it is not to be supposed that the race can improve."[1]

The insistence by the Negroes on all those things "necessary to their self-respect," and the determination on the part of some whites to deny them to the Negroes is seen in the following two incidents. A Negro alderman in a North Carolina town resented one of the town's white merchants' calling him by his first name and "reminded the merchant that he had a 'handle' to his name, and that the handle was the word mister." As a result of this show of "uppityness" on the part of the Negro alderman, the irate merchant had him forcibly ejected from his store. The Negro alderman instituted a court action in the nature of assault and battery against the merchant. The Negro alderman not only lost his case but also was given a lecture by the judge who pointed out that "there was no law in the state of North Carolina . . . by virtue of which one man could be compelled 'to mister another.' "[2]

On a visit to the Western Insane Asylum at Morganton with fellow white assemblymen, R. C. Ward and another Negro member were not allowed to eat at the same table with the white members of the committee, but were offered a "private dining room." Upon his return to Raleigh and the legislative chamber, Ward "complained that his dignity had been grossly insulted by his treatment" at the asylum. The House, however, took no notice of his complaint. A white newspaper editor, perhaps answering Ward's grievance, voiced the sentiments not only of the Democratic controlled House of 1887 but also a majority of the white people of the state when it replied

1. Charles D. Warner, *On Horseback: A Tour in Virginia, North Carolina, and Tennessee* (New York: Houghton-Mifflin and Co., 1892), p. 123.
2. *Recollections of the Inhabitants, Localities, Superstitions and Ku Klux Outrages of the Carolinas* (1880), p. 225.

that white North Carolinians "are not yet prepared for social equality between the two races even if two of the parties are members of the legislature."[3]

White Democrats of the state were quick to protest "social leveling" practices occurring outside North Carolina also. The purported actions of President Grover Cleveland in this regard were especially disconcerting. On August 18, 1888, the Chairman of the Chatham County Democratic Executive Committee wrote Senator Matt Ransom's private secretary:

Colonel [Oliver] Dockery, the Republican candidate for governor of this state, in a speech at this place [Pittsboro] a few days ago, charged that the President had invited Fred Douglas and his white wife to dine with him, and that at such a dining, they were seated respectively on his right and left. That Mr. Cleveland invited Negroes to the White House on terms of intimacy, and on one such occasion kissed a Negro wench. . . . I would be glad if you think it proper to do so, if you would give us an emphatic and authoritative denial of these dirty charges.[4]

In addition to expressing concern and distaste at President Cleveland's reportedly receiving Negroes in the White House as "guests" on social occasions, the Democrats of the state were told by gleeful Republicans that in some instances white women held positions under Negroes in several departments of the federal government.[5] Whether these reports were true or false, there can be no doubt but that they adversely affected the Democratic party in North Carolina in the election of 1888.[6]

The civil rights question was most sharply focused when it revolved around the segregation of Negroes on public carriers and in hotels and restaurants. As is generally known, the civil rights law, passed by the Federal Congress on March 1, 1875, was supposed to secure, among other things, the privilege of riding in public conveyances and of accommodation at hotels without discrimination on account of color or previous condition of servitude. The reaction of a Democratic newspaper of North Carolina perhaps sums up the general attitude of the majority of whites of the state towards the law: "It is done. Hereafter there shall be no discriminating prohibitions against the 'man and brother,' but he shall pay his money and take his

3. New Bern *Daily Journal*, February 12, 1887; Chatham *Record*, February 17, 1887.
4. T. B. Womack to Daniel Lamont, August 18, 1888. Ransom Papers, University of North Carolina Library, Chapel Hill.
5. W. Crawford to Matt Ransom, August 17, 1888: C. B. King to Matt Ransom, October 5, 1888. Ransom Papers.
6. W. L. Saunders to Matt Ransom, September 20, 1888. Ransom Papers.

choice, and walk disinthralled into the dress-circle as well as the cockloft of theatres, and ride in cars, steamboats; put up at hotels, and sit on juries just like white folks. The Civil-Social Levelling Rights bill is an accomplished fact. . . ."[7] The hope, however, of most North Carolina whites was that Negroes would feel disinclined to intrude upon the society of white men; that if the Negroes would not force themselves into places where their presence would provoke trouble, the civil rights law would be for all practical purposes a nullity. Their hopes were not to be realized. Negroes in various parts of North Carolina sought to enjoy all of the privileges accorded white people on railroads, steamboats, in hotels and theaters. In short, every place of public accommodation witnessed visitations by Negroes. On March 7, 1875, for example, a Negro waiter at the Exchange Hotel in Raleigh departed that city for Savannah, Georgia. According to the *Sentinel,* he had announced before leaving Raleigh that he intended to ride unsegregated and to dine at a "white" eating establishment. The *Sentinel* reported further that the Negro accomplished his aims.[8] Shortly after the passage of the law, James E. O'Hara, Negro lawyer and future United States Congressman from North Carolina, took passage on a steamer at Greenville destined for Tarboro. When he "ensconced" himself in the saloon, the captain of the steamer objected, and O'Hara appealed to the Mayor of Tarboro, who told the captain the civil rights bill had become law. O'Hara was permitted to enjoy the privileges of the saloon.[9]

Not every Negro who attempted to exercise his "civil rights" was as successful as O'Hara or the Raleigh waiter. A Negro woman, Elsie L. Britton, was forcibly ejected from a "white coach" of the Atlanta and Charlotte Air-Line Railway Company in 1881 by a white man after she had been informed by the conductor that she might sit there. The Negro woman instituted a civil action in the Mecklenburg Superior Court in January, 1882, for damages sustained by her. The verdict of the jury was for the railroad company, and Elsie Britton appealed. Associate Justice Thomas Ruffin delivered the decision. He declared that it was well settled, both upon principle and authority, that among the reasonable regulations that railroad companies had a right to adopt was the one classifying their passengers and assigning them to separate, though not unequal, accommodations. However, when the Negro woman and her friends took seats in the "white

7. Greensboro *Patriot,* March 3, 1875.
8. Raleigh *Sentinel,* March 8, 1875.
9. Raleigh *Daily News,* March 13, 1875.

coach," they did so in the exercise of a right and a discretion expressly left to them by the Atlanta and Charlotte Air-Line Railway Company's own regulation. Therefore they were clothed with every privilege that appertained to any other passenger in the coach and were entitled as fully as any other to be protected from injuries arising, as well as from the neglect of the company's servants as from the unprovoked assaults of their fellow passengers; and more especially was this so, after the conductor had been appealed to and had assured them of their "rights to the seats." Ruffin then declared that Elsie Britton was entitled to a venire de novo.[10]

In spite of the court's decision, Ruffin was quick to emphasize that he and his fellow justices adhered to the right of a railroad company to assign white and Negro passengers to separate, "though not unequal," accommodations. This was necessary he declared in order "to prevent contacts and collisions arising from natural and well known antipathies, such as are likely to lead to disturbances from promiscuous intermingling."[11]

Even after the declaration by the United States Supreme Court in the fall of 1883 that the civil rights law was unconstitutional, however, the "civil rights business" would not stay down. In the state elections of 1884, for example, Frank Winston, a white Republican candidate for the office of state superintendent of public instruction, in speaking before a Negro audience in Washington, North Carolina, expressed the view that Negroes were entitled "to whatever your money will buy," such as "a first-class ticket . . . first-class fare . . . to ride in first-class cars and steamboats, and to stop at first-class hotels." This brazen and outspoken support of civil rights for Negroes brought an immediate retort from the Washington *Gazette* in the form of an editorial entitled "A Bad Man." The editor raised and discussed two questions. First, "Do the white people of North Carolina desire such a man to preside over the public schools of the State?" Second, "Are you ready for Civil Rights?"[12] Needless to say, Winston was soundly defeated at the polls.

It is of interest to note that much of the civil rights agitation after 1883 was placed at the feet of the Negroes of the state. "Since the Supreme Court of the United States declared the Civil Rights bill unconstitutional," wrote the Tarboro *Southerner* on November 15, 1883, "the colored people and their papers have been raising a 'howl.'"

10. *Britton vs. R. R. Co.,* 88 N.C. 542 (1883), pp. 543-44.
11. *Ibid.*
12. Washington (N.C.) *Gazette,* September 26, 1884.

The newspaper went on to say that all the justices of the highest tribunal had been abused and slandered save Justice Harlan, who filed a dissenting opinion. The latter justice was lauded by the Negroes "for all the English language is worth." In answer to the complaint of most Negroes, which was the refusal of many transportation lines to allow whites and Negroes to ride together in the same compartment, the *Southerner* continued: "This is no civil right. It is simply a matter of business. If transportation lines consider their business is injured by permitting Negroes to ride with the whites, they have a perfect right to say they shall not, and nobody has a right to complain. The truth of the matter is, that it is not the civil rights, that the colored man thinks are in danger; he is looking further at social rights!"[13]

Since the Negroes were not *legally* segregated on the trains in North Carolina during the period, the editor of the Charlotte *Home-Democrat,* apparently concerned by the dissatisfaction of the Negroes over the decision of the United States Supreme Court, wondered "why any intelligent colored man should want a Civil Rights Bill." He continued by saying that during his travels over the state he had seen "big black Negro men and women sitting in *first-class cars* among white people, *and no one interfered with them—*they were simply left alone in what they considered glory—but if there was a law (passed by Northern radicals for the purpose of degrading Southern white people) compelling admission of Negroes into first-class cars among white ladies, men and children, it would then, in many cases be resisted, and the Negro would get hurt, law or no law."[14]

This absence of a North Carolina law segregating Negro and white passengers on railroad cars elicited strong complaint from some of the whites of the state, particularly toward the end of the period. The editor of a Greensboro weekly declared that "it would be a good thing if our North Carolina legislature would follow the examples of Mississippi and Louisiana and require the R. R. companies to provide separate accommodations for the white and Blacks. . . . The white man will not submit to social equality."[15] A similar protest was voiced by a white woman who said that it should not be difficult for a white person to know how a white lady "feels to get up from a first-class berth in one of the sleepers on the main lines passing Greensboro, to find that a Negro man has occupied the next berth during the night." She wondered if there was a remedy for "this

13. Tarboro *Southerner,* November 15, 1883.
14. Charlotte *Home Democrat,* October 31, 1884.
15. Greensboro *Patriot,* January 8, 1891.

enforced social equality."[16] There was an additional reason given for the necessity of segregating the Negroes. An editorial in the Greensboro *Daily Record* demanded the separation of the races on railroad passenger cars because "while a few colored people know how to behave themselves on the cars, a great many take particular pains to make themselves objectionable."[17]

Apparently the objections on the part of some white citizens of the state prompted a move in the North Carolina legislature of 1893 to enact a law segregating the races on trains. It was this action that led Joseph C. Price, President of Livingstone College and one of the great Negro orators of the state, to head a delegation of the race which appeared before the legislature to protest the passage of the "Jim Crow" coach law. He reportedly received from the speaker of the House, Lee Slater Overman of Salisbury, positive assurances that no such legislation would ever pass that body while he was speaker. The measure died in committee.[18]

Thus, North Carolina did not enact a law separating the races in public conveyances during the period under study. The first state to pass a comprehensive law in this regard was Tennessee in 1881. Other southern states soon fell in line: Florida in 1887, Mississippi in 1888, Texas in 1889, Louisiana in 1890, Alabama, Kentucky, Arkansas, and Georgia in 1891. It is interesting to observe, moreover, that when North Carolina finally enacted a Jim Crow car law in 1899, it did not apply the law to Pullman cars or to through express trains.[19]

In addition to the agitation for a Jim Crow car law, the whites of North Carolina urged that separate waiting rooms should be provided for the races. As in the case of Jim Crow cars on the railroads, their demands were stimulated by the enactment of such legislation in Arkansas, Louisiana, Mississippi, and South Carolina.[20] North Carolina, in spite of these protestations and urgings, failed to follow the lead of other southern states in providing separate waiting rooms at railroad stations. Whatever the reasons, economic or humanitarian, the state was free of Jim Crow in public transportation and railroad stations between 1876 and 1894.

16. Greensboro *Daily Record*, January 23, December 4, 1891.

17. *Ibid.*, December 22, 1890.

18. "Lessons from the Life of J. C. Price," address by John C. Dancy at the State Normal School, Elizabeth City, May 25, 1899. MSS in hands of Mrs. Lillian D. Reid, Salisbury, North Carolina.

19. Gilbert T. Stephenson, *Race Distinctions in American Law* (New York: D. Appleton and Co., 1910), pp. 208, 216, 220.

20. See, for example, the Greensboro *Patriot*, January 8, 1891, and the Greensboro *Daily Record*, December 22, 1890; Stephenson, *Race Distinctions*, pp. 220, 228, 351.

As in the case of public transportation, there was no North Carolina law barring Negroes from hotels and restaurants. The presence of a Negro in an "exclusively" white hotel or restaurant was nevertheless strongly resented and resisted by many North Carolina whites. The following examples are cases in point. In August of 1883, while traveling on a steamer on North Carolina's inland waterways, several Negro women, one reportedly the wife of the former United States senator from Mississippi, Blanche K. Bruce, declined to accept the separate meal accommodation that had been prepared for them and took their meals in the main saloon at the general table along with the white passengers. Despite the fact that they behaved "with propriety," it caused "considerable excitement among the white passengers." A number of white women refused to go to the table until the Negroes completed their meals and left the room.[21] Joseph Weaver, a liveryman, was pushed from the porch of the Battery Park Hotel in Asheville, North Carolina, by the manager, John B. Steele. Weaver subsequently instituted criminal action against the hotel manager in the Criminal Court of Buncombe County. The court decided for the hotel manager, and Weaver appealed to the Supreme Court of North Carolina. Associate Justice Alphonso C. Avery, in writing the opinion reversing the decision of the lower court, held among other things, that

Guests of a hotel, and travelers or other persons entering it with *bona fide* intent on becoming guests, cannot be lawfully prevented from going in, or be put out by force, after entrance, provided they are able to pay the charges and tender the money necessary for that purpose, if requested by the landlord, unless they be persons of bad or suspicious character, or of vlugar habits, or so objectionable to the patrons of the house, on account of the race to which they belong that it would injure the business to admit them to all portions of the house. . . .[22]

In the town of Weldon, considerable agitation and alarm was voiced over the purported action of the Atlantic Coast Line officials in seating a Negro man "as black as hades" in a dining room that was "supposed to be for the use of white guests only." The incident was denied by the hotel manager who said that "at great expense" the Atlantic Coast Line Hotel has "guarded against outraging the sentiments of Southern white people." He emphasized the point that the Negroes who patronized the hotel ate "behind a screen out of

21. Tarboro *Southerner*, August 23, 1883. Bruce denied that his wife was involved in the incident. (See the Wilson *Advance*, September 7, 1883.)
22. *State vs. Steele*, 106 N.C. 782 (1890).

sight of the white passengers."[23] Five years later the screen must
have been removed, for the Weldon *News,* in a simmering editorial,
blistered the non-segregated policy of the hotel:

Perhaps the only place in the United States which claims to be first class,
where Negroes and white people are admitted to the same room and seated
at the same tables is at the Atlantic Coast Line Hotel, Weldon, North
Carolina. In that hotel, one man's money is as good as another's and all
are admitted on the same footing, no attention being paid to the inherent
objections which Anglo-Saxons have to their being mixed up on a pepper
and salt style with all sorts and conditions of men.

Does the Atlantic Coast Line think it can with impunity ignore the
prejudices of the white people and obliterate instincts implanted by the
Almighty Himself in their breasts? Does the Atlantic Coast Line think
it can ride roughshod over these instincts which have resisted the influences of ages and the operations of partisan power? If so, the Atlantic
Coast Line overestimates its power.[24]

Another white newspaper of that section of the state urged all "good
white people" not to "patronize that hotel."[25] Although the manage-
ment again apologized for "outraging the sentiments of Southern white
people" the *Southerner* was editorializing about "this mixed races
business" at the Atlantic Coast Line Hotel months later.

The Knights of Labor aroused the ire of a segment of the whites
of North Carolina as a consequence of the "race-mixing" incident
at the annual national meeting of that organization in Richmond in
1886. As a result of the refusal of the white hotels of that city to house
an interracial delegation from New York, that delegation took accommodation in a Negro hotel. Terence V. Powderly, the Grand
Master, in his opening-day speech on October 4, 1886, not only
publicly commended the New York delegation for standing "by the
principles of our organization which recognizes no color or creed in
the division of men" but also explained in no uncertain terms why
he selected from that delegation, Francis J. Ferrel, a Negro, to introduce him. "I made the selection of that man . . . to introduce me," he told the assembled delegates, "so that it may go forth
from here to the entire world that we practice what we preach."[26]
Many white editors of North Carolina, viewing Powderly's selection of Ferrel as a deliberate attack upon southern laws and social

23. Raleigh *News and Observer,* September 25, October 1, 1886.
24. Weldon *News,* quoted by the Tarboro *Southerner,* April 16, 1891.
25. Tarboro *Southerner,* April 16, 1891.
26. *Record of Proceedings of the General Assembly of the Knights of Labor of
America.* Tenth Regular Session, Richmond, Va., October 4-20, 1886, X-XI, 12.

equality, angrily denounced the Grand Master. In answer to Powderly's statement that the Knights of Labor knew no social distinctions
that were maintained by color, the *News and Observer* of Raleigh
retorted, "We know that scores of the best men in our community,
who are Knights of Labor, do recognize and will continue to recognize that there are, always have been and will continue to be social
distinctions between the races."[27]   Another white newspaper of the
state predicted that Powderly, because of his social-equality policy,
would never regain the confidence of "the thinking people of the
South, whose judgement and prejudices he has offended."[28]   The
mere presence of the Negro delegates "right in among the whites a la
Republican convention" brought strong protests from the Goldsboro
Argus.[29]   In the absence, then, of the act of choosing Ferrel to introduce him, Powderly and his organization would not have been
spared the ire of some of the white newspapers of the state for his
"blatant" attempts at "social leveling."

As in the case of an absence of laws separating the races in public
conveyances, in hotels and restaurants, and at public gatherings, interestingly enough there was no law prohibiting interracial marriages.
The lack of statutory provisions, however, did not mean that the whites
of North Carolina were not opposed to such unions. Commenting on
a report in the *Carolinian* of Hickory, North Carolina, that "a nice
pretty and educated white girl" of Wheeling, West Virginia, had
married "an ugly, uneducated nasty black nigger," the Wilson *Advance*
thought it inconceivable that any white woman of sound mind could
be in love with a Negro. In a heated outburst, it declared, "The
woman . . . is ignorant in spite of her education, and should have been
in an asylum. The fact that she consented to live with the Negro as
his wife proves her insanity. All right thinking people will agree
with us that such demented persons ought not to be allowed unre-
strained freedom. The speediest and severest punishment possible
ought to be visited upon the Negro."[30]   The marriage of several white
women to Negro men in North Carolina prompted the *Advance* to
lift a voice of warning against "this tendency of permitting these
things to go on at our doors without protestations and without any
effort to check them or to punish the parties." The paper went on to
say that the "horrors of miscegenation" ought to cause North Carolina

27. Raleigh *News and Observer,* October 12, 1886.
28. Quoted in the Greensboro *North State,* October 21, 1886.
29. *Ibid.*
30. Wilson *Advance,* August 10, 1883.

statesmen to adopt a policy that would prevent forever any approach to social equality or intermarriage of the races.[31]

Even though there was determined opposition against interracial marriages, there appears to have been no serious concerted action taken against the illegitimate relationships of white men and Negro women. This type of association, although receiving practically no mention in the press, was sufficiently widespread to prompt George A. Mebane, a Negro member of the 1876-1877 legislature, to propose a bill for its discouragement. He sought to make it unlawful for any white man and colored woman "to lewdly and lasciviously associate, bed, or cohabit together." For so doing Mebane urged a fine of not less than fifty dollars nor more than five hundred dollars, or imprisonment in the county jail from six to twelve months. In not recommending the bill, the legislative committee to which it was referred declared that adequate legislation was found in chapter 32, section 46, of the North Carolina *Code*. It is interesting to note, however, that the *Code* simply stated that it was unlawful "if any man and woman, not being married to each other," engaged in such relationships.[32] Thus it would seem that there was little will to bring the power of the law to bear against those who participated in such activities.

A white minority, on the other hand, while not approving interracial marriages, or illegitimate relationships, did encourage social intermingling. At the marriage reception of a well-to-do Negro couple in Waughtown, North Carolina, on December 28, 1882, some of the white *elite* of Winston and Salem were present. Among the distinguished white guests was the president of the National Bank of Winston. "All fared sumptuously and everything went on merrily as a marriage ball." A white reporter present observed that such "social intermingling" would do much towards removing the prejudice that existed between the races.[33]

The most frenzied manifestation on the part of the whites to combat social equality was through mob violence. It would seem that a general pattern of interracial violence has been an outstanding characteristic of southern life. It must be remembered that violence created as well as maintained the institution of Negro slavery. As one Southern historian observes, the triumvirate of force, violence, and

31. *Ibid.*, September 14, 1883.
32. Legislative Papers, 1876-1877. State Department of Archives and History, Raleigh. See also *Battle's Revisal of the Public Statutes of North Carolina, 1872-1873.* chapter 32, section 46.
33. Winston *Union-Republican*, January 4, 1883.

terror was the South's accepted mode of meeting Negro-white con-
flicts that whites felt could not be resolved in any other way.[34]

The years following the Reconstruction era were years in which a
campaign of force, violence, and terror was directed against the Negro
group. This was not only because of the determination of the southern
whites to undo the general work of the Reconstructionists but because
of the special fear of Negro equality. Thus, the dread of slave insur-
rections that plagued the ante-bellum South was replaced in the years
after 1876 with an even greater horror, equality of the races in all their
social relationships. The one conspicuous characteristic in the interracial violence of the period was the conviction by the whites that the
Negro must be "kept in his place" at all costs. As one Southerner
wrote,

The conviction that the black man must now and then be intimidated, in
order to keep him from forgetting the bounds which Southern tradition
have set for him, is firmly rooted in the consciousness of many Southern
people. So unquestioned is this philosophy that at times lynchings are
planned and carried through—not under the fierce compulson of mob
hysteria—by men who have calmly resigned themselves to the performance
of a painful duty, which, according to their lights, is necessary for the
good of society.[35]

It is, therefore, interesting to observe that between 1881 and 1894,
thirty-three Negroes were reported victims of mob rule in North
Carolina. Thirty-one were lynched between 1881 and 1888. In
every case, the Negro was charged with murdering a white person or
with rape or attempted rape of a white woman. The larger number,
by far, was found in the former group.[36] The all too frequent appeal
to "lynch law" prompted one North Carolina newspaper to warn in
1883 that "should many more cases . . . occur the State will lose her
reputation for strict conservatism and love of law and order."
In urging the whites to abide by the law, it declared that "any other
course is full of wrong and danger."[37] Although the newspaper's
concern over the increase in lynchings was warranted, in no other
southern state of the former Confederacy did Negroes live in com-

34. George B. Tindall, *South Carolina Negroes, 1877-1900* (Columbia: University
of South Carolina Press, 1952), p. 233.

35. Clarence Cason, *90° in the Shade,* quoted in Maurice R. Davie, *Negroes in
American Society* (New York: McGraw-Hill Book Co., 1949), p. 348.

36. Much of this data was compiled by the writer from Turner's *North Carolina
Almanac, 1880-1894.* See also *Thirty Years of Lynching in the United States, 1889-
1918* (New York: National Association for the Advancement of Colored People,
April, 1919), p. 84.

37. Tarboro *Southerner,* November 15, 1883.

parative safety from lynchings than they did in North Carolina. While only twelve Negroes were reported lynched in North Carolina between 1889 and 1894, thirty-three were mob victims in Virginia during the same period. In Tennessee, fifty-eight were lynched, while in Louisiana, seventy-nine died in this manner. The number was greater in Mississippi—ninety-nine.[38] This figure for Mississippi appears to be a conservative one. One Mississippi historian has declared that it was impossible to make any reliable estimate of the number of Negroes lynched by whites in that state because "such matters attracted little or no attention in the press."[39]

Despite the fact that Negroes of North Carolina lived in comparative safety from lynch law, the brutality and public approval that characterized these acts in many of the southern states can be found in the lynching of a Negro at Tarboro in 1887. The Negro, accused of attempted assault on a white girl, was lodged in the Tarboro jail. The jail officials, because of the highly charged emotional atmosphere, recommended that the Negro be removed from the Tarboro jail to Williamston. A protest meeting of white citizens in Tarboro resulted. As a consequence of this meeting, a mob of some two hundred men went to Williamston, smashed the jail door, and took the unfortunate Negro back to Tarboro and lynched him at the scene of his attempted assault. A placard found upon the victim read "We hang this man, not in passion, but calmly and deliberately, with a due sense of the responsibility we assume. We take executive power in this case and hang this man in accordance with the unwritten law of the land, because the written law provides no penalty adequate to the crime. And be it understood, we who have done this act will repeat it under similar circumstances."[40]

The white press of the state, committed to a policy of white supremacy, very rarely before the late eighties spoke out against mob violence. Indeed, press notices of lynchings usually condoned the act and described the participants as "the better class of citizens" performing a painful but necessary duty to society. An indication of the beginning of a shift in the prevailing white attitude was an editorial in the Greenville *Eastern Reflector* following the lynching of three Negroes by a white mob. On January 29, 1888, when a mob took Jack Blount, Matthew Blount, and Patterson Spruill from the Plymouth jail, lashed them to trees, and riddled their bodies with bullets,

38. *Thirty Years of Lynching*, pp. 68-70, 74-76, 91-100.

39. Vernon L. Wharton, *The Negro in Mississippi, 1865-1890* (Chapel Hill: University of North Carolina Press, 1947), p. 224.

40. Raleigh *State Chronicle*, May 12, 1887.

the *Eastern Reflector* "deplored the fact that mobsters over-looked the supremacy of the law." The paper went on to say that it was most unfortunate "that so many lynchings are blotting the history of the Old North State."[41] On October 24, 1889, following another lynching, the Chatham *Record* warned: "It is high time that the law abiding citizens of North Carolina were arousing themselves to a sense of their great danger. If one set of men can with impunity unlawfully take the life of a fellow-man, why cannot another and another do likewise? This spirit of mob law if persisted in must produce a state of anarchy, where might makes right and license takes the place of liberty!"[42] The Negro press, naturally, raised a protesting voice. The editor of the *African Methodist Episcopal Zion Church Quarterly,* John C. Dancy, for example, characterized lynchings as "the true inwardness of the demon-like frenzy of the presumed protectors of Southern virtue." He urged "all lovers of justice and liberty to . . . stop the degrading crime of lynching by earnest protest against it."[43]

Despite these and other pleas, mob violence continued throughout the period. In 1893 the state legislature took cognizance of the widespread opposition to lynching and passed an act, weak though it was, "to protect prisoners confined in jail."[44]

The Negroes of the state were not always contented to be the recipients of white mob violence. On occasions they were themselves infected with the spirit of mob law. In Elizabeth City on July 16, 1881, a white man had a dispute with his Negro washerwoman about some allegedly missing clothing. She called him some opprobrious names, and he knocked her down. News of the incident quickly spread through the Negro section, and a group of one hundred Negroes collected and "threatened summary vengeance" on the offending white man, even going so far as to defy openly the mayor after he had ordered them to disperse. Arrests were subsequently made which ultimately led to the white man's being fined. In summing up the incident, the local newspaper made the interesting observation that "All the parties did wrong, the woman in grossly insulting the man, the man in striking the woman, and all who attempted to take the law in their own hands."[45]

At Fayetteville in late August, 1888, two Negro youths were ar-

41. Greenville *Eastern Reflector,* February 1, 1888.
42. Chatham *Record,* October 24, 1889.
43. *A.M.E. Zion Church Quarterly,* II (July, 1892), 418.
44. *Public and Private Laws and Resolutions of the State of North Carolina, 1876-1894,* c. 461. Act of March 6, 1893.
45. Elizabeth City *North Carolinian,* July 20, 1881.

rested for allegedly assaulting a young white girl. Rumors circulated among the Negroes of that city that the girl's friends would lynch the two boys under cover of night. As a consequence the jail was placed "under a close watch of armed Negroes."[45] The rumored lynching did not occur.

46. A. A. McKethan to Governor Alfred M. Scales, August 22, 1888. Governors' Papers, State Department of Archives and History, Raleigh.

18

"From Three to Ten Years"

. . . if a man of color is brought before a court, it is no difficult matter to prove him guilty. The jury is composed of all white men—perhaps one or two colored; they all say guilty; the judge sentences the prisoner to from three to ten years in the State Penitentiary, when had it been a white man, if found guilty at all, would have been sent to the county work-house or jail for sixty or ninety days.

Coleman Twining, in the FIRST ANNUAL REPORT OF THE NORTH CAROLINA BUREAU OF LABOR STATISTICS, 1887.

North Carolina Negroes in the post-Reconstruction period were made to realize that before the bar of justice a white skin was a decided advantage. More often than not Negroes were often the recipients of harsher punishments than were meted out to whites. Indeed, evidence that convicted a Negro failed in many instances to convict a white person charged with a similar offense. This practice followed the theory generally believed by many whites of the South that the Negro group possessed a natural addiction to crime. This assumption by whites as well as their unwavering determination to curb that tendency goes far in explaining why the prisons and jails were generously populated with Negroes.

The state of the city and county jails in which Negroes and whites charged with trifling offenses were lodged deserve some attention. In many of these structures across the state there was no effort to separate the accused from the convicted, nor the young and first offenders from the hardened and frequently convicted criminals. The Negro prisoners, by virtue of sheer numbers, were the greatest sufferers from these practices. In 1892, for example, inmates in the county jails of North Carolina numbered 188 whites and 392 Negroes. By far the majority of the latter group was confined for larceny, assault, and battery.[1] As to the sanitary condition of the jails and inmates, the *News and Observer* painted this picture of a Wake County jail: "In and around the cells or cages ... we find the building very filthy, with a stench that indicates great neglect of cleanliness. The prisoners are sorely afflicted with body lice and filthy. .... This suggests that ... other jails in North Carolina are in a condition more or less like that described."[2] As has already been indicated, since the Negro population made up the large proportion of the jail population, it was this group who suffered the most from the neglect and indifference of the jail officials with respect to sanitation and cleanliness of the jail houses.

The presence of Negroes on juries did little by way of reducing the number of commitments. The records reveal the hostility of whites with regard to jury duty by Negroes. A state meeting of "representative colored men" in Raleigh in 1880, for example, complained that in many of the counties across the state Negroes were not permitted to act as jurors.[3] Even in the "Negro counties" effort was made to restrict the number of Negro jurors to a figure considerably less than whites on the jury panel. Halifax, a county with a large Negro majority, had on its list of jurors for one term of court in 1876 the names of twenty-three whites and thirteen Negroes.[4] In Craven County in 1886 the county commissioners drew fifty-four whites and only five Negroes for jurors at the fall term of the Superior Court.[5] It would appear, then, that the middle and late eighties witnessed the decreasing frequency of the use of Negroes on juries.

There is conflict of evidence when it comes to the matter of the Negroes' position in the administration of justice. In some instances

---

1. *Biennial Report of the Board of Public Charities of North Carolina, 1893-1894,* pp. 202-32.
2. Raleigh *News and Observer,* November 20, 1886.
3. Raleigh *Signal,* January 21, 1880.
4. Warrenton *Gazette,* August 11, 1876.
5. New Bern *Daily Journal,* November 6, 1886.

justice was slow in coming their way. In 1878 a white man in Monroe shot and killed a Negro who was running from him. For this cowardly act the jury failed to convict him. "Though if it had been a white man who had been shot," observed one member of that race, "it would have went [*sic*] hard with him."[6] On the other hand, in 1892 a large number of citizens, white and Negro, petitioned the solicitor of the Second Judicial District, George H. White, himself a Negro, to induce Governor Thomas M. Holt to offer a reward for the capture of two white men who "without cause" shot and killed a Negro in Warren County.[7]

In spite of instances such as those cited above, the all too common tendency to show little compassion toward Negro offenders not only increased the annual consignment of Negroes to the state penitentiary but also it contributed to an excess of Negro over white admissions. In 1876 there were 676 Negro prisoners in the state penitentiary.[8] Four years later the number had increased to 979.[9] In 1890 there were only 408 whites, but 1,623 Negroes, in the state prison.[10]

The question may well be asked, "How is the increase of the Negro prison population to be explained?" In addition to the white-held theory of natural criminality among Negroes was the growing demand for abundant, cheap labor brought on by the expansion of railroad construction in the state. It is not fruitful to go into a detailed discussion of the rapid expansion of this mode of transportation, which was quite marked throughout the period under observation; nor a recapitulation of the findings of Hilda J. Zimmerman and Herbert Stacy McKay relative to the convict lease system as practiced in North Carolina between 1876 and 1894. Suffice it to say that it is reasonably safe to conclude that the need for an ever-ready, cheap supply of manpower to do the laborious and hazardous work of rail construction contributed to a large degree toward the increase of the Negro prison population.[11] Without a doubt, Negro prisoners were

6. C. Austin to Governor Zebulon B. Vance, November 15, 1878. Governors' Papers, State Department of Archives and History, Raleigh.

7. J. R. Rodwell to George H. White, December 7, 1892. *Ibid.*

8. Turner's *North Carolina Almanac, 1877*, p. 36.

9. U.S. Bureau of the Census. *Tenth Census. Delinquent Classes* (1880), XXI, 479.

10. *Ibid., Eleventh Census. Crime* (1890), Vol. III, Part ii, p. 3.

11. For excellent studies on the convict and convict system, see Hilda Jane Zimmerman, "Penal Systems and Penal Reforms in the South Since the Civil War" (Unpublished Ph.D. dissertation, University of North Carolina, 1947), and Herbert Stacy McKay, "Convict Leasing in North Carolina" (Unpublished M.A. thesis, University of North Carolina, 1942).

responsible for most, if not all, of the 3,582 miles of railroad track laid between 1876 and 1894.[12]

As Monroe Work explains, "The use of prisoners as convicts enabled this group to become a source of revenue for the state, or a reduction of cost by their employment, rather than the employment of free labor."[13] The inevitable result, then, was that North Carolina officials took an active part in increasing the number of convicts. Coleman Twining, a machinist from Wilmington, describes one method of enlarging the Negro prison population:

. . . we have two races in our State who are nearly equally divided as to numbers, and while we find race prejudice prevalent throughout the white population, and while it does not stop and rest with the common citizen, but goes further, and, I am sorry to say, extends to and enters our courts of justice, so called. Therefore, if a man of color is brought before a court, it is no difficult matter to prove him guilty. The jury is composed of all white men—perhaps one or two colored; they all say guilty; the judge sentences the prisoner to from three to ten years in the State Penitentiary, when had it been a white man, [he] if found guilty at all, would have been sent to the county work-house or jail for sixty or ninety days.

Now in hiring out convicts . . . they are hired to some railroad or canal contractor, who are both, in nine cases out of ten, inhuman and void of conscience. Now to give action to this feeling of prejudice spoken of, the unfortunate man is put at work in the worst places that are on the work. Why? Because he is a convict, and if he dies it is a small loss, and we can make him work there, while we cannot get free men to do the same kind of labor for say six times as much as the convict costs.[14]

Twining suggested that instead of sending to the penitentiary for three to ten years a Negro who "perhaps did not steal five dollars' worth—probably two or three chickens—send him to the county work-house for sixty or ninety days, or more, as the magnitude of the crime."[15]

John Nichols, a white Republican congressman from the Fourth District in North Carolina in 1886, commenting on the large number of Negro prisoners in the State Prison in Raleigh, bluntly declared

12. U.S. Bureau of the Census, *Eleventh Census. Report on Transportation Business* (1890), Vol. XIV, Part I, p. 34. See also the *Eighth Annual Report of the North Carolina Bureau of Labor Statistics, 1894*, p. 257.

13. Monroe N. Work, "Negro Criminality in the South," *Annals of the American Academy*, XLIX (September, 1913), 74-80.

14. *First Annual Report of the North Carolina Bureau of Labor Statistics, 1887*, pp. 198-99.

15. *Ibid.*

that "the evil is in our present system of law."[16] Nichols was referring to the practice of the North Carolina courts to disregard or ignore any distinction between petty and grand larceny. Both carried a penalty of ten years, there being no minimum sentence. Significantly, in this regard, North Carolina was the only state demanding such a penalty for petty larceny; the average sentence for the other forty-seven states was six months to one year.[17]

Negro members of the state legislature throughout the period attempted to restore the distinction between petty and grand larceny. The purpose of the bills advanced by them in the General Assembly was to prevent excessive punishments for minor crimes, and thus to reduce the prison terms of a large number of the Negro prison population. James Wilson, a member of the legislature of 1876-1877, for example, sought the appointment of a committee to report a general bill classifying all criminal offenses according to their "proper grade and degree," and affixing as far as practicable the terms of imprisonment or other punishment proportionate to the grade and degree of such offenses. Wilson correctly reasoned that since there were grades and degrees of crime, there ought also to be grades and degrees of punishment. His proposal was summarily rejected.[18]

If the above factors are not considered when one examines the number of prison commitments between the years 1876 and 1894, it would appear beyond any question that the Negro was obviously more criminal than the white.[19] But the sometime subtle operation of race prejudice, accentuated by the demands of railroad construction for laborers, accounted to a great degree for the rapid and increased growth of the Negro prison population throughout the period under observation.

From the outset it was generally an accepted practice that the system of convict leasing was to be confined in the main to the use of Negro prisoners. As has been noted, most of the whites of the state approved the farming out of such convicts even if for only their subsistence rather than the inadvertent forcing of taxpayers to support the Negroes in the state penitentiary. That prisoners in private hands would suffer from maltreatment was a foregone conclusion, and Negro

16. *Ibid.,* p. 185.

17. U.S. Bureau of the Census, *Eleventh Census. Crime* (1880), Vol. III, Part I, pp. 394-95.

18. Legislative Papers, 1876-1877. State Department of Archives and History, Raleigh. See also *House Journal, 1879,* p. 233; *House Journal, 1883,* p. 590.

19. See Nathaniel Cantor, "Crime and the Negro," *Journal of Negro History,* XVI (January, 1931), 61-66.

state legislators were constantly advocating legislation aimed at improving the condition of the prison population. As early as 1877, William H. Moore, a Negro state senator from New Hanover, proposed a bill to inquire into the complaint that convicts had been "mutilated by shooting them down" and that other convicts were made to witness such shootings. Moore also emphasized the fact that the convicts did not have sufficient fires in winter to warm them. The Committee on Penal Institutions, to which the bill was referred, decided that it should not pass since there was no evidence to sustain the allegations of Moore. The committee went on to say that it was satisfied that the convicts were comfortable. Indeed, the convicts were so comfortable, the committee chairman in an obiter dictum statement observed, "that one old [Negro] woman who had visited her son in there went home so well pleased that she said she was going to try to get the old man . . . in there also."[20]

Such a light-hearted reply to the serious charges of Negro legislators did not appease the latter group. Henry C. Rogers, in the 1876-1877 General Assembly, was such a Negro. Since he had received information from apparently reliable authorities that in some instances the Negro convicts farmed out by the state had been subjected to personal abuse and punishment unwarranted by the law, Rogers proposed a joint committee of one from the Senate and two from the House to make a thorough inquiry of such charges. His proposal was rejected.[21]

Nevertheless, to the damaging charges that Negro convicts were fatally abused was added a report on December 30, 1882, that nineteen Negro convicts lost their lives in crossing the Tuckasegee River while working on the Western North Carolina Railroad. The report indicated a complete disregard of human life by the overseers and guards. The superintendent of the state penitentiary in Raleigh categorically denied this report and insisted that every precaution had been taken to assure the safety and well-being of the convicts. His statement apparently satisfied state officials inasmuch as no more was heard of the incident.[22]

Mismanagement and brutality was not confined to Negro convicts. It extended to and within the walls of the state penitentiary. Stewart Ellison, a Negro member of the 1879 legislature, attempted to prohibit the "whipping or mal-treatment" of convicts in the Raleigh prison.

20. Legislative Papers, 1876-1877.
21. *Ibid.*
22. Governors' Papers, January 9, 1883.

The measure was defeated.[23] The beating and hospitalization of several Negro prisoners in 1887 by one of the white guards at the Raleigh institution resulted in a strong protest by three prominent Negro leaders of the period. James H. Harris, Stewart Ellison, and James H. Young wrote Governor Alfred M. Scales that "the recent unfortunate occurrence at the State Penitentiary in which a number of our race were involved has in no small degree excited the colored people of this community [Raleigh]. A recurrence of the scenes then and there enacted might incite an open violation of the law. This, all good citizens, white and colored, alike, would regret."[24] The records do not reveal whether Governor Scales consented to the interview that they requested.

Despite these and other evidences of brutality, Negro prisoners continued to be hired out as convicts.[25] Private contractors, naturally, were interested chiefly in the exploitation of the prisoners' labor. Since there was little pressure on them to provide in a most elemental way for the welfare of the Negro convicts, it is surprising that the miserable conditions of the convicts were not worsened by official indifference.

23. *House Journal, 1879*, p. 151.
24. Governors' Papers, April 20, 1887.
25. See *House Journal, 1893*, p. 29.

19

"Down Every Alley"

I have visited scores and hundreds of houses huddled in festering heaps under every hill and down every alley; it is impossible to look . . . in any direction and not be nauseated by them.
E. B. Emery, LETTERS FROM THE SOUTH, 1880.

The living conditions of the Negro population in regard to sanitation and health are revealing. In both country and town life, whole families lived in small houses, often containing but one room. Especially was this true of the poorer classes of Negroes in the towns of North Carolina. A New England woman, visiting Wilmington in 1880, noted the outside appearances of these houses. "I have visited scores and hundreds of houses," she declared, "huddled in festering heaps under every hill and down every alley; it is impossible to look . . . in any direction and not be nauseated by them."[1] The interior offered little by way of contrast with the exterior, as the following picture will show:

The shanty is black within and without through age and weather, but more through dirt and grime; and the decaying floor is filthier than the ground outside. . . . There is no chair or stool—nothing to sit upon but the wreck of a bedstead, which holds a nest of what was once straw, a feather pillow which trots itself, and rags of wool and cotton which are equally smutty and frisky. The only bit of furniture besides the bed is a small table, and three children are rubbing off the slime of it with potato skins left yesterday—for they get a meal some days—and these parings furnish

1. E. B. Emory, *Letters from the South* (Boston: Todd Printers, 1880), p. 8.

their only meal today. Under the table is a battered wash-dish in which they stir their hoecake . . . and a broken skillet in which they bake it; but wood is scarce to them, and only now and then can they steal a bit.[2]

Akin to the undesirable housing as a health menace was the contaminated drinking water. In Wilmington in 1880, for example, almost all the drinking water came from wells, springs, and creeks. A water analysis, conducted in that year by the North Carolina Board of Health, found it to be "almost uniformly bad," and that some was "positively dangerous from distinct sewage contamination." The drinking water of Durham was also listed as unhealthy and dangerous.[3]

One of the major causes for the contamination of the drinking water was the privy. In many cases there was direct communication between it and the well. For example, many of the wells of Wilmington were dug only twenty or thirty feet from the privies. In some instances, they were only two to four feet from them. But even had the wells been dug thirty or more feet from the privies, the soil upon which Wilmington is located was described as being "nearly as white as the seashore and as permeable;" and, therefore, they would still have been exposed to continued contamination.[4] The situation was worsened by the fact that in one area of that city approximately one mile square, there were 1,309 privies, most of which were shallow in depth, "sometimes with no exterior protection."[5] The question may well be asked, "Did not the city furnish drinking water to all its inhabitants?" The answer is in the affirmative, but the yearly water tax of fifteen or twenty dollars prevented many of the more destitute Negroes from taking advantage of the more sanitary facilities. And when the plumber's fee is taken into consideration, the possibility for the introduction of water to the premises was even more remote.[6]

A comparison of the death rates of the whites and Negroes in North Carolina for selected years in selected areas shows most effectively the latter group's plight. Among the Negroes of Wilmington in 1879 there were 341 reported deaths. For the same year, there were 154 white deaths.[7] Therefore, the death rate among the Negro population was more than double that of the whites; while the number of Negroes was only one-third greater than the whites (10,288 Negroes to 6,776 whites). And so, although the Negro population

2. *Ibid.*, p. 9.
3. *First Annual Report of the North Carolina Board of Health, 1879-1880*, pp. 16-19.
4. *Ibid.*, p. 62.
5. *Bulletin of the North Carolina Board of Health* (March, 1890), pp. 195-96.
6. *Second Biennial Report of the Board of Health, 1887-1888*, p. 176.
7. Wilmington *Morning Star*, January 3, 1880.

exceeded that of the whites by more than 30 per cent, their death rate surpassed that of the whites by more than 100 per cent. In 1890, F. W. Potter, a white physician of Wilmington, listed pneumonia and tuberculosis as the chief killers "among our colored population."[8] The mortality of the Negroes in Asheville in 1887 was unusually high. In January of that year, it was 64.0 per 1,000; in February, it was a phenomenal 88.0 per 1,000; in March there was a slight decrease, 72.0 per 1,000. The causes of deaths among the Negro population of this city were mainly acute bronchitis, pneumonia, and measles.[9] The destitute condition of the majority of Negroes of Asheville, coupled with the cold winters, accounted, to a large degree, for this excessive death rate.[10]

A mortuary report made from the record in the city clerk's office of New Bern for six years, 1882 to 1887 inclusive, shows the number of interments in the white and Negro cemeteries.

Year	Cedar Grove (white)	Greenwood (Negro)
1882	85	132
1883	67	118
1884	60	146
1885	46	158
1886	55	176
1887	53	179

The interments in the white cemetery with one exception regularly decreased, while those in the Negro cemetery increased—and with one exception increased regularly. The editor of the white daily newspaper disagreed with those who held that the distribution of shells on the streets, the whitewashing of the trees, and general cleanliness of the white districts caused the decrease in white deaths. "We think," he added, "that there are many causes that tend to the increase of mortality among the colored people other than the lack of lime and disinfectants."[11] The editor, though failing to elaborate, could have had in mind the socio-economic disabilities under which the Negro citizens of New Bern labored.

An examination of the mortalities among the Negro population in New Hanover County reveals the extent to which water contamination from nearby privies affected the death rate. Because New Hanover County is located on the southeastern coast of North Carolina in

8. *N.C. Health Bulletin* (February, 1890), p. 187.
9. *Second Biennial Report of the Board of Health,* pp. 52-63.
10. *Asheville City Directory,* (Asheville: Southern Directory Co., 1887), pp. 18-19.
11. New Bern *Daily Journal,* May 31, 1888.

relatively flat, low country, with highly porous soil, exposure to typhoid fever, dysentery, diarrhea, and related diseases resulting from cess pools and contaminated drinking water would be the greatest single factor in any explanation of the high death rate. Nearly one-half of the Negro deaths in 1879 occurred during the rainy months between July and October. Of the total number of deaths, the majority were from malarial fever, typhoid fever, and other fevers, with tuberculosis, pneumonia, and whooping cough following in that order.[12]

However, the accuracy of these death statistics was doubted by the North Carolina Board of Health. "On account of their poverty and obscurity as a class," the Board of Health felt that all the deaths among the Negroes were not recorded; hence the mortality rate given for that group was relatively too low.[13]

Although the official statistics of Negro deaths might have been "too low," an examination of the diseases that caused Negro deaths in twenty-eight towns and cities of North Carolina in 1893 reveals the chief killers to be tuberculosis, diarrheal diseases, brain diseases, heart diseases, pneumonia, malarial fever, and typhoid fever.[14] It is interesting to note that the large death rate from tuberculosis was attributed to a number of causes. Among them were insufficient clothing during the winter months; the lack of fire wood in winter; the want of an abundance of good, nutritious food; the lack of proper care in sickness; and overcrowding in the most unhealthy parts of the towns or cities.[15]

Thus the greatest killers among the Negroes of North Carolina, whether city, county, or state-wide, were tuberculosis, diarrheal diseases, fevers (typhoid, scarlet, and malarial), pneumonia, and brain and heart diseases. The factors contributing to the high tubercular mortality have already been alluded to; and as to the deaths from diarrheal diseases, typhoid, diphtheria, "and certain interic fevers," the North Carolina Board of Health concluded that they were caused by "bad wells, foul yards, privies, and cess-pools." The above diseases, it might be added, were classed by the health authorities as "filth diseases," commonly found in the larger towns of the state.[16]

A contrast of the decrease in the death rates of the Negroes of North Carolina with that of other southern states will suggest the extent of the interest of the states in reducing Negro mortality. Be-

12. *First Biennial Report of the Board of Health*, pp. 164-65.
13. *Fifth Biennial Report of the Board of Health, 1893-1894*, p. 91.
14. *Ibid.*, p. 105.
15. *Ibid.*
16. *Ibid.*, p. 73.

tween 1880 and 1890 the death rate per 1,000 in North Carolina fell
from 17.61 to 12.88, a decrease of 4.73 per 1,000. In no other southern
state except Arkansas was there a greater reduction in Negro mortality
for the ten-year period.[17] This not only indicated evidence of the
growing concern with which North Carolina viewed the health of its
Negro population but it also gives evidence of the rising social status
and improved well-being of the Negroes of the state.

17. U.S. Bureau of the Census. *Eleventh Census. Vital and Social Statistics* (1890),
IV, 7.

20

Social Life:

High and Low

> ... *I shudder to think of exposing my children to the social ... proscription to which I have been a victim.*
> Helen M. Chestnutt, *Charles Waddell Chestnutt,* pp. 16-17.

Social activities among the Negroes of the state, both rural and urban, were not unlike those of the whites. The range of such activities was as wide as their socio-economic conditions. Farm hands, for example, were more prone to Saturday afternoon fights and drinking binges. The social life of the more sophisticated Negro urban dwellers, on the other hand, was considerably more conservative and less ostentatious.

The pleasures of the mass of the Negro working class, whether rural or urban, came not only from the "Sa'ddy" afternoons in town, but also from experiences of visiting or attending meetings of organizations to which they belonged. A common sight at these meetings, be it a church gathering, a picnic, or simply an informal group get-together, is vividly described by a young Negro school teacher in 1879:

Among both white and black tobacco . . . and snuff are used to a fearful extent. Both races and both sexes partake of [them] freely, women chewing the weed as well as the men and also smoking it. I daily see women having in their mouths little slender sticks, one end chewed into little fibers with which they convey snuff to their mouths and apply it vigorously from the grinders on one side of the mouth to the remotest grinder on the other. Mothers frequently, after use of their tooth-brushes, give them to their suckling babes, and thus allow [them] to taste and cultivate a relish for the black powder. I have seen little boys and girls between the years of four and five using the brush as expertly as their parents.[1]

Negro church leaders constantly railed against the use of tobacco during church service. Only in this way could they keep their congregations from abusing the churches by spitting on the floors.[2]

One of the more popular forms of Sunday entertainment among urban Negroes was the excursion, or inter-city visitation. The various Negro social groups chartered special trains at reduced prices for transportation. Although Wilmington was a favorite visitation spot, other cities also attracted the excursionists. Despite the fact that white newspapers reported them, the editors, apparently, did not approve of them. A Greensboro newspaper, for example, in referring to one of these excursions, observed that "a black cloud swept over South Elm Street. . . . Every colored person in town went to High Point. . . ."[3] The sarcasm of the editor, evidently had little effect on curtailing the inter-city visits, for a similar excursion left Greensboro a month later for Wilmington.[4] According to I. Garland Penn, at least one Negro editor, W. C. Smith, of the Charlotte *Messenger,* a newspaper that reportedly catered to the taste of "the better class" of Negroes, was also opposed to Negro excursions.[5] It is probable that opposition of the Negro editor was motivated by a conviction that the only beneficiary from these trips was the railroad company.

Emancipation Day celebrations were eagerly looked forward to by the Negroes of North Carolina. Every January 1 after 1863 they gathered in the towns across the state to celebrate with pomp and merriment the emancipation of their race from bondage. A typical celebration would go like this. Replete with brass band, a Negro militia company, a Negro fire company, and several social organizations, Negroes "hundreds strong," all carrying United States flags, would march through the principal streets of the town to the courthouse. Here the procession would gather to hear the reading of the

1. Hampton *Southern Workman,* September, 1879.
2. *Minutes of the Fourteenth Session of the North Carolina Annual Conference of the A.M.E. Zion Church,* p. 20.
3. Greensboro *Daily Battle-Ground,* July 23, 1881.
4. *Ibid.,* August 14, 1881. See also the New Bern *Daily Journal,* July 6, 1893.
5. I. Garland Penn, *The Afro-American Press* (Springfield, Mass., 1891), p. 273.

Emancipation Proclamation, followed by an address from a prominent Negro or from a white man sympathetic to the aspirations of the Negro group. Sometimes the speeches urged the assembled Negroes to pledge themselves to insist upon equal rights and not to cease demanding until they were secured; sometimes the addresses were "advice speeches," urging frugality and thrift and greater attention to morals, while others were markedly conservative in urging the Negroes to harbor no ill will towards the white people.

The Negroes of the state looked upon their fraternal organizations and benevolent societies with a great deal of pride. In most of the major towns and cities were local lodges of either the Masons or Odd Fellows. Their titles suggest the spirit and partisanship of the members. In Durham in 1887, the Masons were organized into Doric Lodge, No. 28; the Odd Fellows had in the same city in 1892 the Pride of Durham Lodge, No. 2095, and Reliable Lodge, No. 2970.[6] The Odd Fellows of Charlotte in 1893 could boast of the Star of Hope Lodge, No. 1719, and the Rising Star Lodge, No. 1655.[7] Raleigh had two Masonic lodges, Widow's Sons, No. 4, and Excelsior; the Odd Fellows one, Virtue Lodge.[8] The local branches of both the Odd Fellows and Masons were organized into state-wide Grand Lodges that met annually in one of the larger cities of the state. At these meetings, which lasted several days, the delegates, in addition to dinners, parties, and other social activities, concerned themselves with social and cultural interests. At the 1890 session of the Grand Lodge of Masons, held in Asheville in early December, a resolution was passed urging the state legislature to establish a colored state agricultural college similar to that already established for the whites.[9]

The Negroes of the state also found it to their interest to organize themselves into secret benevolent societies for social and cultural advancement as well as mutualized relief. As in the case of the fraternal organizations, the titles of these societies reflected the purposes behind their *raison d'être,* such as the United Order of True Reformers and the Household of Ruth.[10]

Throughout the period under study the state maintained companies of Negro militia. In 1877 after the Democratic gubernatorial and legislative victory of that year, the latter body on March 12 re-

6. *Durham City Directory* (Raleigh: Levi Branson, 1887), p. 200; *Durham City Directory* (1892), p. 167-68.
7. *Directory of Charlotte, N.C.* (Charlotte: Blakely Printing House, 1893), p. 27.
8. *Raleigh City Directory* (Raleigh: Edwards, Broughton and Co., 1880), pp. 190-91.
9. New Bern *Daily Journal,* December 16, 1890.
10. *Durham City Directory* (1892), pp. 167-68.

voked all commissions and at the same time established a new State
Guard. North Carolina was divided into three military districts, and
the various companies were required to enlist for a term of five years.
The whites were organized into three infantry battalions and two
artillery battalions, a total of 1,305 men. Two Negro infantry bat-
talions were formed. The Fourth was composed of four companies:
Oak City Blues, New Bern Rifle Cadets, New Bern Guards, and the
Oberlin Vance Guards. The Fifth was made up of five companies:
Hanover Light Infantry, Cape Fear Light Infantry, Howard Light
Infantry, Fayetteville Rifle Guard, and the Charlotte Blues. Field
officers were all Negroes. The two battalions aggregated about 500
enlisted men.[11]

Negro National Guard units steadily declined in number and
personnel during the eighties and nineties. In 1878 there were
11 Negro militia companies with a total of more than 800 officers
and enlisted men. Five years later, the Adjutant General's office
reported 5 companies and 205 officers and enlisted men. In 1894,
out of a total of 1,512 officers and enlisted men in the State Guard,
there were 40 Negro officers and enlisted men.[12]

This rapid decrease in the Negro personnel of the State Guard
was in part attributable to white opposition. W. J. Yates, one of the
editors of the Charlotte *Democrat,* strongly objected to the formation
of a Negro militia company in that city and wrote scathingly of "the
intelligent white men who encouraged and recommended Negro
companies."[13] A letter voicing opposition to the establishment of a
Negro company in Wilmington "from the better class of citizens" was
sent to Governor Alfred M. Scales by the mayor of that port city.[14]
Many protests by white citizens stemmed from the conviction that it
would be dangerous to arm Negroes. The editor of the Durham
Tobacco Plant, for example, wrote Governor Scales that it was wrong
to arm and equip a colored militia company because the majority of
Negroes "have no good feeling for white people." Similar grounds
for opposition came from the mayor of Fayetteville.[15]

Although the whites feared that the Negro militia men would use
their weapons against them, the primary function of the Negro

11. *Annual Report of the Adjutant General* (1877), pp. 5-7, 24.
12. *Ibid.,* p. vi; *ibid.* (1882), p. 28; *ibid.* (1894), p. 92.
13. W. J. Yates to Governor Alfred M. Scales, June 21, 1887. Governors' Papers, State Department of Archives and History, Raleigh.
14. John Fowler to Governor Alfred M. Scales, June 28, 1887. *Ibid.*
15. C. B. Green to Governor Scales, August 18, 1887; A. A. McKethan to Governor Scales, August 22, 1887. *Ibid.*

companies throughout the period appeared to be ceremonial and social. Emancipation Day, Decoration Day, the Fourth of July, and the annual fair sponsored by the North Carolina Industrial Association featured parades by the Negro units of the State Guard. At the Negro state fair of 1885, for example, one of the high points was the competitive drill for colored companies of the State Guard. "Twenty-five dollars in gold" was the first prize; a gold helmet was the second prize.[16]

The Negro militia, however, as already noted, suffered from the growing intolerance of Democratic administrations and a hostile white citizenry between 1876 and 1894. Thus from the ten armed and fully equipped Negro companies that sprang into existence between 1874 and 1876 under Republican auspices, the number steadily decreased throughout the eighties and nineties. Indeed, by 1894 the only unit left was an unattached one, the Charlotte Light Infantry, numbering forty enlisted men and three officers.

Resembling the militia in function were the Negro volunteer fire companies that were organized in some of the towns of the state before the advent of professional fire-combatting organizations. Many of the Negro fire companies had rather eye-catching names such as the Rough and Ready Hook and Ladder Fire Company of New Bern, the Reliance Engine Fire Company of the same city, and the Neptune Fire Company of Charlotte. An annual event of the North Carolina Industrial Association at its yearly fair in Raleigh was the competition among the Negro fire companies to determine which of the competing companies was the most thorough in extinguishing a supposed fire.[17]

The colored fire companies were perhaps more useful than the militia. They served not only as a means of entertainment through their firemen's balls, banquets, and picnics but also as valuable adjuncts to the white fire companies. A Negro team in Greensboro in February, 1891, for example, saved a hardware store and its merchandise.[18] James Sprunt mentions "a fire company composed entirely of Negroes . . . which did splendid work" in Wilmington.[19] According to the Wilmington *Morning Star* of January 7, 1880, "several colored fire companies" were active in that city. New Bern, in 1880, had two Negro fire companies. Charlotte also boasted of

16. *North Carolina Gazette,* September 26, 1885.

17. See Raleigh *Evening Visitor,* November 10, 1886; *North Carolina Gazette,* September 26, 1885.

18. Greensboro *Daily Record,* February 2, 1891.

19. James Sprunt, *Chronicles of the Cape Fear River, 1660-1916* (Raleigh: Edwards, Broughton and Co., 1916), 538.

two.[20]   There can be no doubt but that the yeoman work of these
and other Negro fire companies mitigated somewhat the rising white
hostility to the race.

Groups of Negro singers found it a profitable activity to present
concerts before public audiences made up of both races.   In great
demand throughout eastern North Carolina, the Star Concert Troupe,
composed of Negroes of New Bern and Raleigh, presented a concert
in New Bern on July 10, 1888.   The concert consisted of vocal and
instrumental music as well as recitations, and the *Daily Journal* said
that "some of the pieces were creditably rendered, and especially fine
were some of the voices."[22]   As a result of the town-wide acclaim of
the July 10 appearance, by request, the Star Troupe returned on July 23
for a repeat performance.[23]   Another singing group, the Black Dia-
mond Quartet, made up of four men, all natives of Raleigh, was
well known inside and outside North Carolina.   On May 20, 1887,
the quartet gave a concert in Greensboro; of that performance, a white
Greensboro newspaper declared that the singing was of "a superior
order . . . and well received by a large audience."   Among the songs
rendered were "Rocked in the Cradle of the Deep," and "One Hundred Fathoms Deep."[24]

There appeared to be little concerted effort to form social groups
based purely on common professional interests.   On the other hand,
many of the prominent Negroes of the state were members of the
Masonic or Odd Fellows lodges.   Apparently, some of these lodges
were affiliated with international bodies, for in 1879 John C. Dancy,
editor of the *Star of Zion,* went to England as a delegate of the Right
Worthy Grand Lodge of Good Templars.[25]   George H. White, a
prominent lawyer-politician, was elected Grand Master for the State
of North Carolina at the 1890 session of the Negro Grand Lodge of
Masons in Asheville in early December.[26]

The most popular social activity among the wives of the Negro
professional and businessmen was the literary club.   The Ladies
Pansy Literary Club of Raleigh was typical of such social organizations.   Listed among its membership were "many of the most beautiful, refined and cultured colored ladies of that city."   On November 5,

20. *New Bern City Directory* (Raleigh: Edwards, Broughton and Co., 1880), p. 138;
ibid., p. 13.
22. New Bern *Daily Journal,* July 11, 1888.
23. *Ibid.,* July 21, 1888.
24. Greensboro *Morning News,* May 24, 1887.
25. Penn, *The Afro-American Press,* p. 197.
26. New Bern *Daily Journal,* December 16, 1890.

1891, it gave what was described as "one of the most unique entertainments of the season." The newspaper reporting the event praised it as "both a literary and social event of the highest order. . . ."[27]

Marriages of the Negro elite were events of major social interest and attracted considerable attention in the Negro newspapers. The wedding on November 10, 1880, of Sophia Ellison, eldest daughter of Stewart Ellison, a prominent Raleigh politician and businessman, for example, was described by the *North Carolina Republican* as follows:

The bride was elegantly attired in white cashmere, trimmed with lace and satin bows to match; in her hair she wore white flowers, which were very becoming. Gold ornaments, ear-rings with pearl settings, necklace and chain, over all of which was gracefully worn the customary bridal veil of white tulle. . . . At the conclusion of the ceremony at St. Paul's AME Church the invited guests repaired to the handsome residence of the bride's father, where a splendid collation was in waiting. . . .[28]

Among the gifts received by the couple were silver, fine linens, and crystal.[29]

Marriages of upper class Negroes were sometimes reported in white newspapers. Thus a wedding in Waughtown involving two prominent Negro families of that town not only brought out "the better people" of the Negro group, but, according to a white newspaper, the white elite of Winston and Salem were also there. Among the distinguished white guests was the president of the National Bank of Winston. "All fared sumptuously . . . [and] there was nothing left undone on the part of the host to make his guests feel at home." "The mothers of the bride and groom," observed the paper, "graced the occasion with their presence to the delight of all."[30] Needless to say, social intermingling of the elite of the two races in North Carolina was the exception rather than the rule.

The prevailing social proscription against such general socializing of white and Negro upper classes greatly restricted the latter group's enjoyment of numerous events and programs of a cultural nature. Charles W. Chestnutt, during his stay in Fayetteville, faced the dilemma of many upper class Negroes. Although he had studied and practiced to the point where he could appreciate public concerts of classical music, Chestnutt in 1878 observed ruefully that he "never

27. Raleigh *Gazette,* November 7, 1891.
28. Raleigh *North Carolina Republican,* November 12, 1880.
29. *Ibid.*
30. Winston *Union-Republican,* January 4, 1883.

hears what little there is to be heard."[31] Four years later the stultified social order led Chestnutt to declare despairingly: "I get more and more tired of the South. I pine for civilization and companionship. . . . And I shudder to think of exposing my children to the social and intellectual proscription to which I have been a victim."[32]

The "social and intellectual proscription" referred to by Chestnutt was ameliorated somewhat in North Carolina towns possessing institutions of higher learning for Negroes. These schools frequently sponsored for the general public literary and musical entertainments of a high order. Bennett Seminary (now Bennett College), for example, on March 19, 1891, presented such a program. Included were a piano duet, "Il Trovatore," a discussion on "Resolved, that an illiterate man should be disfranchised," and an address entitled "Aim High."[33]

The musical and literary programs presented by Negro colleges, churches, and social organizations emphasized the evolutionary change in the social position of the Negro which had occurred after 1865. The intensification and hardening of racial segregation, particularly after 1890, left the Negroes with no alternative except to develop compensatory social relationships within their own group.

31. Helen M. Chestnutt, *Charles Waddell Chestnutt* (Chapel Hill: University of North Carolina Press, 1952), pp. 16-17.
32. *Ibid.*, p. 31.
33. MS in the Archives, Holgate Library, Bennett College.

21

Conclusion

*We desire to become good citizens. We would add
to the peace and dignity, the glory and greatness of
our state by every means in our power. All we want
is a settlement upon the principles of justice and
Christianity, and a practical acknowledgement and
enforcement of our rights under the Constitution
and the laws.*
Charles N. Hunter, December 26, 1888.

In the foregoing pages an attempt has been
made to inquire into the conditions of the Negroes in North Carolina
from the return of Bourbon Democracy in 1876 to its defeat in 1894
by the combined forces of the Populists and Republicans. Concentrated
in the eastern part of the state where the majority of the white population also lived, the Negroes, who at the end of the period numbered
561,018, showed a willingness equal to or surpassing that of the whites
to congregate in the towns and cities of North Carolina. Indeed, in
1890 Negroes comprised nearly 50 per cent of the population in the
twelve major urban centers of the state.

In spite of the city-ward movement, the vast majority of Negroes
throughout the period continued to live in the rural areas. In 1890,
for example, there was a total of only 55,695 urban Negroes, while
505,325 still lived in the rural areas. The percentage of Negroes in the
total urban population was considerably larger than the percentage of
Negroes in the rural population. In 1890, Negroes made up 48.1 per

cent of the total urban population of the state, while they constituted only 33.6 per cent of the total rural population.

The tendency of the Negroes to continue to be rural dwellers, but at the same time to maintain approximately an equal percentage in the total urban population, presents a marked contrast to the situation in other southern states. This paradoxical situation in North Carolina prompts an interesting observation. The rural habitation of the Negroes of the state, although it caused them to suffer from disadvantages that resulted from limited economic and educational opportunities and inadequate social contacts, should have made their presence in North Carolina less objectionable. At the same time, however, the inclination of the Negroes of the state to migrate to the towns and cities in proportion equal to or in excess of the whites had the effect of offsetting or minimizing the comparatively calm race relations that their stay in the rural areas might have insured.

The exodus of the Negro rural dweller to the town and city within and without the state not only affected the character and prospects of North Carolina agriculture but also tended to increase the hardships of the Negroes themselves. In the towns of North Carolina, whole families, including the father, mother, brothers, and sisters, lived in small houses often containing but one badly ventilated room. Especially was this true of the poorer classes of Negroes. Often situated in the more undesirable sections, in the "bottoms" or "basins," many of the homes were indescribably filthy inside and out.

Akin to the undesirable housing as a health menace in the towns and cities was the contaminated drinking water. Since most of the drinking water came from wells, springs, and creeks located within a few feet or yards of the privy, exposure to contamination was an ever-present threat. When the plumber's bill was added to the expense of the yearly tax necessary to obtain purified water furnished by the city, the possibility for the introduction of safe water to the premises was even more remote.

These factors, combined with a high illiteracy rate and with a lack of proper food and clothing brought on by low wages or unemployment, caused many Negroes to become the easy victims of the many diseases that rage among any poverty-stricken class. Deaths among the Negro population in Wilmington in 1879, for example, were more than double those of the whites, while the number of Negroes was approximately one-third greater than the number of whites (16,788 Negroes to 6,776 whites). The Negro population of that coastal city, then, while exceeding that of the whites by more than 33 per cent, had a death rate that surpassed that of the whites by more than 100 per cent. The greatest killers among the Negro population were tuberculosis, diarrheal diseases, pneumonia, and "the fevers"—typhoid, diphtheria, and malaria.

A comparison of the decrease in the death rate of the Negroes of North Carolina with that in other southern states suggests the extent of the interest of the former Confederacy in reducing Negro mortality. Between 1880 and 1890, the death rate per 1,000 in North Carolina fell from 17.61 to 12.88, a decrease of 4.73 per 1,000. In no other southern state except Arkansas was there a greater reduction in Negro deaths for the ten-year period.

Although North Carolina provided institutional care for its Negro defectives and dependents, the accommodations were inadequate. The Eastern Hospital for the Negro Insane in 1880 could accommodate 100 patients; yet in the same year there were 437 insane Negroes reported in North Carolina. Lest the emphasis here upon the Negroes should obscure contemporaneous conditions among the white defectives and dependents, it should be observed that there was a similar lack of accommodations for the latter group, although not quite as acute.

The Negroes comprised by far the larger proportion of the prison population of the state. In 1890 there were 408 whites and 1,625 Negroes in the state prison in Raleigh. Several factors accounted for the excessive number of Negro prisoners. In the first place, the development of the railroad and public road systems of the state stimulated a demand for abundant cheap labor. In the second place, as a result of this need for an ever-ready cheap supply of manpower to do the laborious and hazardous work of rail and public road building, many North Carolina officials took an active part in increasing the number of convicts in the state penitentiary. Negroes were often sentenced from three to ten years for stealing two or three chickens. Such was possible under North Carolina law, for there was no distinction between petty and grand larceny in that both carried a maximum penalty of ten years. Therefore, racial prejudice, accentuated by the demands of railroad and county road construction, swamp drainage, and canal building for laborers, accounted to a great degree for the rapid and increased growth of the Negro prison population throughout the period under observation. It is imperative that these special factors be considered when the number of prison commitments between the years 1876 and 1894 are examined.

The Negro farm population, vis-à-vis the town and city population, made up the larger percentage of the Negroes of North Carolina. In fact, 43.6 per cent of all employed Negroes of the state were agricultural laborers. This situation, incidentally, was common to all of the southern states, with the possible exception of Tennessee and Virginia. Significantly, many white landlords, tenants, and farm laborers of eastern North Carolina evidenced an obviously unfavorable attitude towards Negro tenants and farm workers. They contended that Negroes were unreliable, dishonest, and inefficient. There is little doubt that a goodly number were improvident and slovenly. However, the shortcomings of the Negro farm workers were primarily the result of malpractices in the wage scale, the mortgage and lien bond system, and the practice of paying part of the wages in supplies.

Negro farm workers, for the most part, were employed at wages lower than those paid to white farm workers. The whites justified the lower wage scale for Negroes on the premise that the Negroes could "live on less." The truth of the matter is that the white landlords, realizing the occupational restrictions placed upon the Negroes generally, were convinced that this group, in order to subsist, would work at any price. The Negroes themselves, keenly and uncomfortably aware of the economic obstacles against them, as well as their lack of training in other pursuits, accepted the low agricultural wages or migrated to the towns and cities where a similar situation faced them—to work at severely depressed wages. This condition prevailed at the beginning of the period and continued to be so to the end. The mortgage and lien bond system was favorable to the interests of the landlord group. Although there were denials that many of the laws governing the system were aimed at Negro tenants, evidence seems to support the contrary view. In the heavily Negro-populated eastern counties, the landlords demanded about 60 per cent of the annual crop. This situation obtained in no other section of the state. As to the practice of paying wages to farm hands and tenants in supplies by the landlord or in orders upon the merchants, there is considerable question as to whether the landlords or the merchants were the greatest exploiters of the Negro farm dwellers. Certainly, both were guilty of profiteering at the expense of the Negro agricultural workers of North Carolina.

When we turn from an examination of Negro rural economic life to that of the town and city, we see a group that had no more satisfactory status. Despite the glowing accounts of expanding industrial development in North Carolina during the period, the majority of the Negroes in the towns and cities of the state earned their living in domestic and personal service. Indeed, instead of escaping from the menial jobs, town and city Negroes found themselves, toward the close of the period, confined almost exclusively to these pursuits. The comparatively small number of Negroes engaged in other economic endeavors, such as manufacturing and mechanical industries, trade, and transportation, were found in occupations requiring little or no skill but much physical strength and stamina. The above reasons partly explain the sizable concentration of Negroes in the tobacco industry of the state. The work in the leaf factories was mainly a hand process, performed under very bad working conditions.

Between 1876 and 1894 Negro professional men and women constituted the smallest percentage of the total number of Negroes employed in North Carolina. Of equal significance is the fact that of the number engaged in the professions in 1890, 95.2 per cent, were either clergymen or teachers. This may be attributed to one principal cause: as a result of segregation, the Negro minister and school teacher enjoyed an almost complete monopoly, being relatively free from white competition. Such was not the case with the Negro lawyer, physician, or dentist. However, as the period came to an end, even the snail-like increase in the number of Negro professionals evidenced hope for the future. Similar to the Negro professional, the Negro businessman experienced slow but steady growth. In 1880 there were 80 Negro business establishments, with a combined estimated worth of $79,000; nine years later there were 175 such concerns with an estimated worth of $129,000. A factor contributing to the rise of the Negro entrepreneur was the refusal by white businessmen to employ Negroes in other than menial occupations. Some Negroes, then, in an effort to free themselves from the wage earning class became their own employers. Predominantly small businessmen, the Negroes concentrated upon owning general stores and grocery stores and upon manufacturing and selling liquor.

During the period under study, the right of Negroes to own real property was never questioned. Nevertheless, the poverty of this group between 1876 and 1894 can be seen unmistakably in a study of the value of the property they owned. The Negroes of North Carolina possessed in 1893 an aggregate wealth of $8,018,446. When it is considered that 561,018 people had to share in this wealth of slightly more than eight million dollars, their plight is most apparent. By studying the value of the property owned by Negroes in Wilmington, one realizes the extent of the poverty of Negroes in the towns and cities of North Carolina. In that city, in 1879, a Negro population of

10,462 possessed an aggregate wealth of $207,385—a per capita wealth of only $19.08.

The same factors that hampered the Negroes of North Carolina in the economic sphere were present as they sought a place in the cultural and social life of the state. In comparison with the Negroes of other southern states, the Negroes of North Carolina were still in a relatively favorable position. Despite spirited opposition by a segment of the whites of the state, equality of educational facilities, for example, was more nearly realized between the races in North Carolina than in most of the other states of the former Confederacy. The relatively satisfactory educational facilities offered by the state, combined with the determination of the Negroes to learn, resulted in a sharp decrease in Negro illiteracy from 77.4 per cent in 1880 to 47.6 per cent in 1900.

Although the state made commendable progress in decreasing Negro illiteracy between 1876 and 1894, it offered scant instruction beyond the secondary school level for Negroes. The responsibility for advanced training was assumed almost solely by the various Negro religious denominations, which established such institutions as Shaw, St. Augustine, Biddle (now Johnson C. Smith), Barber-Scotia, Bennett, and Livingstone. These schools primarily, though not exclusively, were concerned with the creation of an educated ministry and missionaries. Despite the growing number of young, educated clergymen in North Carolina between 1876 and 1894, the large number of uneducated preachers continued to control the masses of Negro church-goers. Although figures on the number of Negroes in the various religious denominations of the state are sketchy, it is clear that the Baptists claimed the bulk of the Negro church members and that the Methodists ranked next. Emotionalism found in the Baptist churches of that day as well as the democratic organization and administration possibly accounted for the popularity of that denomination among the masses of illiterate and semi-literate Negroes.

Between 1876 and 1894, too, the growth of the Negro press of the state gave further evidence of the rising literacy among the Negroes of North Carolina. Similar to the *raison d'être* of all Negro newspapers in the United States was the desire of editors of the Negro newspapers of North Carolina "to uplift the race" and at all times "to take an uncompromising stand against those who outrage, oppress and malign the Negro." Negro editors of the state published weekly, semi-monthly, and monthly periodicals. Unfortunately, between 1876 and 1894, Negro newspapers as a general rule did not survive long enough to build up a sizable subscriber group. During the period, at least twenty were founded in the state, but most failed to sustain two years of publication. The long lives of the *Star of Zion,* of Salisbury, the Charlotte *Messenger,* and the Raleigh *Gazette* were unique among Negro journals of North Carolina. The Negro newspaper, of a size similar to that of its white contemporary, was usually made up of four pages devoid of headlines and pictures. The editor devoted a respectable amount of space to such items of local interest as those pertaining to social functions, religious and fraternal activities, schools, health, and business. Despite its limitations, the Negro press of North Carolina was instrumental in demonstrating the intellectual capacity of the race and represented one of the best means of informing the public at large of the Negroes' development, achievements, aspirations, and progress.

There was little organized recreation for the Negroes of North Carolina during the period. Their pleasures came from the relatively commonplace experiences of visits, excursions, or meetings of organizations to which they belonged, especially the fraternal and secret benevolent societies. In most of the major towns and cities there were local lodges of either the Masons or Odd Fellows. Fire fighting was a form of civic recreation as well as of service performed by the Negroes in the larger towns and cities. The yeoman work of these fire companies perhaps mitigated to some extent white people's hostility to the race.

As in the earlier periods, the social relationship between the Negroes and whites of North Carolina was governed by both legal and extra-legal practices. The most effective limitations, however, on the relationship between white and Negro were the unwritten agreements among the whites that any approach to "social equality" should be resisted at all costs. The matter of social equality was most sharply focused upon when it revolved around the segregation of Negroes on public carriers, in waiting rooms, and in hotels and restaurants. Although spirited and indignant protests came from many whites, North Carolina did not enact any Jim Crow laws in these areas during the period under study. Other southern states did enact such laws between 1876 and 1894.

Unfortunately, North Carolina, similar to other southern states, had its lynchings. Over a five-year period, 1889-1894, twelve Negroes died at the hands of lynch mobs. This aspect of Negro life in North Carolina, gruesome though it is, presents a commendable contrast to the situation in other southern states. Tennessee, Mississippi, Alabama,

Louisiana, Virginia, and Georgia far outstripped North Carolina in this activity. The fact that relatively few Negroes were lynched in North Carolina can be attributed partly to a vigorous, outspoken anti-lynch press. From one end of the state to the other, editors deplored mob law. The anti-lynch bill of 1893 was enacted partly as a result of their insistence for such a statute.

This praiseworthy piece of legislation, regrettably, reflects most clearly the inconsistency in the legislative record of North Carolina in safeguarding the rights of all its citizens. This contradiction is, though, perhaps, understandable. With few exceptions, the members of each session of the General Assembly had lived all their lives among the people whom they represented and, therefore, had been exposed to all the influences of local environment and mores. When they thought of Negroes, these officials naturally affirmed the general views of their communities, which were, if judged by the political campaigns between 1876 and 1894, anti-Negro and anti-Republican. Although in 1876 the Democratic leaders and the Democratic press of the state attempted to assure the apprehensive Negroes that no rights would be taken from them, the first Bourbon Democratic legislature enacted the county government law that abolished the right of the people to elect all local officials. This enactment, in effect, nullified the strength of the Negroes at the ballot box in eastern North Carolina by denying them the right to elect county officials who controlled their personal and civil liberties. Since the law applied to all the counties in the state, there was considerabe opposition to it not only by the Negroes in eastern North Carolina but also by the whites in the sparsely Negro-populated regions of western North Carolina. Such opposition persisted throughout the period and eventually contributed to the Populist-Republican fusion in the 1890's.

In addition to establishing the county government law, the North Carolina legislature between 1877 and 1894 took even more drastic steps to decrease the voting power of the Negroes in the state. Early in the period, the passage of a series of election laws gave the judges and registrars almost unlimited power in determining the qualifications and eligibility of voters. In 1889, the General Assembly enacted an even more stringent election law ostensibly aimed at further reducing the Negro electorate of the state. Similar legislation was passed during the period to restrict the political power of Negroes in the towns and cities in which that race had a larger percentage of eligible voters than did the whites.

As in the case of suffrage laws enacted by the North Carolina legislature between 1877 and 1894, it is possible to see a decided reflection of the racial attitude of the white citizens of the state in the passage of laws dealing with public education. In spite of the pleas of the Democratic governor, Zebulon B. Vance, in 1877, to deal justly with all school children of the state, three years later, in 1880, the legislature passed the first of a series of acts providing that all tax money collected from the property and polls of white persons was to support white schools and that all tax money collected from Negroes was to be used for the support of Negro schools. This doctrine that each race should be held responsible for the education of its children was received enthusiastically by a large portion of the white press of the state. Some white newspapers felt that it was not only unfair to tax whites to educate Negroes, but that it was wrong per se to educate Negroes.

Because of these suffrage and education restrictions, Negroes were able to retain some of the privileges and rights which they had enjoyed between 1865 and 1876 only because the North Carolina Supreme Court interpreted the news laws liberally. That body, in spite of an occasional adverse decision, as in the case of *Harris vs. Scarborough,* in which the court refused to declare unconstitutional the election law of 1889, was the single conspicuous protector of the suffrage and education rights of the Negroes of the state. The illiberal spirit of a large majority of the white citizens of North Carolina and the adverse, sometimes intolerant, laws enacted by the General Assembly of the state were, fortunately, frequently offset by the rulings handed down by the North Carolina Supreme Court. Without Supreme Court justices like Smith, Merrimon, and Clark, the lot of the Negroes in North Carolina between 1876 and 1894 would have been more precarious than it was.

In other respects the period was notable for the number of Negro office holders in the local, state, and national legislatures. In the General Assembly of North Carolina the overwhelming majority of the fifteen Senate and fifty-two House members between 1876 and 1894 were elected from predominantly "Negro counties." Though the Negroes of the state were elated to see members of their race in both houses of the state legislature, they were especially proud of the fifteen who served in the upper house during the period under consideration; for, similar to membership in the United States Congress, membership in the state Senate carries with it greater prestige, affluence, and stature than does membership in the house.

When one reviews the legislative careers of these Negro members, several factors should be borne in mind. First, a sizable portion of them had college and normal school training; a still larger number possessed a public school education; and the few who had no formal schooling had become educated to the extent that they were fairly literate. Second, as a result of their learning, there was a generous sprinkling of teachers, preachers, and lawyers among them. Third, with few exceptions, they had enjoyed long years of public service preceding their election to the General Assembly.

An over-all analysis of the type of legislation sponsored or supported by the Negro representatives deserves some note. First, as a result of the widespread illiteracy among the Negro population of the state, much of the energy of the Negro representatives was expended on efforts designed to improve and expand the educational facilities available to the Negroes of North Carolina. Their proposals, whether in the form of bills or resolutions, were intended to remove or alleviate what they considered to be some of the more pronounced weaknesses. Among these were the dearth of normal schools for the training of Negro teachers, the somewhat lower salaries paid to Negro teachers, the absence until 1891 of state-supported college training for Negroes, the discriminatory provisions in the school laws, and the lack of compulsory school attendance laws. The proposals to compel regular school attendance, although motivated by a desire to educate the Negroes, were calculated to place the state on a higher educational level by decreasing the illiteracy among the whites as well as the Negroes.

Second, since the vast majority of the convicts were Negroes, the Negro members of the General Assembly throughout the period were continually introducing proposals for the protection and welfare of the Negro prison population. These bills and resolutions can be divided into three categories: those seeking better treatment of convicts, both in the penitentiary and on the railroads and public roads of the state; those attempting to modify, repeal, or amend the existing laws providing excessive punishment for petty crimes and thereby to reduce the Negro prison population; and those intended to abolish indirectly convict labor on the public roads by substituting the practice of "working" them by taxation. That these proposals and resolutions were all ultimately defeated or summarily rejected does not imply that they lacked merit. On the contrary, it would seem to indicate that a large proportion of the white legislators ignored the welfare and the protection of the Negro prison population.

Finally, the largest single group of bills and resolutions introduced by the Negro representatives attempted either to amend or to repeal the county government and election laws. Although these proposals, for the most part, were intended to remove certain franchise restrictions under which the Negroes suffered, the Democrats in the General Assembly, blinded by partisanship and white supremacy, ignored or failed to sense their genuinely democratic spirit.

In the face of economic, social, and political disabilities, the interest of the Negroes in emigration and colonization persisted throughout the period. Some Negroes, particularly during the first ten years of Democratic rule, evinced interest in Liberia; however, fewer than four hundred actually went to that African country. For several reasons the movement of Negroes from North Carolina to Liberia was inconsiderable. In the first place, Negro leadership was generally hostile to such movement, and in the second place, many whites, especially those with agricultural interests, opposed, for obvious reasons, emigration to Liberia. In the third place, the bulk of the dissatisfied Negroes of the state, despite their approval of emigration, preferred to remain in the United States.

Opinions of the North Carolina whites regarding the exodus of Negroes from the state were divided. The landlords of the eastern part of the state were extremely alarmed over the movement since the Negroes were the main source of their labor supply. Other whites, however, were pleased to see the Negroes leave the state because from their viewpoint such emigrations meant a reduction in the friction between the races caused by "malicious men at the North and wicked designing men in the South." In a class analysis of Negro reaction to colonization and emigration, it is clear that the Negroes who were economically dependent on other Negroes, and not on the whites to any comparable degree, tended to oppose such schemes. Negro politicians, clergymen, merchants, and businessmen, therefore, adopted a conservative, if not hostile, view toward any movement designed to remove the Negroes from North Carolina. The illiterate and semi-literate tenant farmers and day laborers—underpaid, overworked, deprived of material goods—comprised the larger percentage of the "emigrating Negroes."

Although a continuing stream of Negroes throughout the period left the state for a more salubrious racial or economic climate, and thousands more were anxious "to shake the North Carolina dust from their heels," by far the largest number clung tenaciously to the land of their birth. By 1894, in spite of economic, social, and political proscriptions, the Negroes who remained in the state were optimistic; yet at the same time they were acutely conscious of the obstacles in the path of their advancement.

Bibliography

I. PRIMARY SOURCES

A. MANUSCRIPTS

American Colonization Society Papers, 1876-1894. In the Manuscript Division, Library of Congress.

Ashe, Samuel A. Papers, 1876-1894. In the State Department of Archives and History, Raleigh.

Baptist Associations. Minutes and Records, 1790-1933. In the Manuscript Collection of the Duke University Library.

Butler, A. Papers, 1854-1937. In the Southern Historical Collection of the Library of the University of North Carolina.

Eppes, Henry. Papers, 1887. In possession of R. Faulkner Eppes, Greenville, North Carolina.

Governors' Papers, 1876-1894. In the State Department of Archives and History, Raleigh.

Hawkins, Marmaduke J. Papers, 1892-1894. In the State Department of Archives and History, Raleigh.

Hunter, Charles N. Papers and Scrapbook, 1866-1929. In the Manuscript Collection of the Duke University Library.

Legislative Papers, 1877-1894. In the State Department of Archives and History, Raleigh.

Minute Book of Local Assembly No. 3606 (Raleigh) of the Knights of Labor, 1886-1890. In the State Department of Archives and History, Raleigh.

Ransom, Matt W. Papers, 1876-1894. In the Southern Historical Collection of the Library of the University of North Carolina.

Russell, Daniel L. Papers, 1876-1894. In the Southern Historical Collection of the Library of the University of North Carolina.

Scales, Alfred M. Letter Book, 1885-1889. In the State Department of Archives and History, Raleigh.

Smith, Edward Chambers. Papers, 1892. In the Manuscript Collection of the Duke University Library.

Smith, Peter Evans. Papers, 1882. In the Manuscript Collection of the Duke University Library.

Thorpe, Benjamin Peter. Papers, 1837-1889. In the Manuscript Collection of the Duke University Library.

Vance, Zebulon Baird. Papers, 1880. In the State Department of Archives and History, Raleigh.

B. OFFICIAL RECORDS AND DOCUMENTS

1. Publications of the United States Government

Second Annual Report of the Commissioner of Labor, 1886. Washington: Government Printing Office, 1887.

Third Annual Report of the Commissioner of Labor, 1887. Washington: Government Printing Office, 1888.

Bulletin of the Bureau of Labor. No. 54 (September, 1904). Washington: Government Printing Office, 1904.

Bulletin of the Department of Labor. Vol. II (1897). Washington: Government Printing Office, 1897.

U.S. Bureau of the Census. *Tenth Census of the United States: 1880. Defectives, Dependents and Delinquent Classes.* Vol. XXI. Washington Government Printing Office, 1888.

U.S. Bureau of the Census. *Tenth Census of the United States: 1880. Population.* Vol. I. Washington: Government Printing Office, 1883.

U.S. Bureau of the Census. *Eleventh Census of the United States: 1890. Crime.* Vol. III, Part 2. Washington: Government Printing Office, 1895.

U.S. Bureau of the Census. *Eleventh Census of the United States: 1890. Population.* Vol. I, Part 1. Washington: Government Printing Office, 1897.

U.S. Bureau of the Census. *Eleventh Census of the United States: Report on Transportation Business in the United States.* Vol. XIV, Part 1. Washington: Government Printing Office, 1895.

U.S. Bureau of the Census. *Negro Population, 1790-1915.* Washington: Government Printing Office, 1918.

U.S. Bureau of the Census. *Twelfth Census of the United States: 1900. Statistical Atlas.* Washington: U.S. Census Office, 1903.

U.S. Bureau of the Census. *Thirteenth Census of the United States: 1910. Abstract of Census.* Washington: Government Printing Office, 1913.

U.S. Department of Labor. *History of Wages in the United States from Colonial Times to 1928.* Washington: Government Printing Office, 1929.

2. *Publications of North Carolina State and County Government*

Code of North Carolina, 1883. 2 vols. New York: Banks and Brothers, 1883.

Code of North Carolina, Revisal of 1905. 2 vols. Raleigh: E. M. Uzzell and Co., 1905.

Colonial Records of North Carolina. Edited by William L. Saunders. Raleigh, 1890.

Colored Marriage Register of Guilford County, 1867-1886. In the Guilford County Courthouse, Greensboro, North Carolina.

Executive and Legislative Documents of the State of North Carolina, 1885. Raleigh: P. M. Hale, Printer, 1885.

Handbook of North Carolina, 1879, 1883, 1886, 1893. Raleigh: Edwards, Broughton and Co.

Journal of the House of the General Assembly of the State of North Carolina, 1876-1893. Published by the State.

Journal of the Senate of the General Assembly of the State of North Carolina, 1876-1893. Published by the State.

Manual of North Carolina, 1913. Edited by R. D. W. Connor. E. M. Uzzell and Co., 1913.

Marriage Register of Guilford County, 1886-1897. In the Guilford County Courthouse, Greensboro, North Carolina.

North Carolina *Supreme Court Reports, 1877-1894.* Published by the State.

Public and Private Laws and Resolutions of the State of North Carolina, 1876-1894. Published by the State.

Register of Deeds and Mortgages, 1876-1894. In the Guilford County Courthouse, Greensboro, North Carolina.

C. BOOKS

African Repository, 1876-1892. Washington: McGill and Withers Co.

Appleton's Annual Cyclopedia, 1880-1894. New York: D. Appleton and Co.

Emery, E. B. *Letters from the South.* Boston: Todd Printers, 1880.

Mebane, George A. *The Negro Problem.* New York: Alliance Publishing Co., 1900.

North Carolina as Told by Contemporaries. Edited by Hugh T. Lefler. Chapel Hill: University of North Carolina Press, 1934.

North Carolina Sermons. Vol. I. Edited by Rev. Levi Branson. Raleigh: Branson House, 1893.

Penn, Garland I. *The Afro-American Press.* Springfield, Mass., Willey and Co., 1891.

Paul, Hiram V. *History of the Town of Durham, North Carolina.* Raleigh: Edwards, Broughton and Co., 1884.

The Negro Artisan. Edited by W. E. B. Du Bois. Atlanta: Atlanta University Press, 1902.

Thompson, Holland. *From the Cotton Field to the Cotton Mill: A Study of Industrial Transition in North Carolina.* London: The Macmillan Co., 1906.

Warner, Charles D. *On Horseback. A Tour in Virginia, North Carolina, and Tennessee.* New York: Houghton-Mifflin and Co., 1892.

Zeigler, Wilbur G., and Grosscup, Ben S. *The Heart of the Alleghanies or Western North Carolina.* Raleigh: Alfred Williams and Co., 1883.

D. AUTOBIOGRAPHIES, BIOGRAPHIES, MEMOIRS

Andrews, R. McGants. *John Merrick.* Durham: Seeman Printery, 1920.

Assembly Sketch Book, 1885. Raleigh: Edwards, Broughton and Co., 1885.

Biographical History of North Carolina. Vol. II. Edited by Samuel Ashe. Greensboro: Charles L. Van Noppen, Publisher, 1905.

Brooks, Aubrey L. *Walter Clark: Fighting Judge.* Chapel Hill: University of North Carolina Press, 1944.

Chamberlain, Hope S. *This Was Home.* Chapel Hill: University of North Carolina Press, 1937.

Daniels, Josephus. *Editor in Politics.* Chapel Hill: University of North Carolina Press, 1941.

————. *Tar Heel Editor.* Chapel Hill: University of North Carolina Press, 1939.

Dowd, Clement. *Life of Zebulon Vance.* Charlotte: Observer Printing House, 1897.

Fonvielle, W. F. *Reminiscences of College Days.* Raleigh: Edwards, Broughton and Co., 1904.

Hunter, Charles N. *Review of Negro Life in North Carolina with My Recollections.* Raleigh: n.d.

Jones, May (ed.). *Memoirs and Speeches of Locke Craig.* Asheville: Stockney and Maale, 1923.

Legislative Biographical Sketch Book, 1887. Raleigh: Edwards, Broughton and Co., 1887.

Pegues, A. W. *Our Baptist Ministers and Schools.* Springfield: Willey and Co., 1892.

Recollections of the Inhabitants, Localities, Superstitutions and Ku Klux Klan Outrages of the Carolinas. Cleveland? 1880.

Rippy, Fred (ed.). *Furnifold Simmons, Statesman of the South: Memoirs and Addresses.* Durham: Duke University Press, 1936.

Shotwell, R. A., and Atkinson, Natt. *Legislative Record, Sketches of the Lives of the Members, 1877.* Raleigh: Edwards, Broughton and Co., 1877.

Simmons, William J. *Men of Mark.* Cleveland: George H. Rewell and Co., 1890.

Sinclair, D. F. *Biographical Sketches of the Members and Officers of the General Assembly, 1889.* Raleigh: Edwards, Broughton and Co., 1889.

Tomlinson, J. S. *Tar Heel Sketch Book: A Brief Biographical Sketch of the Members of the General Assembly, 1879.* Raleigh News Steam Book and Job Print, 1879.

———. *Assembly Sketch Book, 1883.* Raleigh: Edwards, Broughton and Co., 1883.

Tomlinson, W. G. *Biography of the State Officers and Members of the General Assembly, 1893.* Raleigh: Edwards, Broughton and Co., 1893.

Waddell, Alfred M. *Some Memories of My Life.* Raleigh: Edwards, Broughton and Co., 1908.

Winston, Robert W. *It's a Far Cry.* New York: Henry Holt and Co., 1937.

E. ALMANACS, YEARBOOKS, DIRECTORIES

Annual Catalog, Bennett College, Greensboro, North Carolina, 1900.

Annual Catalog, Scotia Seminary, Concord, North Carolina, 1887-88, 1889-90, 1890-91, 1891-92, 1893-94.

Asheville City Directory, 1887. Asheville: Southern Directory Co., 1887.

Blum's Farmer's and Planter's Almanac, 1881. Salem: E. T. Blum, Publisher, 1881.

Branson's North Carolina Business Directory, 1884, 1890. Raleigh: Levi Branson, Publisher.

Chataigne's North Carolina State Directory and Gazeteer, 1883-1884. Raleigh: J. H. Chataigne, Publisher, 1883.

Chataigne, J. H. *Raleigh City Directory, 1875-1876.* Raleigh: Edwards, Broughton and Co., 1875.

Directory of Charlotte, North Carolina, 1893-1894. Charlotte: Blakely Printing House, 1893.

Directory of the City of Wilmington, 1889. Wilmington: Messenger Steam Presses, 1889.

Durham City Directory, 1887. Raleigh: Levi Branson, Publisher, 1887.

Greensboro City Directory, 1887. Newburgh, New York: Thompson, Breed and Crafutt Co., 1887.

The Mercantile Agency Reference Book, January, 1880. New York: Dun, Barlow and Co., 1879.

The Mercantile Agency Reference Book, January, 1889. New York: Dun, Barlow and Co., 1888.

The Mercantile Association of the Carolinas Reference Book, July, 1889, January, 1890, January, 1891. Wilmington: Jackson Co.

Negro Year Book, 1818-1819. Tuskegee: Negro Year Book Publishing Co., 1919.

New Bern City Directory, 1880-1881. Raleigh: Edwards, Broughton and Co., 1880.

North Carolina Baptist Almanac, 1882. Raleigh: Edwards, Broughton and Co., 1882.

North Carolina Baptist Almanac, 1891. Raleigh: C. T. Bailey, Publisher, 1891.

North Carolina Tobacco Belt Directory, 1886. Raleigh: Edwards, Broughton and Co., 1886.

Raleigh City Directory, 1880-1881. Raleigh: Edwards, Broughton and Co., 1880.

Raleigh City Directory, 1888. Raleigh: Observer Printing Co., 1888.

Raleigh City Directory, 1883. Raleigh: Edwards, Broughton and Co., 1883.

Ramsey's Durham Directory, 1892. Durham: N. A. Ramsey, Publisher, 1892.

Randolph County Business Directory, 1894. Raleigh: Edwards, Broughton and Co., 1894.

Scotia Seminary, Concord, North Carolina, Twenty-fifth Anniversary, 1870-1905.

Turner's *North Carolina Almanac,* 1880-1894.

F. REPORTS

Annual Report of the American Colonization Society, 1876-1895. Published by the American Colonization Society.

Annual Report of the North Carolina Bureau of Labor Statistics, 1887-1894. Published by the State.

Biennial Report of the Attorney General of North Carolina, 1886-1894. Published by the State.

Biennial Report of the Board of Public Charities of North Carolina, 1889-1894. Published by the State.

Biennial Report of the North Carolina Board of Health, 1879-1894. Published by the State.

Biennial Report of the Superintendent of Instruction of North Carolina, 1879-1894. Published by the State.

Biennial Report of the Treasurer of North Carolina, 1890-1892. Published by the State.

Minutes of the Twelfth Session of the North Carolina Conference of the A.M.E. Zion Church. Concord, North Carolina, November 24-December 1, 1875.

Minutes of the Thirteenth Session of the North Carolina Conference of the A.M.E. Zion Church in America. Washington, North Carolina, November 22-29, 1876.

Minutes of the Fourteenth Session of the North Carolina Annual Conference of the A.M.E. Zion Church in America. Salisbury, North Carolina, November 28-December 4, 1877.

Minutes of the Fifteenth Session of the North Carolina Annual Conference of the A.M.E. Zion Church in America. Goldsboro, North Carolina, November 28-December 4, 1878.

Minutes of the Sixteenth Session of the North Carolina Annual Conference of the A.M.E. Zion Church in America. Lincolnton, North Carolina, November 26-December 3, 1879.

Minutes of the First Session of the Central North Carolina Conference of the A.M.E. Zion Church in America. Fayetteville, North Carolina, November 10-18, 1880.

Presbyterian Church, *North Carolina Synod Minutes, 1882.* Wilmington: Jackson and Bell, Printers, 1882.

Record of Proceedings of the General Assembly of the Knights of America. Tenth Regular Session, Richmond, Virginia, October 4-20, 1886.

G. NEWSPAPERS

Charlotte *Chronicle.* Scattered copies.
Charlotte *Home Democrat,* 1883-1885.
Chatham *Record,* 1876-1891.
Clinton *Caucasian,* 1890-1892.
Elizabeth City *North Carolinian,* July 20, 1881.
Fayetteville *Observer,* 1888.
Greensboro *Daily Battle-Ground,* 1881.
Greensboro *Daily Bugle,* 1887. Scattered copies.
Greensboro *Daily Record,* 1891-1893.
Greensboro *Morning News,* May 24, 1887.
Greensboro *North State,* 1888.
Greensboro *Patriot,* 1877-1878.
Greenville *Eastern Reflector,* 1882-1886.
Hampton *Southern Workman,* September, 1879.
Kinston *Journal,* 1879-1880.
Lenoir *Topic,* 1877-1880.
New Bern *Daily Journal,* 1880-1894.
New Bern *New Bernian,* November 29, 1879.
*New Bern *People's Advocate,* 1887. Scattered copies.
*New Bern *Republican,* 1887. Scattered copies.
New York *Age,* 1887-1889.
New York *Daily Tribune,* 1882-1894.
*Raleigh *Banner-Enterprise,* May 31, 1883.
Raleigh *Daily News,* March 13, 1875.
Raleigh *Evening Visitor,* November 10, 1886.
Raleigh *Farmer and Mechanic,* 1877-1883.
*Raleigh *Gazette,* 1890-1891. Scattered copies.
Raleigh *Journal of Industry,* 1879-1881. Scattered copies.
Raleigh *News and Observer,* 1880-1894.
Raleigh *North Carolina Republican.* Scattered copies.
Raleigh *Observer,* 1877-1878.
Raleigh *Register,* 1877-1878, 1884, 1885.

Raleigh *Sentinel,* 1876.
Raleigh *Signal,* 1880, 1886-1889.
Raleigh *State Chronicle,* 1889.
Salisbury *Carolina Watchman,* 1877-1889.
Tarboro *Southerner,* 1876-1885.
Warrenton *Gazette,* 1877-1881.
*Washington *Bee,* 1882-1886, 1892.
Washington (N.C.) *Gazette,* September 26, 1884.
Wilson *Advance,* September 8, 1882.
Wilmington *Daily Review,* 1876-1881, 1884-1889.
Wilmington *Journal,* 1876-1878.
Wilmington *Morning Star,* 1876-1881.
Wilmington *Post,* 1876-1881.
Winston *Union-Republican,* 1876-1894.

* Negro newspapers.

H. PAMPHLETS

"A Disgruntled Republican." North Carolina State Democratic Executive
Committee, 1888.
"Address to the Voters of North Carolina." Republican State Executive
Committee, 1876.
Blacknall, O. W. "New Departures in Negro Life," 1883.
Crummell, Rev. Alexander. "The Black Woman of the South: Her
Neglect and Her Needs." Washington, D.C., n.d.
Dockery, Oliver H. "Life and Times."
Douglass, Frederick. "Address on the Lessons of the Hour." Delivered
in the Metropolitan AME Church, Washington, D.C., January 9, 1894.
Finger, Sidney M. "The Educational and Religious Interest of the Colored
People of the South." Address to the Department of Superintendence
of the National Educational Association, Washington, D.C., February
24, 1886.
"Raleigh State Chronicle Supplement," 1888.
"To the Democratic Party of North Carolina." Democratic State Execu-
tive Committee, 1880.

I. ARTICLES

Bassett, A. L. "Going to Housekeeping in North Carolina," *Lippincott's
Magazine,* XXVIII (August, 1881), 205-8.
Cable, George W. "The Convict Lease System in the Southern States,"
Century Magazine, XXVII (February, 1884), 582-99.
Collins, Plato. "The Negro Must Remain in the South," *North Carolina
University Magazine,* N.S., X (1890-1891), 144-53.

"The Colored Fair at Raleigh, N.C.," *Frank Leslie's Illustrated Newspaper,* XLIX (December 6, 1879), 242-43.

Dowd, Jerome. "Cheap Labor in the South," *Gunston's Magazine* (February, 1900), 113-21.

————. "Rev. Moses Hester: Sketch of a Quaint Negro Preacher in North Carolina," *Trinity Archives,* IX (February, 1896), 283-96.

"The Exodus into Indiana," *Frank Leslie's Illustrated Newspaper,* XLIX (January 17, 1880), 362.

Hart, Albert B. "A Cross-Section through North Carolina," *Nation,* LIV (March 17, 1892), 207-8.

Thompson, Holland. "Some Effects of Industrialism in an Agricultural State," *South Atlantic Quarterly,* III (January, 1905), 71-77.

Winston, Robert W. "An Unconsidered Aspect of the Negro Question," *South Atlantic Quarterly,* I (July, 1902), 265-68.

J. PERSONAL INTERVIEWS

Mrs. Alice Dean, daughter-in-law of James Dean, Greensboro, North Carolina, July 30, October 4, 1952.

Mr. R. Faulkner Eppes, son of Henry Eppes, Greenville, North Carolina, December 29, 1952.

Rev. John Mebane, son of George A. Mebane, Tarboro, North Carolina, December 27, 1952.

Mrs. Lillian D. Reid, daughter of John C. Dancy, Salisbury, North Carolina, February, 1960.

II. SECONDARY WORKS

A. BOOKS

Aptheker, Herbert. *A Documentary History of the Negro People in the United States.* New York: Citadel Press, 1951.

Ashe, Samuel A. *History of North Carolina.* Vol. II. Raleigh: Edwards, Broughton and Co., 1925.

Boyce, W. Scott. *Economic and Social History of Chowan County, North Carolina, 1880-1915.* ("The Columbia University Studies in History, Economics and Public Law," Vol. LXXXVI.) New York: Columbia University Press, 1917.

Boyd, William Kenneth. *The Story of Durham.* Durham: Duke University Press, 1927.

Brown, Cecil K. *A State Movement in Railroad Development.* Chapel Hill: University of North Carolina Press, 1928.

Brown, Roy M. *Public Poor Relief in North Carolina.* Chapel Hill: University of North Carolina Press, 1928.

Chestnutt, Helen M. *Charles Waddell Chestnutt.* Chapel Hill: University of North Carolina Press, 1952.

Connor, R. D. W. *North Carolina: Rebuilding an Ancient Commonwealth, 1584-1925.* Vol. II. Raleigh: Edwards, Broughton and Co., 1925.

Dowd, Jerome. *The Negro in American Life.* New York: Century Co., 1926.

Edmonds, Helen G. *The Negro and Fusion Politics in North Carolina, 1895-1901.* Chapel Hill: University of North Carolina Press, 1951.

Foner, Philip S. *History of the Labor Movement in the United States.* New York: International Publishers, 1947.

Franklin, John Hope. *The Free Negro in North Carolina, 1790-1860.* Chapel Hill: University of North Carolina Press, 1943.

————. *From Slavery to Freedom.* New York: Alfred A. Knopf, Inc., 1947.

Frazier, E. Franklin. *The Negro in the United States.* New York: Macmillan Co., 1949.

Fries, Adelaide. *Forsyth County.* Chapel Hill: University of North Carolina Press, 1949.

Hale, P. M. *In the Coal and Iron Counties of North Carolina.* Raleigh: P. M. Hale, Publisher, 1883.

Hamilton, J. G. de Roulhac. *North Carolina Since 1860.* Vol. III of the *History of North Carolina.* New York: Lewis Co., 1919.

Henderson, Archibald. *North State: The Old and the New.* Vol. II. Chicago: Lewis Publishing Co., 1941.

King, Henry T. *Sketches of Pitt County, 1804-1910.* Raleigh: Edwards, Broughton and Co., 1911.

Kinzer, Robert H., and Sagarin, Edward. *The Negro in American Business.* New York: Greenberg, Publisher, 1950.

Knight, Edgar W. *Public School Education in North Carolina.* New York: Houghton-Mifflin Co., 1916.

Lemert, Ben F. *The Tobacco Manufacturing Industry in North Carolina.* Raleigh: National Youth Administration of North Carolina, 1939.

Mabry, William A. *The Negro in North Carolina Politics Since Reconstruction.* Durham: Duke University Press, 1940.

Mangum, Charles S. *The Legal Status of the Negro.* Chapel Hill: University of North Carolina Press, 1940.

Mitchell, Broadus. *The Rise of the Cotton Mills in the South.* Vol. 39 of the *Johns Hopkins University Studies in Historical and Political Science.* Baltimore: John Hopkins Press, 1921.

Pope, Liston. *Mill-hands and Preachers: A Study of Gastonia.* New Haven: Yale University Press, 1942.

Porter, Kirk H. *A History of Suffrage in the United States.* Chicago: University of Chicago Press, 1918.

Quick, W. H. *Negro Stars in All Ages of the World.* Richmond: S. B. Adkins and Co., 1898.

Sherrill, William L. *Annals of Lincoln County, North Carolina.* Charlotte: Observer Printing House, Inc., 1937.

Smedes, H. R. *Agricultural Graphics, North Carolina and the United States, 1866-1922.* Chapel Hill: University of North Carolina Press, 1923.

Smith, Samuel D. *The Negro in Congress, 1870-1901.* Chapel Hill: University of North Carolina Press, 1941.

Sprunt, James. *Chronicles of Cape Fear River, 1660-1916.* Raleigh: Edwards, Broughton and Co., 1916.

Stephenson, Gilbert T. *Race Distinctions in American Law.* New York: D. Appleton and Co., 1910.

Thirty Years of Lynching in the United States, 1889-1918. New York: National Association for the Advancement of Colored People, April, 1919.

Tindall, George B. *South Carolina Negroes, 1877-1900.* Columbia: University of South Carolina Press, 1952.

Turner, J. Kelly and Bridgers, J. L. *History of Edgecombe County, North Carolina.* Raleigh: Edwards, Broughton and Co., 1920.

Wesley, Charles H. *Negro Labor in the United States, 1850-1925.* New York: Vanguard Press, 1927.

Williams, George W. *History of the Negro Race in America.* New York: G. P. Putnam's Sons, 1882.

Woodson, Carter G. *A Century of Negro Migration.* Washington: The Association for the Study of Negro Life and History, 1918.

Whitted, J. A. *A History of the Negro Baptists of North Carolina.* Raleigh: Edwards, Broughton and Co., 1908.

B. ARTICLES

Cantor, Nathaniel. "Crime and the Negro," *Journal of Negro History,* XVI (January, 1931), 61-66.

Coon, Charles L. "The Beginnings of the North Carolina City Schools, 1867-1887," *South Atlantic Quarterly,* XII (July, 1913), 235-47.

Douty, H. M. "Early Labor Organization in North Carolina, 1880-1910," *South Atlantic Quarterly,* XXXIV (July, 1935), 260-68.

Edwards, Thomas. "The Tenant System and Some Changes Since Emancipation," *Annals of the American Academy of Political and Social Science,* XLIX (September, 1913), 38-46.

Eutsler, Roland B. "The Cape Fear and Yadkin Valley Railway," *North Carolina Historical Review,* II (October, 1925), 427-41.

Farmer, Hallie. "The Economic Background of Southern Populism," *South Atlantic Quarterly,* XXIX (January, 1930), 77-91.

Fleming, Walter L. " 'Pap' Singleton, the Moses of the Colored Exodus," *American Journal of Sociology,* XV (July, 1909), 61-82.

Garner, James W. "Recent Agitation of the Negro Question in the South," *South Atlantic Quarterly,* VII (January, 1908), 11-22.

Jolley, Harley E. "The Labor Movement in North Carolina, 1880-1922," *North Carolina Historical Review,* XXX (July, 1953), 354-75.

Kessler, Sidney H. "Organization of Negroes in the Knights of Labor," *Journal of Negro History,* XXXVII (July, 1952), 273-74.

Logan, Frenise A. "The Colored Industrial Association of North Carolina and its Fair of 1886," *North Carolina Historical Review,* XXXIV (January, 1957), 58-67.

————. "The Movement in North Carolina to Establish a State Supported College for Negroes," *North Carolina Historical Review,* XXXV (April, 1958), 167-80.

————. "The Economic Status of the Town Negro in Post-Reconstruction North Carolina," *North Carolina Historical Review,* XXXV (October, 1958), 448-60.

Mabry, William A. "The Negro in North Carolina Politics Since Reconstruction," *Trinity College Historical Society Papers,* XIII (1940), 12.

————. "Negro Suffrage and Fusion Rule in North Carolina," *North Carolina Historical Review,* XII (April, 1935), 79-102.

Miller, Kelly. "Professional and Skilled Occupations," *Annals of the American Academy of Political and Social Science,* XLIX (September, 1913), 10-18.

Padgett, James A. "From Slavery to Prominence in North Carolina," *Journal of Negro History,* XXII (October, 1937), 433-87.

Taylor, Joseph H. "The Great Migration from North Carolina in 1879," *North Carolina Historical Review,* XXXI (January, 1954), 18-33.

Thompson, Holland. "The Southern Textile Situation," *South Atlantic Quarterly,* XXIX (April, 1930), 113-25.

Weeks, Stephen B. "The History of Negro Suffrage in the South," *Political Science Quarterly,* IX (December, 1894), 671-703.

Work, Monroe N. "Some Negro Members of Reconstruction Conventions and Legislatures and of Congress," *Journal of Negro History,* V (January, 1920), 63-119.

Wright, R. R. "The Negro in Unskilled Labor," *Annals of the American Academy of Political and Social Science,* XLIX (September, 1913), 19-27.

Van Deusen, John G. "The Exodus of 1879," *Journal of Negro History,* XXI (April, 1936), 111-29.

C. UNPUBLISHED MATERIAL

Brinton, Hugh P. "The Negro in Durham." Unpublished Ph.D. dissertation, Department of Sociology, University of North Carolina, 1930.

Byrd, Ruth E. "The History of the Force Bill of 1890." Unpublished Master's thesis, Department of History, University of North Carolina, 1930.

Califf, Charlotte. "Wage Differentials Between Negro and White Workers in Southern States." Unpublished Master's thesis, Department of Public Administration, University of North Carolina, 1934.

Douty, Harry M. "The North Carolina Industrial Worker, 1880-1930." Unpublished Ph.D. dissertation, Department of Economics, University of North Carolina, 1936.

Jones, Theron Paul. "The Gubernatorial Election of 1892 in North Carolina." Unpublished Master's thesis, Department of History, University of North Carolina, 1949.

McKay, Herbert S. "Convict Leasing in North Carolina." Unpublished Master's thesis, Department of History, University of North Carolina, 1942.

Noblin, Stuart. "Leonidas Lafayette Polk." Unpublished Ph.D. dissertation, Department of History, University of North Carolina, 1947.

Rice, John Donald. "The Negro Tobacco Worker and His Union." Unpublished Master's thesis, Department of Sociology, University of North Carolina, 1941.

Steelman, Joseph F. "The Immigration Movement in North Carolina, 1865-1890." Unpublished Master's thesis, Department of History, University of North Carolina, 1947.

Zimmerman, Hilda J. "Penal Systems and Penal Reforms in the South Since the Civil War," Unpublished Ph.D. dissertation, Department of History, University of North Carolina, 1947.

Index